THE ANNALS OF
THE KING'S ROYAL RIFLE CORPS

BY THE SAME AUTHOR

THE ANNALS OF THE KING'S ROYAL RIFLE CORPS

Vol. I. "The Royal Americans."
With Portraits, Illustrations and Maps.

Vol. II. "The Green Jacket."
With Portraits and Maps.

APPENDIX, DEALING WITH UNIFORM, ARMAMENT, AND EQUIPMENT

By Major-General Astley Terry and S. M. Milne.
With numerous illustrations.

All rights reserved.

F. Mortimer Savory, Cirencester.

LIEUT.-GENERAL R. B. HAWLEY, C.B.

Frontispiece.

THE ANNALS OF THE KING'S ROYAL RIFLE CORPS

BY
LIEUTENANT-COLONEL LEWIS BUTLER

VOLUME III
THE 60TH: THE K.R.R.C.

WITH ILLUSTRATIONS AND MAPS

LONDON
JOHN MURRAY, ALBEMARLE STREET, W.
1926

PREFACE

TO

THE THIRD VOLUME

THE publication of Vol. III., bringing the story down to 1873, concludes the task undertaken at the instance first of Sir Redvers Buller, afterwards of Lord Grenfell, by the present writer, who will now hand it over to some abler exponent of regimental history. In the course of his work he has, however, accumulated a considerable number of papers dealing with more recent events, and hopes that they may prove valuable material for his successor. A single volume may suffice to bring the continuation of the story up to the eve of the Great War; but in view of the magnitude of that convulsion, and its innumerable incidents, one can hardly estimate the number of volumes that will be needed in order to do justice thereto.

In the first Volume of these Annals was described the principles on which Henri Bouquet, the first of our great battalion commanders, laid the foundation of the system upon which the whole Regiment was by degrees built up.

Volume II. described the introduction of a new arm and a new uniform by Colonel de Rothenburg.

Volume III. will attempt to show how the principles of his distinguished predecessors were adapted by Colonel Robert Beaufoy Hawley to the conditions of modern warfare. Each Volume may therefore be said to give a résumé of the work of one of these three great Commanding Officers. It is possible that there may be in the Army regiments which have never had the good fortune to be commanded by a great master of his art. There are certainly few that have had the advantage of such a trio as Bouquet, de Rothenburg, and Hawley; and it may be remarked that, despite the fact that not one of the Battalions which they respectively commanded is still in existence, the spirit of the three pervades, guides, and develops our Regiment of to-day.[1]

The writer thinks it important to invite attention again to the deficiencies of the information given in the battalion 'Digests of Services.' Trifles such as the issue of a new cap, or the arrival of a Corporal and half a dozen men are duly recorded, but the historian seeks in vain for the intelligence which he might fairly expect to find in their pages. Thus in that of the 1st Battalion there is no indication either of the Companies or their Officers who took part either in the Siege of Delhi or the Red River Expedition; and at the present day, after the long lapse of time, it is almost impossible to give the information with complete accuracy.

The details given in the records of the 2nd Battalion are much better, although even these—the only records of our Regiment printed and nicely bound up as a volume —leave much to be desired; *e.g.* the 'deathless story' of the *Birkenhead* receives three lines only, and these— interpolated as an after-thought two years after the event—contain three mis-statements of fact.

The early entries in those of the 3rd Battalion may

[1] The memory of a great C.O. may be perpetuated for upwards of a century after his death. Thus the 7th Dragoon Guards still appeal to the traditions of Lord Ligonier. In other cases a good system, due no doubt to some outstanding Colonel, remains, although the name of its founder is lost in the mists of antiquity.

PREFACE

be said to reach the nadir of fatuity. When this Battalion was raised in 1855 it was considered unnecessary to mention in its official record the name of even the Commanding Officer! The record begins—*de nubibus*—with the announcement of the arrival of a draft of about a dozen men. Later on a flash of intelligence among the Orderly Room authorities produces the observation—entered as a sort of interlineation—that five or six hundred men had previously been sent from the Depôt. Of so little importance appeared to be the document that not long afterwards it was lost. A new book was then begun, but after a long interval the missing volume turned up again; the result *inter alia* being considerable labour to the inquirer into the facts of the Battalion's history and the need of search through two books, the contents of which he will probably find equally useless.

It is, however, but fair to give credit for the comparative fullness of detail with which the thrilling story of the Battalion in a Cyclone on board the *Star of India* and the *Devonport* is narrated. It is unknown whether at the present date (1925) any officer or man on board is still alive. Although one of the most heroic episodes in our Annals, it is all but forgotten; and were it not for the record in question and a brief note by the Honourable Walter Pepys, who was in the *Devonport*, would have been entirely lost.

These remarks will show that in matters of important detail the historian is often obliged to rely much upon the recollections of surviving officers—if there happen to be any—and although these may be of great value they are not always accurate. The institution of the 'Chronicle' at the beginning of the present century will be the greatest help to the historian of the future, and will go far to minimise the disadvantages under which his predecessors have laboured.

It may, however, be pointed out that the Annual record of events furnished to the Editor of the 'Chronicle' by the various battalions and by the Rifle Depôt ought invariably to contain a list of the Officers with their distribution by Companies at the beginning of each year. This list should also show all alterations, arrivals, and departures which have taken place during the course of the same year. In cases when detachments are furnished the Companies—and their Officers—should be specified.

Information supplementing the narrative given in Vols I. and II., but received after their publication, is given in Appendices.

CONTENTS

	PAGE
Preface	v
List of Illustrations	xiii
Lists of the Regiment in 1830, 1850, and 1873	xv
Regimental Succession of Colonels-in-Chief, Colonels Commandant, and Lieut.-Colonels, 1830–1873	xxv
Synopsis of Contemporary Events	xxvii

CHAPTER I

The term Colonel Commandant—Inception of the Regimental Records   1

CHAPTER II

Members of the Regiment in Parliament—Capture of Officers by Brigands—1st Battalion at Malta—Colonel H. R. Molyneux takes command—The Battalion in the Ionian Islands—Returns to England—Death of Colonel Molyneux—The Battalion in the north of England—Sir W. Davy appointed Colonel Commandant —The Battalion in Ireland   8

CHAPTER III

2nd Battalion at Manchester—Fall of the Broughton Suspension Bridge—The Battalion in Ireland—At Gibraltar—In the Ionian Islands—At Jamaica—Outbreak of Yellow Fever—Death of Colonel Ellis—Conflagration at Kingston—The Battalion in Canada   18

CHAPTER IV

Colonel Dundas takes command of 1st Battalion—Embarkation for India—The Army of the Indus—Sir Charles Napier—The 2nd Sikh War—The Battalion at the Siege and Capture of Mooltan—Battle of Goojerat—Pursuit of the Afghans—Euzuffzye Expedition—Exploit of M. Burke at Pullee Zoormundee—The Centrepiece in the Officers' Mess—Expedition to Kohat—Death of Lieut.-Colonel Bradshaw—Duke of Wellington's last compliment to the Regiment —Lord Melville relinquishes command   30

CONTENTS

CHAPTER V

2nd Battalion at Royal Review in Hyde Park—In Lancashire—The Chartist Movement—The Battalion in Ireland—Embarks for the Cape of Good Hope—The Kaffir War, 1851-3—Wreck of H.M.S. *Birkenhead*—Colonel Nesbitt drowned—Major Adrian Hope—3rd Battalion raised—4th Battalion raised 60

CHAPTER VI

1st Battalion at Jullundur—At Meerut—Issue of the Enfield Rifle—Discontent in the Native Army—Active insubordination . . 86

CHAPTER VII

Outbreak of the Indian Mutiny at Meerut and Delhi—A column from Meerut marches against the rebels—Actions of the Hindun . . 94

CHAPTER VIII

Advance on Delhi—Action of Budlee-ka-Serai—Occupation of The Ridge—Siege of Delhi—Anniversary of Plassey—Incessant fighting—Arrival of the Siege train—The Rifles reinforced from Meerut 113

CHAPTER IX

Assault on Delhi—Its capture—Award of seven V.C.'s to the Battalion—Comments 140

CHAPTER X

Affairs at Meerut—General position in India—Roorkee field force—Campaign in Rohilcund—Capture of Bareilly—Campaign in Oudh—End of the rebellion—Complimentary order of the Governor General—The Battalion returns to England 160

CHAPTER XI

2nd Battalion moved from Cape Colony to India—Its field operations—The Battalion embarks for China—Capture of the Taku forts and Peking—Winter quarters—The Battalion sails for England . 188

CHAPTER XII

The Rifle Depôt—Changes in Colonels-in-Chief and Colonels Commandant—The 1st Battalion at the Tower of London—Marriage of H.R.H. Prince of Wales—Complimentary order by G.O.C. the Brigade of Guards—The Battalion despatched to Ireland—Sails for Malta—Life in the island—The Battalion sent to Canada—The 2nd Battalion at Aldershot—Moves to Ireland—Fenian outbreak—The Battalion sails for India 214

CONTENTS

CHAPTER XIII

3rd Battalion at Dublin—Sails for India—Quartered in the Madras Presidency—Moves to Burma—Ordered back to Madras—The Battalion at Sea in a Cyclone—Gallant conduct of Ensign Lindesay—Colonel Kennedy in command—Battalion sails for England . 231

CHAPTER XIV

4th Battalion at Winchester—The Civil War in America—The Battalion ordered to Canada—Episode on the S.S. *Trent*—The Fenian movement—Colonel Hawley's principles of battalion training—Return to England 243

CHAPTER XV

H.R.H. George Duke of Cambridge Colonel-in-Chief—Rebellion in Canada—1st Battalion ordered on service—Colonel Garnet Wolseley and the Red River Expedition—A strenuous voyage—Occupation of Fort Garry, the modern Winnipeg—The Battalion returns to Montreal—At Quebec—All British troops withdrawn from the Dominion of Canada—The Battalion at Halifax, N.S.—Embarks for England 260

CHAPTER XVI

The 4th Battalion at Aldershot—Incident at the manœuvres in Salisbury Plain—Termination of Colonel Hawley's command—His subsequent career 290

EPILOGUE

General remarks—Men of note in the book—Conclusion . . . 303

APPENDICES

A. SUMMARY OF REGIMENTAL EVENTS, 1873-1918 . . . 312
B. REGIMENTAL INSTITUTIONS :—Celer et Audax Club—Riflemen's Aid Association—Greenjackets' Cricket Club—The 'Chronicle'—Point-to-Point Races—Ladies' Needlework Guild—The Veterans' Dinner 319
C. BATTLE HONOURS 322

APPENDIX TO VOL. I

i. THE REGIMENTAL ARMY LIST 323
ii. ADDITIONAL NOTES 323

CONTENTS

APPENDIX TO VOL II

		PAGE
i.	BARON FERDINAND VON HOMPESCH	326
ii.	REFERENCES TO THE 60TH, BY A GERMAN COMMISSARY IN THE PENINSULAR WAR	326
iii.	CAPTAIN HORACE B. SEYMOUR	328

INDEX 329

LIST OF ILLUSTRATIONS

PORTRAITS, ETC.

LIEUT.-GENERAL R. B. HAWLEY, C.B.	*Frontispiece*	
LIEUT.-COLONEL THE HON. R. H. MOLYNEUX	*Facing page*	18
LIEUT.-COLONEL THE HON. A. F. ELLIS	,, ,,	26
SIEGE OF MOOLTAN	,, ,,	46
VILLAGES OF PULLEE AND ZOORMUNDEE	,, ,,	50
CENTRE-PIECE IN OFFICERS' MESS OF 1ST BATTALION, REPRESENTING THE CAPTURE OF A FLAG IN EUZUFFZYE COUNTRY	,, ,,	54
GENERAL LORD MELVILLE, G.C.B.	,, ,,	60
COLONEL SIR JOHN JONES, K.C.B.	,, ,,	184

MAPS

THE IONIAN ISLANDS	*page*	31
THEATRE OF OPERATIONS, KAFFIR WAR, 1851–3	,,	41
PLAN OF DELHI	,,	131
NORTHERN INDIA	*facing page*	191
NORTHERN CHINA	,, ,,	213
ROUTE OF RED RIVER EXPEDITION	,, ,,	287

ERRATA

List of Illustrations : The Ionian Islands *should read* page 23.
Page 39, *l.* 11 *from bottom,* Bigham *should read* Bingham.
   ,,   95, *footnote, last line,* Keare *should read* Keane.
   ,,   301, *last line but one,* charm of manners *should read* charm of manner.

LISTS OF THE REGIMENT IN 1830, 1850, AND 1873

1830

COLONELS-IN-CHIEF

FIELD-MARSHAL H.R.H. ADOLPHUS, DUKE OF CAM-
BRIDGE, K.G. . . . . . . Jan. 22, 1827.

COLONELS COMMANDANT

BATT.	NAME.	DATE OF APPOINTMENT.
1.	GENERAL N. C. BURTON	Jan. 9th, 1806.
2.	,, HON. E. PHIPPS	Aug. 23, 1807.

LIEUTENANT-COLONELS

1. THOMAS BUNBURY	Feb. 5, 1824.
2. HON. A. F. ELLIS, M.P.	Dec. 18, 1828.

MAJORS

2. CHARLES CHICHESTER	Aug. 29, 1826.
2. CHARLES SHEE	Oct. 26, 1826.
1. CHARLES LESLIE	Dec. 18, 1828.
1. HON. CHARLES GREY, M.P. . . .	April 23, 1829.

CAPTAINS

1. MELVILLE GLENIE (Bt. Major) . .	Mar. 26, 1812.
1. JOHN STRONGITHARM	Aug. 5, 1813.
2. JOHANN H. ADAIR	Jan. 5, 1824.
2. AMBROSE SPRONG	Nov. 18, 1824.
2. ANDREW ELLISON	Jan. 20, 1825.

LISTS OF THE REGIMENT
CAPTAINS—*continued*.

BATT.	NAME.	DATE OF APPOINTMENT.
1.	JOHN BAXTER CARLOS	April 7, 1825.
1.	JAMES GOLDFRAP	April 9, 1825.
1.	JOSEPH C. S. SLYFIELD	July 21, 1825.
1.	THOMAS R. P. TEMPEST	Dec. 25, 1825.
1.	JOHN CAMPBELL	Dec. 26, 1825.
1.	HON. GEORGE UPTON	Feb. 15, 1826.
1.	WALTER TREVELYAN	April 5, 1827.
2.	CHARLES RAMSDEN	April 12, 1827.
2.	CHARLES MARKHAM	June 7, 1827.
1.	GEORGE BROWNE	Oct. 25, 1827.
2.	ARTHUR, MARQUIS OF DOURO	July 21, 1828.
1.	HON. GEORGE VAUGHAN	Nov. 21, 1828.
1.	COSBY LEWIS NESBITT	Dec. 13, 1828.
1.	HON. GEORGE AUG. SPENCER	Jan. 15, 1829.
1.	GEORGE PIGOTT	Mar. 20, 1829.

FIRST LIEUTENANTS

BATT.	NAME.	DATE OF APPOINTMENT.
2.	MATTHEW FURST	Nov. 4, 1809.
1.	RICHARD PASLEY	Nov. 6, 1809.
1.	PETER EASON	Nov. 4, 1819.
1.	JOSEPH ROBINSON	Nov. 18, 1824.
1.	JOHN S. WILFORD	Dec. 25, 1825.
2.	FRANCIS MARLTON	Dec. 26, 1825.
1.	DAVID FITZGERALD	Jan. 28, 1826.
1.	RICHARD GIBBONS	April 8, 1826.
1.	CHARLES HOWE SPENCE	Sept. 24, 1826.
2.	RICHARD W. CROCKER	April 29, 1827.
2.	WILLIAM KNOX	July 12, 1827.
2.	WILLIAM ANDERSON	Nov. 15, 1827.
1.	JOHN WILLIAM CROSS	Jan. 24, 1828.
1.	CHARLES H. CHURCHILL	May 27, 1828.
2.	WILLIAM TOWNSEND GUNN	July 3, 1828.
	FREDERICK F. L. DAYROLLES	Feb. 5, 1829.
	EDWARD WELCH EVERSLEY	Mar. 20, 1829.
	THOMAS NEALE BRUERE	May 14, 1829.
	GEORGE ARMSTRONG	May 15, 1829.
	ALEXANDER, VISCOUNT FINCASTLE	July 9, 1829.

LISTS OF THE REGIMENT

SECOND LIEUTENANTS

Batt.	Name.	Date of Appointment.
2.	Jonathan Greetham	Jan. 5, 1826.
1.	George Budmam	April 5, 1826.
1.	John Reynolds Peyton	April 9, 1826.
2.	Charles Orgell Leman	April 12, 1826.
2.	Robert Atkins	Aug. 24, 1826.
1.	Martin E. Howarth	Sept. 28, 1826.
1.	James St. J. Munro	Mar. 29, 1827.
2.	Henry Bingham	April 30, 1827.
1.	Samuel Brelsford	Aug. 25, 1827.
2.	Alfred Mundy	Nov. 1, 1827.
2.	Spencer Percival Plumer	Nov. 15, 1827.
2.	Francis Jessop	Jan. 23, 1828.
1.	Thomas Bunbury	Jan. 23, 1828.
2.	Thomas Townsend	Jan. 24, 1828.
1.	William H. Fitzgerald	Jan. 30, 1828.
2.	Hon. Theodore D. G. Dillon	Aug. 28, 1828.
1.	William E. Thompson Corbett	Nov. 24, 1828.
1.	Richard Clarell Bingham	Nov. 25, 1828.
1.	William F. Bedford	Dec. 18, 1828.
1.	Hon. Henry L. Powys	April 2, 1829.
2.	Henry W. Ellis	May 14, 1829.
1.	Hon. George Byng	June 25, 1829.

ADJUTANTS

*1.	Samuel Brelsford	Aug. 25, 1827.
2.	Thomas Townsend.	Jan. 24, 1828.

PAYMASTERS

2.	Henry Higgs	Oct. 22, 1812.
*1.	Edward Coxen	Feb. 9, 1826.

QUARTERMASTERS

1.	Jonathan Booth	May 4, 1826.
2.	John Ottley	Mar. 20, 1828.

* Fought in the Peninsula and at Waterloo.

xviii   LISTS OF THE REGIMENT

1851

COLONEL-IN-CHIEF

FIELD-MARSHAL H.R.H. PRINCE ALBERT, K.G.,
ETC. . . . . Aug. 15, 1850.

COLONELS COMMANDANT

BATT.	NAME.	DATE OF APPOINTMENT.
1.	LIEUT.-GENERAL SIR WILLIAM G. DAVY, K.C.H.	Nov. 2, 1842.
2.	,, SIR W. CORNWALLIS EUSTACE, K.C.H.	April 7, 1843.

LIEUTENANT-COLONELS

1.	COLONEL THE HON. SIR HENRY DUNDAS, K.C.B..	
2.	LIEUT.-COLONEL C. L. NESBITT	July 26, 1844.
1.	,, JOSEPH BRADSHAW, C.B.	Aug. 27, 1841.

MAJORS

1.	BT. LIEUT.-COLONEL M. G. DENNIS	May 2, 1845.
1.	MAJOR C. H. SPENCE	Oct. 20, 1848.
2.	,, JOHN JONES	July 20, 1849.
2.	,, W. F. BEDFORD	Oct. 12, 1849.

CAPTAINS

1.	HENRY BINGHAM	June 25, 1841.
1.	HON. H. LYTTLETON POWYS	Aug. 17, 1841.
1.	F. R. PALMER	Mar. 11, 1842.
2.	J. K. MCKENZIE	April 23, 1842.
1.	WEBBE BUTLER	July 26, 1844.
1.	JAMES DOUGLAS	Sept. 20, 1844.
2.	HON. A. HOPE	Dec. 20, 1844.
1.	H. J. DARELL	Jan. 12, 1844.
2.	C. W. H. SOTHEBY	Aug. 14, 1846.
1.	W. J. YONGE	July 10, 1846.
1.	R. F. W. SIBTHORP	Mar. 5, 1847.
2.	DOUGLAS JONES	Jan. 23, 1848.
2.	A. MOSLEY	Feb. 25, 1848.
1.	H. F. KENNEDY	Oct. 20, 1848.
1.	C. N. NORTH	Dec. 28, 1848.

LISTS OF THE REGIMENT

CAPTAINS—continued.

Batt.	Name.	Date of Appointment.
1.	J. F. Jones	Aug. 26, 1849.
2.	G. W. Bligh	Oct. 12, 1849.
1.	A. C. Meik	May 29, 1849.
2.	G. Rigaud	Aug. 16, 1850.
1.	Sir Edward F. Campbell, Bart.	Dec. 27, 1850.

FIRST LIEUTENANTS

1.	G. Clapcott	Mar. 31, 1843.
2.	S. Kenny	July 26, 1844.
2.	E. H. Rose	July 26, 1844.
2.	P. B. Roe	July 26, 1844.
2.	W. P. Salmon	July 26, 1844.
2.	J. Fraser	July 26, 1844.
2.	J. Warburton	Sept. 20, 1844.
1.	W. Hutchinson	April 26, 1844.
2.	R. J. Feilden	Feb. 25, 1845.
1.	D. D. Muter	Jan. 17, 1845.
1.	H. F. Williams	Dec. 20, 1844.
1.	J. A. McQueen	June 6, 1845.
1.	C. A. B. Gordon	June 13, 1845.
1.	J. Maguire	July 4, 1843.
2.	H. E. Warren	June 20, 1843.
1.	A. Fitzgerald	Feb. 13, 1846.
1.	A. H. Mercer	Nov. 1, 1842.
1.	F. A. St. John	Mar. 5, 1847.
1.	F. Andrews	Dec. 19, 1847.
1.	Francis Dawson	June 7, 1847.
1.	L. C. Travers	June 22, 1847.
1.	J. P. Battersby	June 28, 1848.
1.	J. L. E. Baynes	Feb. 25, 1848.
1.	B. Ward	May 5, 1848.
1.	V. Tongue	Dec. 28, 1848.
2.	R. H. Robinson	July 20, 1849.
2.	A. C. Greville	Aug. 26, 1849.
2.	R. W. Brooke	Oct. 12, 1849.
2.	R. Freer	Dec. 13, 1849.
1.	F. C. Fletcher	Aug. 16, 1850.

LISTS OF THE REGIMENT

FIRST LIEUTENANTS—continued.

Batt.	Name.	Date of Appointment.
2.	E. Bowles	Aug. 16, 1850.
1.	R. J. E. Robertson	Dec. 27, 1850.

SECOND LIEUTENANTS

Batt.	Name.	Date of Appointment.
2.	C. W. Earle	Dec. 24, 1846.
1.	T. Nicholson	June 22, 1847.
1.	G. Clark	Aug. 1, 1846.
2.	W. Mure	Oct. 22, 1847.
2.	J. Du Cane	Nov. 5, 1847.
1.	Conyngham Jones	Feb. 25, 1848.
1.	W. Tedlie	May 5, 1848.
2.	B. V. S. Vernon	Sept. 12, 1848.
2.	H. J. Robertson	Oct. 20, 1848.
2.	H. Cockburn	Nov. 10, 1848.
1.	G. B. McQueen	Mar. 9, 1849.
2.	H. P. Montgomery	Aug. 21, 1849.
2.	F. Fitzpatrick	Sept. 11, 1849.
1.	H. Semple	Oct. 19, 1849.
1.	R. W. Hinxman	Nov. 23, 1849.
1.	T. S. Richardson	Jan. 18, 1850.
2.	Hon. G. B. Legge	Jan. 18, 1850.
2.	C. C. Hale	Feb. 15, 1850.
2.	H. M. Jones	April 10, 1850.
2.	W. W. Fox	Feb. 14, 1851.
2.	C. D. C. Ellis	Jan. 17, 1851.
2.	W. H. Jones	May 15, 1851.
2.	A. C. J. Liddele	May 16, 1851.
2.	C. Williamson	July 11, 1851.
2.	A. H. Gregory	Aug. 19, 1851.
2.	F. S. Travers	Aug. 20, 1851.

ADJUTANTS

Batt.	Name.	Date of Appointment.
2.	S. Kenny	May 9, 1843.
1.	J. Maguire	June 2, 1849.

QUARTERMASTERS

Batt.	Name.	Date of Appointment.
1.	T. Berry	Mar. 29, 1842.
2.	R. Power	May 28, 1847.

LISTS OF THE REGIMENT

1873

COLONEL-IN-CHIEF
FIELD-MARSHAL H.R.H. GEORGE, DUKE OF CAMBRIDGE, K.G.

COLONELS COMMANDANTS

BATT.	NAME.	DATE OF APPOINTMENT.
1.	GENERAL G. F. VISCOUNT TEMPLETOWN, K.C.B.	Oct. 24, 1862.
2.	,, VISCOUNT MELVILLE, G.C.B.	April 1, 1863.

LIEUTENANT-COLONELS

4.	ROBERT B. HAWLEY (Colonel).	May 18, 1860.
3.	PETER B. ROE (Colonel).	Sept. 18, 1860.
1.	CHARLES C. B. GORDON.	Aug. 9, 1871.
2.	GIBBES RIGAUD.	April 21, 1872.

MAJORS

1.	HENRY F. WILLIAMS (Bt. Lieut.-Colonel).	Oct. 28, 1864.
2.	ALFRED J. FITZGERALD.	Jan. 24, 1865.
1.	ROBERT J. E. ROBERTSON.	May 29, 1869.
3.	HUGH P. MONTGOMERY.	Nov. 10, 1869.
3.	WILLIAM TEDLIE (Bt. Lieut.-Colonel).	April 9, 1870.
4.	CHARLES WILLIAMSON.	Aug. 9, 1871.
4.	WYKEHAM L. PEMBERTON.	Oct. 28, 1871.
2.	ROWLEY W. HINXMAN.	April 24, 1872.

CAPTAINS

1.	F. D. FARQUHARSON.	April 24, 1858.
1.	J. D. DUNDAS (Bt. Major).	June 22, 1858.
2.	H. H. DEEDES (Bt. Lieut.-Col.; A.A.G. Bengal).	July 2, 1858.
4.	J. J. COLLINS.	July 19, 1859.
	A. CARLISLE.	May 3, 1860.
1.	F. V. NORTHEY (Bt. Major).	May 18, 1860.
2.	W. F. CARLETON.	Sept. 18, 1860.
3.	C. ASHBURNHAM.	Jan. 23, 1863.
3.	K. G. HENDERSON.	June 30, 1863.
3.	E. C. AINSLIE.	Mar. 1, 1864.
2.	J. S. ALGAR.	May 17, 1864.
1.	C. G. KELLY.	Oct. 6, 1864.
3.	C. C. WILLOUGHBY.	Oct. 18, 1864.
4.	F. H. HAMILTON.	Nov. 1, 1864.
4.	H. R. MILLIGAN.	Nov. 22, 1864.
3.	GEORGE HATCHELL.	Jan. 24, 1865.

xxii LISTS OF THE REGIMENT

CAPTAINS—continued.

Batt.	Name.	Date of Appointment.
	J. K. Watson	May 1, 1865.
2.	W. G. Byron	Jan. 3, 1865.
1.	W. J. Poole (S. Aldershot)	April 3, 1866.
2.	N. J. Pauli	June 5, 1866.
1.	W. L. K. Ogilvy (S. Colchester)	Dec. 11, 1866.
3.	H. St. G. Barton	Mar. 8, 1867.
1.	J. O. Young	July 6, 1867.
2.	W. N. Manners	Sept. 17, 1867.
4.	R. H. Beadon	Oct. 16, 1867.
4.	A. Tufnell, A.D.C.	Oct. 23, 1867.
2.	J. Charley	Aug. 14, 1867.
1.	A. F. Terry	Dec. 8, 1867.
1.	J. G. Crosbie	May 20, 1868.
2.	G. H. Trotman	Jan. 11, 1869.
1.	N. W. Wallace	Jan. 23, 1869.
3.	A. Morris	April 24, 1869.
1.	E. H. Ward	May 20, 1869.
1.	C. M. Calderon	Feb. 9, 1870.
4.	R. H. Buller (S.C.)	May 28, 1870.
3.	C. P. Cramer	May 28, 1870.
2.	L. C. Brownrigs	April 20, 1871.
4.	J. H. Croft	Aug. 9, 1871.
4.	F. W. Grenfell	Oct. 28, 1871.
2.	A. A. Kinloch (Staff)	May 8, 1870.
	A. V. O'Brien	April 24, 1872.
2.	C. L. de Robeck (A.D.C.)	April 24, 1872.

LIEUTENANTS

2.	C. G. Fryer	Oct. 6, 1864.
3.	W. Warren	Nov. 22, 1864.
1.	P. J. Barne	June 12, 1863.
1.	G. T. Whitaker	Jan. 24, 1865.
4.	G. Carpenter	Jan. 31, 1865.
1.	R. C. Robinson	Feb. 7, 1865.
2.	G. L. Farmer (A.D.C.)	Mar. 7, 1865.
2.	E. W. Crofton	May 2, 1865.
3.	D. Bingham	May 26, 1865.
4.	J. T. D. Crosbie	Dec. 1, 1865.

LISTS OF THE REGIMENT

LIEUTENANTS—*continued*.

Batt.	Name.	Date of Appointment.
1.	F. H. Baillie	Mar. 30, 1866.
4.	W. Cowan	April 3, 1866.
1.	F. C. Coulson (A.D.C.)	June 26, 1866.
4.	H. Donald Browne	Aug. 14, 1866.
1.	E. L. Fraser	Aug. 21, 1866.
2.	R. Chalmer	Feb. 21, 1866.
3.	H. R. Lindesay	Oct. 2, 1866.
1.	Hon. A. F. Coventry	Nov. 27, 1866.
2.	W. Tilden	Dec. 11, 1866.
2.	H. B. MacCall	Feb. 19, 1867.
3.	B. Frend	Feb. 27, 1867.
2.	A. H. Bircham	Mar. 8, 1867.
4.	J. W. Finch (A.D.C.)	Mar. 15, 1867.
2.	H. A. Ward	Aug. 7, 1867.
2.	Hon. C. R. Howard	Aug. 7, 1867.
3.	P. A. Hope Johnstone	Nov. 6, 1867.
1.	A. F. Mitchell Innes	Nov. 20, 1867.
3.	C. L. Allen	Dec. 25, 1867.
2.	W. Forster	April 6, 1868.
4.	A. Pepys	April 10, 1868.
1.	R. C. Davies	June 24, 1868.
3.	A. R. Whetham	July 20, 1867.
3.	H. P. Wylie	Oct. 28, 1868.
3.	J. B. Price	Jan. 11, 1869.
1.	F. J. Wood	Jan. 23, 1869.
3.	C. Holled Smith	Feb. 3, 1869.
1.	H. S. Marsham	Feb. 17, 1869.
2.	T. S. Clarke	April 24, 1869.
3.	E. H. Thurlow	May 29, 1869.
1.	J. A. Williams	Nov. 10, 1869.
2.	A. A. Phipps	Jan. 5, 1870.
1.	Hon. K. Turnour	Feb. 9, 1870.
1.	J. H. Burstall	May 28, 1870.
3.	A. G. Bagot	Dec. 14, 1870.
1.	H. S. Riddell	Jan. 4, 1871.
1.	H. Hope Edwardes	Mar. 22, 1871.
2.	T. P. Lloyd	Nov. 29, 1864.
2.	F. B. Dickenson	June 12, 1871.

LISTS OF THE REGIMENT

LIEUTENANTS—continued.

Batt.	Name.	Date of Appointment.
4.	E. T. Hutton	Aug. 9, 1871.
1.	F. W. Archer	Aug. 9, 1871.
1.	H. Walpole	Oct. 27, 1871.
3.	J. D. Howden	Nov. 30, 1871.
4.	C. Michell	Oct. 28, 1871.
2.	A. J. Brander	Oct. 28, 1871.
3.	H. E. Fetherstonhaugh	Oct. 28, 1871.
4.	F. M. Ward	Oct. 28, 1871.
3.	C. R. Thorne	Oct. 28, 1871.
2.	C. Hope	Oct. 28, 1871.
4.	R. S. Fetherstonhaugh	Oct. 28, 1871.
3.	G. Astell	Oct. 28, 1871.
2.	H. P. Okeden	Oct. 28, 1871.
1.	N. E. Fenwick	Oct. 28, 1871.
1.	W. H. Holbech	Oct. 28, 1871.
2.	W. S. Anderson	Oct. 28, 1871
2.	F. A. Beauclerk	Oct. 28, 1871.
3.	C. W. Archer	Oct. 28, 1871.
3.	H. Allpey	Oct. 28, 1871.
3.	C. S. Cotton	Oct. 28, 1871.
1.	H. L. Farmer	Oct. 28, 1871.
1.	R. Henley	Oct. 28, 1871.
4.	A. G. Martin	Oct. 28, 1871.
1.	M. C. Boyle	Oct. 28, 1871.

SUB-LIEUTENANTS

Batt.	Name.	Date of Appointment.
1.	H. R. Mends	Dec. 30, 1871.
4.	M. C. F. Walker	Mar. 6, 1872.
2.	A. P. Vaughan	May 29, 1872.
4.	G. G. Grimwood	July 24, 1872.
4.	H. Vere	Oct. 5, 1872.

PAYMASTERS

Batt.	Name.	Date of Appointment.
2.	F. FitzPatrick (Hon. Major)	Mar. 2, 1855.
4.	E. C. Grant (Hon. Major)	Dec. 28, 1855.
3.	C. H. Hignett	May 10, 1871.

ADJUTANTS

Batt.	Name.	Date of Appointment.
4.	H. D. Browne	May 17, 1871.
3.	A. H. Bircham	June 8, 1867.
2.	R. Chalmer	Nov. 10, 1869.
1.	H. S. Marsham	Nov. 17, 1869.

REGIMENTAL SUCCESSION OF COLONELS-IN-CHIEF, COLONELS COMMANDANT, AND LIEUTENANT-COLONELS, 1830–1873

COLONELS-IN-CHIEF

NAME.	DATE OF APPOINTMENT.
H.R.H. ADOLPHUS, DUKE OF CAMBRIDGE	Jan. 22, 1827.
H.R.H. THE PRINCE CONSORT	Aug. 15, 1850.
GENERAL VISCOUNT BERESFORD	Sept. 23, 1852.
H.R.H. GEORGE, DUKE OF CAMBRIDGE	Mar. 3, 1869.

COLONELS COMMANDANT

GENERAL N. C. BURTON	Jan. 3, 1806.
,, THE HON. E. PHIPPS	Aug. 25, 1807.
MAJOR-GENERAL SIR J. MACLEAN, K.C.B.	Jan. 7, 1835.
LIEUT.-GENERAL THE HON. P. STUART	Sept. 26, 1837.
,, SIR W. G. DAVY, K.C.H.	Nov. 2, 1842.
,, SIR W. C. EUSTACE, K.C.H.	April 7, 1843.
,, T. E. BUNBURY, K.C.H.	Feb. 9, 1855.
,, SIR W. G. MOORE, K.C.B.	Jan. 26, 1856.
,, J. PATERSON	April 14, 1857.
GENERAL VISCOUNT TEMPLETOWN, C.B.	Oct. 24, 1862.
LIEUT.-GENERAL VISCOUNT MELVILLE, K.C.B.	April 1, 1863.

LIEUTENANT-COLONELS

1st Battalion

THOMAS BUNBURY	Feb. 5, 1824.
HON. H. R. MOLYNEUX	April 24, 1835.
J. S. SLYFIELD	May 24, 1841.
WALTER TREVELYAN	Aug. 10, 1841.
HON. H. DUNDAS, C.B. (afterwards Viscount Melville, K.C.B.)	1844.

SUCCESSION OF LIEUTENANT-COLONELS

LIEUTENANT-COLONELS—*continued*.

1st Battalion— continued.

NAME.	DATE OF APPOINTMENT.
HON. G. A. SPENCER	Dec. 20, 1844.
JOSEPH BRADSHAW	1845.
M. G. DENNIS	Oct. 19, 1851.
J. JONES	June 20, 1854.
H. BINGHAM	1861.
R. J. FEILDEN	Mar. 1, 1864.
C. A. B. GORDON	Aug. 9, 1871.

2nd Battalion

HON. A. F. ELLIS	Dec. 18, 1828.
CHAS. C. MARKHAM	Aug. 17, 1841.
W. T. COCKBURN	April 23, 1842.
C. L. NESBITT	July 26, 1844.
C. H. SPENCE	Oct. 2, 1853.
F. R. PALMER	June 23, 1858.
WEBBE BUTLER	Sept. 9, 1858.
G. RIGAUD	April 24, 1872.
H. P. MONTGOMERY	Aug. 13, 1873.

3rd Battalion

W. F. BEDFORD	Mar. 23, 1855.
H. BINGHAM	June 19, 1857.
WEBBE BUTLER	1860.
P. B. ROE	Sept. 18, 1860.
H. F. KENNEDY	Nov. 22, 1869.
P. B. ROE	1873.

4th Battalion

E. J. VESEY BROWN	1858.
W. PRETYMAN	April 29, 1859.
R. B. HAWLEY	May 18, 1860.

N.B.—The occasional repetition of a name in two different Battalions is due to the fact that up to the year 1865 the establishment for units in India allowed two Lieut.-Colonels. Thus, H. Bingham was appointed as second-in-command to the 3rd Battalion in 1857 and C.O. of the 1st Battalion in 1861.

SYNOPSIS OF CONTEMPORARY EVENTS

1830, June	Death of George IV., accession of William IV.
Aug.	Abdication of Charles X. of France. Election of Duke of Orleans as Louis Philippe, King of the French.
1832, Mar.	First Parliamentary Reform Act in England.
1833, May	Separation of Belgium from Holland.
1837, June	Death of William IV., accession of Queen Victoria.
1840, Dec.	The remains of the Emperor Napoleon transferred from St. Helena and buried in 'Les Invalides,' Paris.
1845, Dec.	1st Sikh War in India.
1848, Feb.	Abdication of Louis Philippe.
Dec.	Prince Louis Napoleon elected President of the French Republic.
	Insurrectionary movements in Italy, Austria, Prussia, etc.
1852, Sept.	Death of the Duke of Wellington.
Dec.	Louis Napoleon proclaimed Emperor of the French.
1854, Mar.	France and England at war with Russia.
1856	Peace of Paris.
1857, May	Outbreak of Indian Mutiny.
1859, June	France and Northern Italy at war with Austria. Their victory at Solferino.
1861	Consolidation of Italy.
1861	Outbreak of Civil War in America.
1864	Schleswig-Holstein ceded to Germany by Denmark.
1865, April	Civil War in America ended by the surrender of the Southern States.
1866, June, July	Austria defeated by Prussia at Koniggrätz and excluded from the German Confederation.
	Second Parliamentary Reform Act in England.

1870, July . . War between France and Germany.
Deposition of Napoleon III. Italian troops occupy Rome. Adoption of 'Short Service' in the British Army.
1871 . . . Treaty of Peace under which Prussia secures Alsace and part of Lorraine in addition to an Indemnity of £200,000,000.
Suppressions of the Commune in Paris.

THE KING'S ROYAL RIFLE CORPS

CHAPTER I

COLONELS COMMANDANT

BEFORE continuing our narrative of the Regimental History it may be well to give some explanation of the term 'Colonel Commandant,' which, so far as infantry regiments are concerned, is now confined exclusively to the Rifle Brigade and Ourselves.

In the old Royal Army of France a regiment belonged to an individual termed 'Le Colonel Propriétaire,' whose business it was to clothe, pay, and administer the affairs of the regiment in general. It sometimes happened, however, that this person was unequal to the exercise of executive command; or, for that matter, may have had no military knowledge at all. In such a case it was customary to appoint a professional soldier who exercised actual command, under the title of 'Colonel Commandant,' which denoted the fact that his presence was of a temporary nature only. In the British Army very much the same system held good, and when the 'Colonel Propriétaire,' who in our Army was merely termed 'Colonel,' was deficient in the necessary experience, or otherwise engaged, a Colonel (or on occasion Captain) Commandant was appointed to assume executive command. Thus in 1695 we find from 'Dalton's Commission Regiments,' Volume 4,

Page 57, the following: 'Galway's Horse. D'Aubermorgnes to be Colonel commanding,' while a foot-note explains that this officer commanded the Regiment in Lord Galway's absence.[1]

Although the English word 'Commanding' was occasionally used it was more often displaced by its French equivalent 'Commandant.' In 1756 the Royal American Regiment was raised for service in North America. Each of the three Regiments of Foot Guards and the Royal Scots Regiment had at least two battalions, but every other regiment of the Line consisted of one battalion only. The fact of the 60th being composed of no less than four battalions was a new departure.[2] It was felt that one Colonel could not exercise all the functions of his office over so large a body of men. The title Colonel-in-Chief was therefore invented, in order that (as in the rest of the Army) a single officer should exercise general superintendence over the whole regiment; while four others were appointed under him, one to each battalion, and given the title Colonels Commandant. These four officers in effect exercised nearly all the functions usually associated with the office of Colonel, but the choice of a Firm to act as Regimental Agent has always been made by the Colonel-in-Chief. An additional reason for their appointment lay in the fact that the four battalions of our regiment were not only designed for permanent service out of England, but would, in addition, almost certainly be distributed over large tracts of country far apart from one another. The first Colonel-in-Chief of

---

[1] Lord Galway was not a sham soldier, but on the contrary a very fine General, a pupil of the great Turenne; for he was a Frenchman, a Huguenot, who had come to England after the Revocation of the Edict of Nantes and had been made a Major-General in the British Army.

[2] With one exception. Prior to the birth of the Royal American a regiment of four battalions had been raised. Curiously enough it also bore the numeral 60th, but was very soon disbanded.

the 60th was, as has been shewn, Major-General the Earl of Loudoun. The Colonel Commandant of the 1st Battalion was John Stanwix; of the 2nd, Joseph Dusseaux; of the 3rd, Charles Jefferys, and of the 4th, James Prevost; and there is evidence to show that at the outset they not only paid, clothed, and administered, but actually commanded their respective battalions; the other field officers being one Lieut.-Colonel and one Major per Battalion. At the end of a year or two it happened, however, that all four Colonels Commandant were made Brigadier-Generals; and, being thus removed from their Battalions, command of the latter naturally fell to the Lieut.-Colonel, an arrangement which has held good ever since.

A little later in the eighteenth century double battalion Regiments became more common in the British Army, and it was the practice to appoint a Colonel Commandant for the second of the two battalions; but, excepting in the case of the 60th, the practice did not, as regards the Infantry, survive the Peace of Amiens in 1802.

In 1800 the 95th Regiment (at the present day known as the Rifle Brigade), under the Colonelcy of General Coote Manningham, was formed. In 1805 it received a 2nd Battalion, and in 1809 a 3rd Battalion; but during Manningham's life that officer alone bore the title of Colonel, and exercised its duties over all three battalions. On his death, General Sir David Dundas, the Commander-in-Chief, determined to place the Regiment on the same footing as the 60th, whose 5th Battalion was at that period serving under Wellington in Spain and Portugal.

General Dundas evidently thought that the 95th Rifles, which had recently joined Wellington's army, would, like the 60th, be split up and dispersed among its

Brigades. He accordingly wrote the following letter to the Secretary of War :—

'Horse Guards, 1st September, 1809.

'MY LORD,—In consequence of the death of Major-General Manningham the command of the 95th Rifle Regiment has become vacant, and as it is at present composed as follows, viz. 3 battalions . . . and is the description of force continually called for and usually obtainable in small detachments. I have to inform your Lordship, that under these circumstances . . . His Majesty has been pleased to approve that each battalion should be handed to a separate Colonel, one battalion being ample for one Colonel, but all representatives to be similar to the Colonels Commandant of the 60th Regiment and the whole to be placed under the command of a Colonel-in-Chief, the latter without pay or emolument.

'I have the honour, etc.,

'(*Signed*) DAVID DUNDAS.

'To the Rt. Hon. Secretary at War.'

It so happened that Sir David Dundas himself became the new Colonel-in-Chief of the 95th, but it was not until he had resigned the office of Commander-in-Chief that he received an emolument of fourteen shillings per day, as the pay of his office.

It also happened that when in 1809 the 95th joined Wellington's Army the battalions sent were maintained intact; and one reason for the creation of its Colonels Commandant disappeared. Nevertheless the main principle laid down by Dundas that the performance of a Colonel's duties should be limited to one battalion was in itself sufficient reason for accepting his suggestions. In 1815, when the Rifle Regiments were each reduced to two battalions, the number of Colonels Commandant was proportionately diminished. When, after the Crimean War, the 3rd and 4th Battalions of each Regiment were re-raised no further Colonels Commandant were at first made, and it was not until about the year 1903 that the number of Colonels Commandant was raised to four per Regiment. In the interval administrative powers had been taken out of the Colonel's hands and his duties had in consequence almost entirely died away. Since 1877 the duties of the Colonel-in-Chief or Colonel Commandant have been almost nominal and purely of an honorary character.

At the moment of writing (1924) there is some reason to believe that the Army Council intends to utilise the services of regimental Colonels and of Colonels Commandant to a greater extent, but time alone can show whether such intention will be carried out. In our own Regiment for some years past certain duties have been actively performed by the Colonels Commandant to the great advantage of the Corps. They have taken a leading part in the administration of the funds of our branch of the Riflemen's Aid Association, in that of the Celer et Audax Club, with its manifold committees, and have invariably presided at the annual dinner of the Veterans' Association. To this number must be added the very important and indeed sometimes arduous work of sifting the qualifications of the many applicants for commissions in our regiment, and of submitting to H.M. the Colonel-in-Chief the names which appear to be the most suitable in the long list.

These examples, which might easily be multiplied, serve to indicate that nowadays the position of Colonels Commandant is the reverse of being a sinecure.

Possibly through ignorance of its historical derivation the Army Council has now also conferred the title of Colonel Commandant on the Commander of a Brigade.

Inception of Regimental Records

On November 9, 1922, a Circular Letter was forwarded by the Adjutant-General, Horse Guards, to O.C. regiments and battalions, instructing them to compile and forward to him the records of their unit since it was originally raised.

Of this letter the O.C. our 2nd Battalion took no notice, but in the 1st Battalion the Commanding Officer (presumably Lieut.-Colonel Alexander Andrews, or, in his absence through illness, Lieut.-Colonel J. F. FitzGerald, C.B.) took the matter in hand by writing the following :—

'MEMORANDUM—RECORDS OF 60TH RIFLES

'Copy of a Circular to be addressed to the undermentioned officers :—

'Major-General :   Edward Codd.[1]
'   ,,   G. Mackie, C.B.[1]
'Lieut.-General :   Baron de Rothenberg.
'Colonel :   Sir William Williams, K.C.B.
'Major-General :   Sir John Kearn, K.C.B.
'Colonel :   W. G. Davy.

'Having it in command from His Royal Highness the Duke of York, Colonel-in-Chief of the 60th Rifle Corps, to have the history of the Regiment recorded, and particularly that of the late 5th, now the 1st Battalion 60th Rifles : I beg to observe that in order to comply with H.R.H.'s intentions I find it necessary to collect such documents as can be procured from those who have served in the different Battalions, and who from their rank and abilities are most capable of affording such information.

'May I therefore request that you would have the goodness to favour me with a short detail of such occurrences, actions, and testimonials (specifying the dates of such as you may deem most important) to forward the views of His Royal Highness.'

Instructions to the person appointed to write and transmit the letters in question.

'In the letter addressed to Baron de Rothenburg he will be requested to state *when*, where, and under what circumstances the 5th or Rifle Battalion was *first raised*, and the nature of their

[1] These General Officers are still shown in the regimental lists as Lieut.-Colonels (supernumerary).

services whilst under his command, with any observations he may be pleased to afford concerning the nature and usefulness of Rifle men, and of Jägers in the foreign service.

'In that to Colonel Davy :—

'He will be requested to give any general information about the Regiment, with the particular service of the 5th Battalion whilst under his command in the Peninsula, with also copies of any orders or other testimonies of their gallant conduct.

'And the same in those addressed to Sir Wm. Williams and to Sir John Keane.

'When General Codd is written to, he may be required to state the services of the different Battalions he has been in, particularly in the West Indies or North America; and General Mackie the same.

'Captain Leslie during his absence will use every endeavour to collect information by taking notes and extracts from public despatches, histories of North America, etc.' [1]

The draft of this Circular is not signed or dated, and although addressed to persons in a position to give full historical information, the results, judging from the exiguous entries in the battalion, 'History of Services' were very small and unsatisfying.

[1] Captain Charles Leslie was author of a work called 'A Military Journal.' It would appear that he compiled the earlier pages of 'The History of Services of the 1st Battalion'; and it is possible that it was while collecting historical information that he met Major Patrick Murray, and received from that officer the narration of events in the American War of Independence, which forms the subject of Appendix I. in Vol. I., p. 288, of these Annals.

CHAPTER II

THE Annals of the Regiment were carried in Vol. II. to the date on which William IV. was pleased to confer on the 60th its present title ' The King's Royal Rifle Corps.' Fifteen years had passed since the termination of the war with France ; and a rather longer period was destined to elapse before the Regiment was again called on for active service. A lengthened period of peace may have great results in strengthening the bonds of discipline, improving the system of interior economy, and numberless other matters, important not only in themselves but as a preparation to future service in the field ; but it does not as a rule call for any prolonged notice on the part of the historian, even though members of the Regiment may, as individuals, perhaps distinguish themselves in the field of politics, art, or science.

In regard to politics, Colonels J. F. FitzGerald and the Hon. A. F. Ellis entered the House of Commons ; but the incident which will excite most interest at the present time is the fact that in 1830 Major the Hon. Charles Grey, a Major in the 60th, contested the Borough of High Wycombe with Benjamin Disraeli and defeated his illustrious opponent. In days prior to the Reform Act of 1832 constituencies were small. After a poll lasting several days the votes were found to have been cast, for Grey 20, for Disraeli 12. The whole number of voters in the Borough was only 34. In later years Major Grey became a General Officer and Private Secretary to Queen Victoria, in which capacity he was brought into confidential relations with his erstwhile adversary, and ever felt the highest regard and admiration for him.

Among other notable persons serving at this period in our Regiment was the Marquis of Douro, elder son of the Duke of Wellington. He joined the 1st Battalion as a Captain in 1828 and quitted it in 1830, when the battalion went abroad.

2

We left the 1st Battalion at Gibraltar. During the period of its stay at that fortress the 'History of Services' is silent. One incident not entirely devoid of interest has, however, been preserved. It would appear that two Officers of the Battalion, Lieutenant J. W. Cross and 2nd Lieutenant J. St. J. Munro, while absent on a few days' leave were captured by brigands near Algeciras. Their further adventures are described in the following official letter from Munro to his Commanding Officer:—

'Gibraltar, 26th December, 1831.

'Sir,—I have the honor to inform you that on the morning of the 24th inst., after the departure of Lieutenant Cross for Gibraltar, Blaydes and myself were taken by the Robbers to a thatched hut on the brow of a hill on the opposite side of the river in the centre of the Sierra de Cassares, not more than a quarter of a mile from the road, where they kept us prisoners till seven o'clock, the owner of the house being apparently in league with them, as he cooked their dinners, etc., etc. As soon as it was dark they made us mount our horses and follow them across the river; then followed the course of the road by keeping along the plough'd fields, avoiding all the Farm Houses. At this time the robbers were twenty in number, all well mounted and armed; two rode on each flank of us to avoid our escaping. We halted after riding two hours, about a mile to the north of the Ford on the road to Manilva, where they bivouacked on the top of a strong mountain, making us sleep on the ground with no covering. During the night scouts were continually coming in, and they had an established system of Sentries. An hour before daylight they made us ride back part of the road till we arrived at the bed of a stream opposite to the Venta, where we remained until Lieut. Cross arrived with money, when the Chief (who styled himself and was addressed by his Band) "José Maria" galloped up, and told them to return everything, which they did but partly, and then trotted off in the direction of the Sierra Bermeza, leaving us to pick up our guns and a few clothes. They appeared much afraid about Troops coming from Algeciras and consulted frequently by themselves what they should do with us, when some who were more savage than "José Maria" we overheard voted for killing us, and escaping without waiting for the money. They treated us indifferently, giving us only some bad bread and our horses only one feed of Barley during the four and twenty hours we were with them; they increased in numbers in the morning to twenty-four, and José Maria on leaving us cautioned us not to speak about them at the Ventas on the Road as he had eight of his men watching us between him and San Roque. During the whole time we were with them they frequently drew their knives across our throats and levelled their guns at us, swearing if Cross did not come alone, or did not arrive by 12 o'clock, they would cut our throats, as it made less noise than shooting us. José Maria is a very short thick-set man with black whiskers, and very light brown eyes, and has great control over his gang, by whom he is much dreaded. He has with him a young Son, who he boasts has already killed twenty-two soldiers besides others. I could swear to any one of the gang. who are all a most rascally looking set of fellowes. José Maria said he saw me buying a hat in a shop at Ronda and was informed of our Road and departure by a young man at the Rasade de las Aminas, and that he had been lying in wait twenty-four hours for us. He kept Cross' and my watch, besides various other things.

    'I have the honor to be, Sir,
     'Your most obedient humble Servant,
      '(*Signed*) W. J. MUNRO,
       '2nd Lieut. 1.60 Rifles.

'Lieut.-Colonel Bunbury,
 'Comm. 1st Batt. 60th King's R.R. Corps.'

3

In October 1834 the Battalion proceeded to Malta, the voyage occupying just six weeks. In the following year General Burton died and was succeeded as Colonel Commandant by Major-General Sir John McLean, who had served under the Duke of York in the expedition to the Helder in 1799, in Egypt under Sir Ralph Abercromby in 1801, and in the Peninsula throughout almost the whole of the campaigns, although not in our Regiment.

In April of the same year Lieut.-Colonel Bunbury, K.H., who had commanded the Battalion for eleven years, exchanged to the 67th Regiment with Lieut.-Colonel the Hon. Henry R. Molyneux, receiving for the exchange no less than £3,500, a sum the whole of which it is said he lost at the first subsequent race-meeting which he attended! Colonel Molyneux assumed command at the St. Elmo Barracks in November.

It will be remembered that at this time the Ionian Islands belonged to Great Britain, either by conquest in the wars with France or by cession at the peace of 1814. In 1836 the 1st Battalion, having been broken up into six Service and four Depôt Companies, embarked for Corfu, and was quartered in the Citadel; but within four months was removed to the Island of Vido, with a view to assisting in the construction of its fortifications, for the British Government had decided that Vido was in future to be the *place d'armes* of the whole island group. In April of the following year it returned to Corfu and was quartered at the Port Raymond Barracks. During January 1838 three Companies were detached to the Island of Zante, and a Subaltern and 43 O.R. were sub-detached thence to the Island of Cerigo, where several

Riflemen distinguished themselves in saving life on the occasion of the wreck of a brig off the Island.

In March of the same year Headquarters proceeded from Corfu to Vido and a few weeks later to Zante. In September the Battalion was still further split up; the three companies at Vido being relieved by our 2nd Battalion, which had recently arrived, and distributed in small detachments among Paxo, Ithaca, and Santa Maura.

In August, 1839, the Battalion was augmented to an establishment of 800 R. and F., distributed as follows:—

6 Service Companies, consisting of 24 Sergeants, 10 Buglers, 600 O.R.
4 Depôt　　,,　　　　,,　　　16　　,,　　4 F.　200 ,,

Such information as the writer has been able to glean of the Battalion's visit to the Ionian Islands [1] was given him by the late Major G. H. Courtenay, who was present with the Battalion at the time and survived till 1914, when he died at the age of ninety-eight. Among other things which he mentioned was the fact that the 'Huntsmen's Chorus' was then known as the 'Yäger Call.' He also mentioned incidentally that it was customary for young Officers to carry knapsacks on the march.

The period spent in the Ionian Islands has always been described as delightful. The Battalion at this time consisted of very young soldiers, and one man who was regarded as a Methuselah and commonly known as 'old Ryan' was in reality only thirty years of age.

Among the Officers who served with the Regiment in the Mediterranean were Randal Rumley, Arthur Cunynghame, Freeman Murray, afterwards Colonels Commandant; Walter Trevelyan, John Jones (known in the Indian Mutiny as the Avenger), Henry Bingham, all of

---

[1] The Ionian, sometimes known as the Seven, Islands (viz. Corfu, Cephelonia, Zante, Santa Maura, Ithaca, Cerigo, and Paxo) were handed over by Britain to Greece in 1864.

1839] ADOPTION OF THE MESS JACKET 13

whom later on commanded the 1st Battalion; Charles Markham, Francis Palmer, Webbe Butler, C. L. Nesbitt, future Commanders of the 2nd Battalion, Sam Nichols, whom some of us remember more than half a century later as Master of the Hursley Hounds, William Bedford, subsequently Colonel of the 3rd Battalion. Adrian Hope, son of the famous General Sir John Hope and himself highly distinguished a few years later in the Crimea and Indian Mutiny, were also in the Regiment, so were Thomas Guy Gisborne, who attained some note as a composer of songs, and Hudson Lowe (son of the notorious Sir Hudson), who later on became a Barrister. Of the Peninsular veterans three only remained—Slyfield, Adair, and Richard Pasley.

Major Courtenay spoke well of the two Commanding Officers, Colonels Molyneux and Ellis. The former he compared to the President of a Republic, the latter to a benevolent autocrat. Colonel Molyneux did a great deal of good work, giving particular attention it would appear to the better preparation of the men's meals and to the establishment of schools for their education. The regimental officers in general seem to have had a reputation for reading. There was a considerable Irish element in the Battalion, and the best N.C.Os. were as a rule Irishmen, being socially of a comparatively high class.

It was during this period that the Mess Jacket was introduced. At dinner officers had previously worn their full-dress jackets buttoned up. In the Ionian Islands the jackets worn in this way became uncomfortably hot. They were therefore unbuttoned and a waistcoat introduced, a custom which, although opposed at the time by higher Military Authority, gradually spread to the remainder of the Army. The large plume of cock's feathers worn in the shako was found to be top heavy and very inconvenient, more particularly during manœuvres in extended order.

4

In 1840 the Battalion was ordered home, and Colonel Molyneux being absent on leave, Headquarters and three Companies under the command of Major W. T. Cockburn embarked on April 17, and after landing at Portsmouth were joined by the four Depôt Companies there stationed. On June 15 Colonel Molyneux rejoined. On the 26th the Battalion proceeded by sea to Woolwich, which was reached on July 2. The three remaining Companies which had quitted Vido on May 20 reached Woolwich on July 9, and were sent on detachment to Deptford under command of Major Cockburn.

On July 30 the Battalion was inspected by Lieut.-General Lord Bloomfield, G.O.C., Woolwich, and the following letter, written by him to the A.G. Horse Guards, is taken from the regimental record of service in the War Office :—

'Woolwich, 31st July, 1840.

'My Dear Macdonald,
  'It is a most agreeable duty to transmit the enclosed copy of an Order issued in this Garrison yesterday, and called forth by the movements referred to.
  'I have seen all the Armies of Europe, and do not hesitate to aver that more efficiency in the peculiar Arms of this Corps I have not met.
  'I pray you to lay this before Lord Hill with the expressions of my high respect.
                    'Yours most sincerely,
                         '(*Signed*) Bloomfield.
'Lieut.-General Sir John Macdonald.'

Enclosure

Garrison Order by Lieut.-General Lord Bloomfield, G.C.B., G.C.H.

'Woolwich, 30th July, 1840.

'Lieut.-General Lord Bloomfield assuring Lt.-Colonel Molyneux of his unqualified approbation and high commendation at the general appearance and steadiness of the 1st Battalion King's Royal Rifles in the field yesterday, cannot adequately convey his gratification at their several movements, which did not fail to impress on the Lieut.-General's mind a conviction of the admirable instruction given and established, and which was evidenced by the zeal, intelligence, and rapidity with which the Lieut.-Colonel's intentions were executed by his Battalion. The Lieut.-General begs to offer his best thanks to all.

'*(Signed)* BLOOMFIELD, Lt.-General.' [1]

In August the Battalion was inspected by its Colonel-in-Chief, H.R.H. The Duke of Cambridge; and a few days later proceeded to Windsor to be reviewed by H.R.H. Prince Albert. During January 1841 the Battalion was re-armed with the Brunswick percussion rifle. In October the whole of the Officers dined by the invitation of their Colonel-in-Chief at Cambridge House. This entertainment may perhaps have led to the introduction a few years later of our Annual Regimental Dinner.

To the deep regret of all ranks Colonel Molyneux died in London on May 23, and was buried at St. George's Chapel, Windsor. He was certainly a great C.O., and the traditions of his period of command, although not very definite, lingered for many years after his death. Colonel Molyneux had the advantage of the aid of Thomas Mitchell, who held the appointment of Adjutant from 1835 to 1844, and in 1842 published a small volume on the ' System of

---

[1] It will be noticed that Lord Bloomfield does not allude to the Regiment by its numeral, which may very possibly have not been in general use at the time. Since its official abolition in 1881 the numeral has been more frequently used than had previously been the case.

Light Drill,' based on the previous works of Colonels de Rothenberg and Charles Leslie.

Colonel Molyneux was succeeded by Major J. S. Slyfield from the 2nd Battalion; but Slyfield never assumed command, for in August he died of yellow fever on the voyage from Jamaica, and Major Walter Trevelyan became Lieut.-Colonel.

In the middle of July the Battalion proceeded to Manchester, where it was broken up into detachments, two Companies being quartered at Bolton, two at Wigan, two at Blackpool, two at Burnley, and one each at Colne and Liverpool. Not until May of the following year was it re-concentrated at Manchester. In consequence of riots which were taking place in the Potteries two Companies, under Major Wilford, proceeded on July 19 to Newcastle-under-Lyne. Other disturbances broke out in various places in Lancashire and Cheshire, and the Battalion was again broken up into detachments for the restoration of order. In April, 1843, it was once more concentrated at Manchester.

Meanwhile our Colonel Commandant, Sir John McLean, had in the previous November been transferred to another Regiment. He was succeeded by Lieut.-General Sir William Gabriel Davy, C.B., K.C.H., whose name will be remembered as commander of the 5th Battalion at Roliça, Vimieiro, and Talavera.

The further stay of the Battalion at Manchester was short. On May 8 it embarked for Dublin, where three Companies under Major Wilford were quartered at Pigeon House Fort, and two under Brevet-Major Temple at Beggar's Bush Barracks; while Headquarters and the remaining eight Companies marched to Newbridge, but on the 29th were brought back to Dublin and quartered in Richmond Barracks. Here a few weeks later they were inspected by Lieut.-General Sir Edward Blakeney, K.C.B., Commander of the Forces in Ireland.

In November two Companies under Major Wilford were detached to Naas.

By January 24, 1844, the Battalion had been completed up to its establishment, viz. 800 R. and F. Recruiting parties were therefore called in with the exception of one left at Aberdeen and another at Swansea with the object of filling future vacancies.

In the first days of March the Battalion quitted Dublin and was broken up as follows: Headquarters and four Companies including the two from Naas were stationed at Kilkenny; three at Waterford; one each at New Ross, Carrick-on-Suir, and Castle Conor.

CHAPTER III

TOWARDS the end of September 1830 the 2nd Battalion, quitting the Isle of Wight, marched to Weedon. Here it remained for about a fortnight, en route for Carlisle. Its destination was, however, altered to Manchester, where it arrived in the first days of November.

The stay of the Battalion at Manchester was marked by a remarkable and unfortunate incident. On April 12, 1831, it had taken part in a Field Day at Kersall Moor. On returning home one Company, commanded by Lieutenant P. S. Fitzgerald, which was on detachment at the Salford Barracks, crossed the Suspension Bridge at Broughton. As the head of the Company reached the bridge the men broke step, but just at this moment some one began to whistle a march tune, whereupon, as if by word of command, the whole Company recovered step. It was soon noticed that the bridge began to vibrate, the vibration increasing as the greater number reached it. The head of the Company had, however, nearly reached the Pendleton side of the river when a loud noise, resembling a continuous discharge of musketry, was heard, and one of the iron pillars on the near side of the bridge broke; whereupon the roadway bolt on losing its support naturally fell into the river which flowed some sixteen or eighteen feet below, carrying with it the greater part of the Riflemen. But a few, including the Officers, though thrown to the ground, were able to scramble up and reach

LIEUT.-COLONEL THE HON. R. H. MOLYNEUX.

the further bank. The Company consisted of 74 Officers and men, of whom over 40 were precipitated into the water or thrown with great violence against the side chains of the bridge. The river fortunately happened to be hardly four feet deep; and the men were able either to wade to the bank or scramble up the inclined plane formed by the chains and the fallen roadway. Four were badly hurt and a large number of the remainder suffered from con tusions.

The Riflemen were marching with arms slung; but a certain number of rifles and swords were lost in the river. Curiously enough, the bridge had been constructed by Lieutenant Fitzgerald's father.

This account is taken from the 'Manchester Guardian' of April 16, 1831, and the 'Manchester Chronicle' of the 12th. The former states that no life was lost. On the other hand the War Office Book of Casualties at the Public Record Office gives the names of ten Riflemen who were killed. Which of these contradictory accounts is correct can hardly be now ascertained; but the writer has found several entries in the W.O. book chronicling the death of individuals who at the date of entry were unquestionably alive.

On December 27 the Battalion embarked for Dublin, where it was quartered at the Royal Barracks. In July 1832 Nos. 3 and 5 Companies under Major Slyfield marched from Dublin to Balbriggan, and the remainder of the Battalion was distributed as follows :—

No. 1. Company at Rathanagan and Allen.
No. 2. ,, ,, Dunlavin.
No. 7. ,, ,, Athy.
No. 8. ,, ,, Maryborough.
No. 10. ,, ,, Baltinglass.
Headquarters with Nos. 4, 5, and 6 to Templemore via Naas.

On August 3 Nos. 3, 5, and 9 Companies under command of Major Thornhill marched for Nemagh.

The detachments appear to have constantly changed stations; but in the middle of August 1833 the Battalion was once more concentrated in Dublin; in the first instance at the Royal Barracks, afterwards at Beggar's Bush, Pigeon House Fort, St. George's Barracks, and Portobello.

Early in May 1834 the Battalion again quitted Dublin, Headquarters and Nos. 1, 2, 3, 5, 8, 9, 10 Companies being ordered to Mullingar, No. 4 to Castletown Delvin, No. 6 to Killucan, and No. 7 to Tullamore.

The stations continued to undergo frequent changes; but early in March 1834 the Battalion was concentrated at Buttevant, where it was organised in six Service and four Depôt Companies. On the 26th the former, viz. Nos. 1, 2, 6, 7, 9 and 10, marched for Cork, the Depôt Companies, Nos. 3, 4, 5 and 8, being left at Buttevant under Major Slyfield.

The Service Companies now received orders to sail for St. Helena and the Cape of Good Hope; but in August the destination was changed for Gibraltar. Nos. 1 and 8 Companies, under command of Captains Spong and Rumley, sailed on October 26, reaching Gibraltar on November 11. Headquarters, consisting of Nos. 2, 6, 7, and 10 Companies, under command of Lieut.-Colonel Ellis, sailed on December 18, landing at Gibraltar on January 10, 1836. Officers present with the Battalion in addition to the Colonel were Captains Spong, Rumley, Nesbitt, Johnson, and Knox; Lieutenants Fitzgerald, Arthur Cunynghame,[1] Everard, and Levitt; 2nd Lieutenants Brandling, Weston, Butler, Jebb, Phipps,

---

[1] Lieutenant Cunynghame is better known as General Sir Arthur Cunynghame, Colonel Commandant in 1876.

the Hon. J. E. Thurloe, Lieutenant and Adjutant Townsend, Paymaster Odell, Quarter-Master Brannan, Surgeon Leigh, Assist. Surgeon Maurice.

2

No record remains of the period spent at Gibraltar, which was probably uneventful. On October 24, 1837, after a complimentary Order from Major-General Sir Alexander Woodford, the Battalion embarked for Corfu, where it arrived in the following November.

At Corfu, as already mentioned, the 1st and 2nd Battalions joined hands, this being the first occasion they had met since 1802, when both were at Tobago. On four subsequent occasions the two Battalions have come together, viz. at Benares in 1858, at Dublin in 1866, at Aldershot for the Jubilee Review in 1887, and in 1914 also at Aldershot.

The stay of the 2nd Battalion in the Ionian Islands was partly made at Corfu, partly at Vido, with small detachments at Fano, Paxo, and a few other islands. As already noticed, it had been decided to construct elaborate fortifications at Vido, and to quote the words of the Record of the Battalion, 'The service of the troops became of a very multifarious and extended nature, furnishing the aforesaid detachment as well as artificers for the public works in Corfu and Vido together with the ordinary duties of the garrison.' In April 1840 Nos. 6 and 9 Companies were detached to Santa Maura.

In October 1840 orders were received to proceed to Jamaica, but the embarkation did not actually take place until March 11, 1841, when the Battalion, about 530 strong, under command of Colonel Ellis, sailed from Corfu in the *Apollo* troopship, the remaining officers present being Major Slyfield, Captains Nesbitt, Hamilton, Stuart, and Munro, Lieutenants Levett and Beresford, 2nd Lieutenants Wood, Hon. Adrian Hope, Sibthorpe, and A. R. Saunders, Adjutant Townsend, Paymaster Fitzgerald, Quarter-Master Brennan, Assistant-Surgeons Maurice and Richardson.

Port Royal, Jamaica, was reached by the Battalion on June 4, and on its arrival the 82nd Regiment, which had lost its C.O. and 140 men from yellow fever, was moved by sea to Maroontown, a healthy station on the northern side of the island. The G.O.C., Sir William Gomm, fully realising the danger of allowing a regiment newly arrived in the hot weather to remain on the low ground, desired to send the Riflemen up to the Blue Mountains. As a hill station he had selected Newcastle, situated at a height of 4,000 feet above the sea. The Generals had made many representations to the Horse Guards as to the criminal folly of quartering troops in a district infected with yellow fever, and—after great difficulty—had got leave to erect hutments for one Company at Newcastle. He felt that men would, however, be better off even under canvas in the hills than in barracks on the plains, but curiously enough was thwarted by the medical authorities, who may perhaps have feared the effect of having men in tents during the approaching rainy season.

The Rifle Battalion arrived in good health. No. 3 Company made up to 130 strong was sent to Newcastle under Captain Nesbitt; but the rest of the Battalion was quartered in the neighbourhood of Kingston on the low ground; Headquarters and Nos. 1, 6, and 10 Companies being stationed at Stony Hall; Nos. 7 and 9 under Major Slyfield at Fort Augusta. Within three weeks 70 out of 90 men at this Fort were struck down by yellow fever.

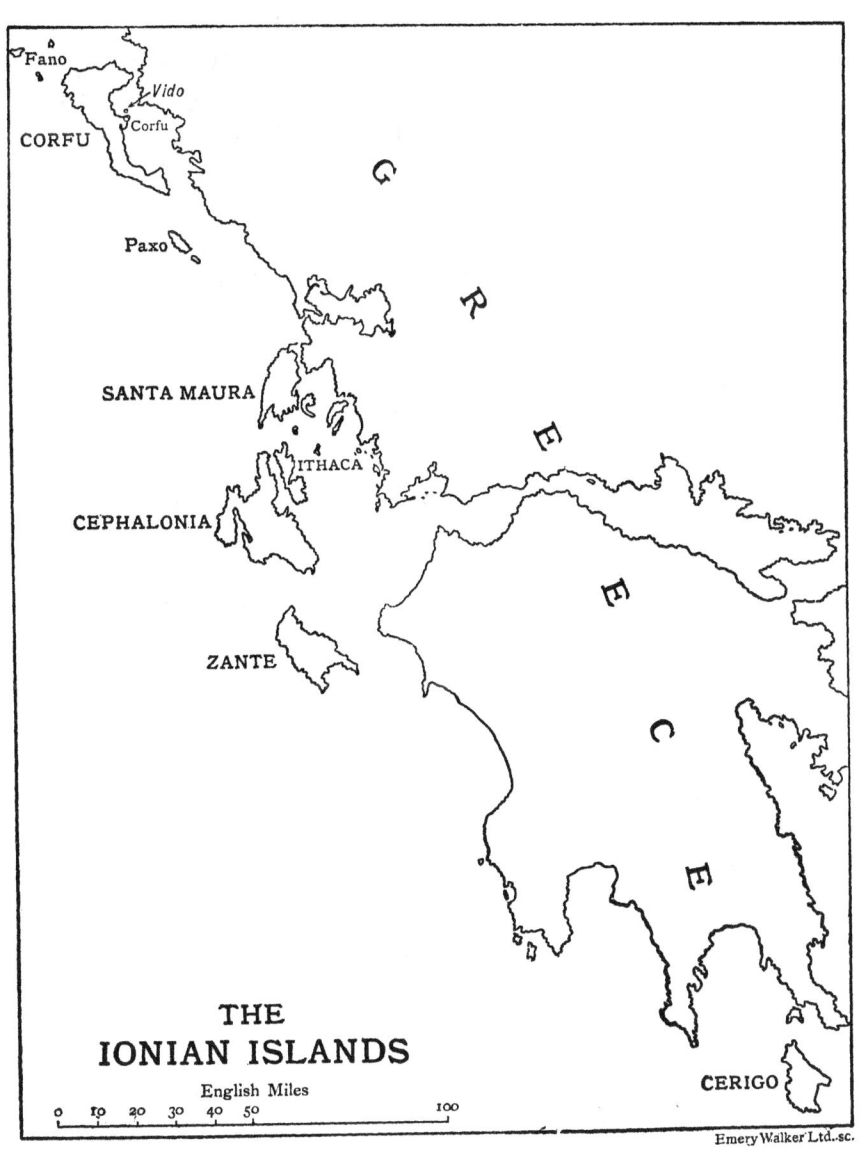

By July 1, 37 Riflemen were dead. A fortnight later the figure was raised to 60.

Sir W. Gomm now insisted on having his own way. But before the remainder of the battalion could be sent to the hills preparations were necessary and delay occurred. Writing on August 9 to Lord FitzRoy Somerset (afterwards Lord Raglan), Military Secretary at the Horse Guards, the General states that the mortality amounted to upwards of 100 : entirely from the 400 men quartered in the plains, for the detachment at Newcastle had incurred no fever.

During the whole of this terrible time Colonel Ellis had never spared himself. He had ridden daily in the hot sun from station to station, visiting the numerous detachments, cheering up the sick in hospital, and doing everything in his power to accelerate the removal of his Battalion to the hills. Early in August the Battalion was entirely at Newcastle and neighbourhood ; but 140 men, 8 or 10 women, and several children had already died. On the 11th the Colonel took up his abode in the hills ; this exertion had unhappily undermined his strength. On the very day following he was attacked by fever and died shortly afterwards.

Of Colonel Ellis, Adrian Hope wrote as follows :—

'Since the arrival of the Regiment in Jamaica it had been very sickly and we had lost a very large number of men. During this time the Colonel's exertions had been unremitting to promote the health of the soldiers and to prepare more healthy quarters for them.

'He was always to be met riding in the sun to visit one or other of his detachments, and hardly a day passed that he did not spend some time in the Hospital endeavouring to raise the spirits of the patients. In fact his only thoughts were for his regiment. In the beginning of August the men were all removed to the mountains, where they were quartered in the coffee plantations ; and on the 11th the Colonel himself went to reside in the Governor's House on the plantation of Middleton belonging to the Agent of his father, Lord Seaford. He then appeared in perfect health, though much hurried and excited. Next morning he was attacked by fever and sent off immediately for Dr. Ferguson, the first Medical Man in Kingston. On the 13th I saw him, when he appeared flushed and in some pain. He spoke quietly, asked me some questions connected with duty, and gave some orders about Court Martial.

'On the 14th he was considered a little better. On the 15th a change took place, but he himself expressed great confidence of recovery. In the afternoon he sent for Capt. Nesbitt, senior Officer, but his mind wandered and he could not explain himself. On the 16th he died, and was burried in St. Andrews Church Yard. The Bishop read the Service.

'His loss will long be felt by this Regiment and all who knew him.'

Writing on August 19 Sir William Gomm remarked:—

'We are already beginning to reap great advantages from our measures, when all heads have been suddenly bowed over the Bier of him who was the warmest and most active friend, and deservedly the pride and idol of his Corps.'

The General followed up his letter by a touching General Order.

Colonel Ellis might have returned to England and assumed command of the 1st Battalion, vacant by the death of Colonel Molyneux, but had decided to remain at what he felt was the post of danger. Major Slyfield was therefore promoted in place of Molyneux, and quitted Jamaica a few days before the death of Colonel Ellis. But in that island he too had contracted the seeds of yellow fever, and died at St. Thomas's on the voyage home.

The total loss of the 2nd Battalion from fever amounted to 2 Officers, 173 other ranks, 10 women and many children: about 33 per cent. of its strength.

But Riflemen have a wonderful power of recuperation. In the autumn a draft from the Depôt arrived, and the General reporting to the Military Secretary on December 7, shows :—

'The best health possible continues to prevail among the troops stationed in the mountain quarters of this island, while sickness of a contagious character is general in the towns and over the plains on both sides of it. The whole of the 60th, numbering 474 in the ranks, are now established at Newcastle. . . . I made a half-yearly inspection of the Corps this morning, and it would have delighted Lord Hill (C.-in-C. at the H.Q.) to note the healthy and thoroughly English appearance of these men after all that has so recently passed over them.'

3

Major C. L! Nesbitt assumed command of the Battalion. In consequence of a disturbance which had taken place at Kingston 300 men of the Battalion under command of Major Nesbitt proceeded on December 28 from Newcastle to Up Park Camp. In the opinion of Sir William Gomm, the General, the circumstances of the case appeared to warrant special approval.

'Kingston, Jamaica, 12th January, 1842.

'The 60th Rifles were at their appointed station at Up Park Camp six hours after receiving the order to leave Newcastle, behaved themselves with the greatest spirit and propriety while in the low ground, and returned to their quarters in the mountain under the command of Capt. Giffard in five hours from station to station, without leaving one man sick and without a defaulter or straggler. An opportunity like that just afforded them was wanted to complete the soldierlike character of the 60th and establish the merits of the mountain station.

'(*Signed*) W. TURNOR, D.A.G.'

LIEUT.-COLONEL THE HON. A. F. ELLIS.

Godfrey Rhodes, at that time a Subaltern in the Regiment, writes of this period as follows :—

'On December 30th, 1841, I embarked for Jamaica with a large draft of ten or twelve officers and 300 men, under command of Lieut.-Colonel Charles Markham.

We encamped on the Newcastle Estate Government Plantation, some 4,000 ft. above sea-level, and out of range of the yellow fever. By degrees the men constructed log huts thatched with long grass and wattle and mud walls, but the officers were for a long period under canvas. Shingle-roofed houses were by degrees constructed by the authorities. The Officers and men were chiefly employed in road making (6 ft. wide only) and constructing huts. The heat never exceeded 80 degrees ; the nights were cool.

'Humming birds built their nests in the coffee-trees. Rock-pigeons were abundant, also ground grouse ran about the roads and ravines, while strawberries grew on the higher hill called St. Catherine's. The coffee trees were cropped twice a year, in April and October. The flowers were white and fragrant. Orange trees were on the hills and produced fruit in abundance.

'Transport for all provisions and materials was on pack mules.'

On January 17, 1842, Lieut.-Colonel Charles Markham, having arrived, assumed command of the Battalion, but died on April 22. Major Nesbitt had by this time returned to England, for his promotion had been into the 1st Battalion, and the temporary command devolved on Major Crombie.

On December 23, 1842, a still larger detachment of the Battalion under Major Crombie marched from Newcastle to Up Park Camp in aid of the Civil Power, and again elicited a Complimentary Order from the G.O.C.

On January 30, 1843, Lieut.-Colonel W. T. Cockburn assumed command. In April the Battalion received the Brunswick Rifle and Swords. In May it was completed to its full establishment, 800 rank and file, of whom 540 were allotted to the Service Companies and the remainder to those of the Depôt.

On August 26 a dangerous fire broke out at Kingston, and the Battalion was sent down thither from Newcastle at a moment's notice. The G.O.C., Major-General Berkeley, congratulated the Battalion on the speed with which it had arrived on the spot and ensured the safety of the city for the night, relieving the 2nd West India Regiment, which was exhausted by its exertions. 'It is satisfactory to the Major-General,' continued the Order, 'to perceive that the usual character of this Corps for discipline and celerity already shown in this command on more than one instance has been fully sustained on this occasion.' A few days afterwards the Battalion returned to Newcastle. The Civic Authorities also expressed their thanks, stating that had it not been for the unceasing exertions of the Regiment the fire would have consumed the greater part of the city. They subscribed $1,000 to be distributed among the troops, but this mark of appreciation was declined with thanks, it being felt that the money would be better spent in relieving the necessities of those whose houses had been burnt to the ground.

On March 28, 1844, the Battalion, in pursuance of orders from the Commander-in-Chief, sailed for Quebec, reaching Halifax on April 25, and disembarking at Quebec on May 17, where they were quartered in the Citadel Barracks.

On February 27, 1845, Lieut.-Colonel Nesbitt arrived and took command of the Battalion in the place of Colonel Cockburn, who retired from the Service. In September the Battalion moved into the Jesuit Barracks. In May 1845 the Battalion was moved from Quebec to St. John's, Canada East. During this year we again come upon the name of De Rottenburg: a son of the General having joined the Battalion.

In July 1846 the Battalion proceeded from St. John's

to Montreal; and the following month to Quebec, en route for Halifax, N.S., where it arrived on August 29.

Early in May 1847 the Battalion embarked in H.M.S. *Vengeance* for England, the list of Officers present being as follows: Lieut.-Colonel C. L. Nesbitt, Major Crombie, Captains Robinson, McKenzie, Holbech, and Mansel, Lieutenants Bligh and Feilden, 2nd Lieutenants Aldworth, Payne, Galton, Dawkins, and Greville, Paymaster Fitz-Gerald, and Quartermaster Brannan. The *Vengeance* reached Portsmouth Harbour on June 5; and the Battalion having disembarked proceeded to Chichester, where the Service and Depôt Companies were once more amalgamated.

During the period of Foreign Service the three Depôt Companies had had varied experiences, having been quartered in turn at Buttevant, Clare Castle, Jersey, Portsmouth, Clonmel, Naas, Dublin, Newry, Belturbet, Stirling, Dundee, Aberdeen, Paisley, and Chatham. Its tour in Scotland from May 21, 1844, until May 25, 1846, is the only period spent in that country by any part of our Regiment. On May 18, 1847, the Depôt proceeded to Chichester awaiting the arrival of the Service Companies.

CHAPTER IV

On June 4, 1844, an order was received by the 1st Battalion to prepare for service in India. As a consequence 369 volunteers, including 38 from the 2nd Battalion, and 47 from the Rifle Brigade, joined from other corps in order to bring the Battalion up to the Indian establishment, which consisted of 2 Lieut.-Colonels, 2 Majors, 10 Captains, 20 1st Lieutenants, 10 2nd Lieutenants, 1 Paymaster, 1 Surgeon, 3 Assistant do., 1 Adjutant, 1 Quartermaster, 58 Sergeants, 21 Buglers, and 1,000 Riflemen. Of these the Paymaster, Edward Coxen, had fought in the 95th Rifles at Waterloo.

On June 9 the Battalion received a route for Fermoy, where it arrived a few days later. On July 1 the Battalion was formed into 1 Depôt and 3 Service Companies. The Depôt was to be quartered at Chatham.

In the same month Colonel the Hon. Henry Dundas, C.B., half-pay 83rd Regiment and previously of the Coldstream Guards, having exchanged with Colonel Trevelyan, took command of the Battalion. During the rebellion in Canada he had seen what amounted to active service, and had become a Brevet-Colonel in 1841.

In consequence of the augmentation to the Indian establishment considerable promotion took place among the officers. Major Nesbitt became the 2nd Lieut.-Colonel; Captain Rumley (nearly 40 years later a Colonel Commandant) became Major; Lieutenant Webbe

Butler, Captain: and no less than 11 2nd Lieutenants received the rank of Lieutenant; their places, says the 'History of Services,' being taken by the appointment of 'young gentlemen' to the regiment as 2nd Lieutenants.

About this time Lieut.-Colonel Cockburn resigned command of the 2nd Battalion, and Major the Hon. G. A. Spencer was appointed his successor. But Colonel Nesbitt, being Spencer's senior, claimed the right to command that battalion: and the matter being referred to the Duke of Wellington, Commander-in-Chief, the Duke allowed Nesbitt's claim. Spencer therefore remained in the 1st Battalion as its second Lieut.-Colonel.

On August 7 a rifle competition took place for the gold medal offered by the C.O. It was won by Rifleman Alexander Geddes of D Company, but his score and other particulars are not known.

During the second week of August two Companies marched for Cork; but notwithstanding their absence the remaining Companies paraded over 1,000 strong for the farewell inspection of the Battalion by the C.-in-C. in Ireland, Lieut.-General Sir Edward Blakeney, a distinguished Peninsular veteran, who expressed deep regret at losing the Battalion from his command.

But after all the Battalion did not at once embark. The condition of Ireland was so much disturbed that it could not be spared. The two advance Companies returned from Cork to Fermoy, and the Battalion was reformed into 10 Companies. A half company, consisting of 2 Subalterns, 3 Sergeants, a Bugler, and 40 Riflemen, was despatched to Michelstown.

Meanwhile the transports had sailed for India with a large quantity of plate belonging to the Regiment and Officers' Mess on board. Whether it was ever recovered does not appear.

In May 1845 Lieut.-Colonel Joseph Bradshaw of the 37th Regiment exchanged with the Hon. G. A. Spencer, and joined our Battalion as second in command. Bradshaw's career was cut short by his untimely death a few years later, but Captain G. Bliss McQueen, his sole surviving brother officer (June, 1924) describes him as 'a first-rate soldier, the ideal of a Rifleman, good drill, smart, always well mounted, and very liberal.' On June 1 the Battalion was once more broken up into 1 Depôt and 9 Service Companies. It marched a few days afterwards, in detachments to Cork, where it embarked for India. On the Sunday previous to embarkation the Riflemen attended Divine Service as usual. The name of the officiating clergyman is lost to posterity, but one sentence of his sermon has been handed down: 'My bones,' observed he, in a passage which must have given great comfort to his hearers, 'will repose in the tombs of my ancestors; yours, my brethren, will be strewn along a foreign shore.'

No less than five transports were occupied by the Battalion, of which one, the *Neptune*, became dismasted in a heavy gale off Mozambique Channel (Lat. 39° 30′ S.; Long. 43° 20′ E.), some hundreds of miles south-west of the Island de Réunion, where half a century later the same Battalion was wrecked in the *Warren Hastings*. On October 6 the *Neptune* succeeded, not without difficulty, in putting into the island of Mauritius. The detachment on board, commanded by Colonel Bradshaw, landed and did garrison duty until the 5th of the following month, when it again embarked for Bombay, where Battalion Headquarters had arrived in the *Stebon Heath* on October 15. From Bombay Headquarters marched to Poona, which was reached on November 1, the other Companies gradually arriving at that station by the end of the year. This was the first Rifle Battalion to arrive in India; the first also in which promotion went through the whole regiment; a fact which seems to have disturbed the military authorities, who had hitherto been accustomed to single battalion regiments only.

The story of this voyage reminds us of many occasions on which the 1st Battalion has met with misfortune at sea; misfortune that has sometimes been shared by its drafts or detachments on their way to join Headquarters. The draft which sailed in 1848 was shipwrecked between Bombay and Karachi. In the following year the Captain of the *Aboukir*, conveying another draft, mistook the lantern of a fishing-boat for that of the Bombay lightship, and ran his vessel on to the dangerous rocks stretching out from the harbour, known as the South-West Prongs. The night was happily fine and the sea calm, for the ship made a heavy list to starboard, and the crew seizing the boats made off, abandoning the Riflemen to their fate. One old boatswain, an ex-man-of-war's man, alone remained on board. At the first shock the Riflemen had quitted their hammocks and a few got into the rigging; but on being recalled by Lieutenant Francis Dawson (an officer of little more than five years' service, but the senior on board) fell in on deck with the remainder of the draft. Despite the difficulty of standing upright, the men—most of them, both officers or other ranks, undrilled boys—were perfectly steady. Not a word was spoken. They were told off in sections to different parts of the ship, and settled down manfully to their allotted tasks. All were eventually taken off in safety. During the voyage the above-named boatswain had treated the Riflemen with unfailing abuse in his choicest naval language; but when all was safe he came up to Dawson as he was about to leave the vessel, saying, ' Well, Sir, I have always abused the soldiers on the voyage out, but I have been an old bluejacket myself, and I must say there is nothing like *The Royals* after all. They are to be depended on for work.'

When the Battalion came back to England in 1860 the voyage was marked by no special incident, but must have been intensely wearisome, for it occupied no less than 140 days.

Its next voyage on return from foreign service took place in December 1877. The Battalion was coming home from Halifax, N.S., in H.M.S. *Tamar*. No casualty occurred, but the weather was terrible.

In 1890 the Battalion embarked for India on the troopship *Crocodile*, which broke its main shaft in the Indian Ocean and had to be towed into Bombay by the *Serapis*.

In 1897 Headquarters with four Companies of the Battalion proceeding to Mauritius from the Cape of Good Hope in the *Warren Hastings* were wrecked on the Réunion Island.

Nevertheless, despite this remarkable succession of naval disasters it does not appear that any Rifleman lost his life.

2

At the time when the 1st Battalion landed in India, Lord Hardinge, the Governor-General, had need to keep a watchful eye in many directions. Several of the Provinces were in a condition of unrest, and lack of discipline was manifest in a considerable proportion of the native regiments. But the most pressing danger was on the side of the Punjaub, that large triangular tract of country watered by the five rivers which gave the state its name, viz. Indus, Jhelum, Chenab, Ravi, and Sutlej, and occupied by a warlike race of Hindoos known as Sikhs. This country, which was not directly under British rule, had been governed by a strong man named Runjit Singh, termed the 'Lion of the Punjaub,' who clearly understood the strength of British power. But on his death in 1839 a succession of weak rulers were murdered by the Sikh army, which, in view of recent disasters to our arms in Afghanistan, believed itself capable of defeating the British Army.

In December 1845 the Sikh army, 60,000 strong with 150 guns, under command of Lal Singh, crossed the Sutlej, and although worsted in the subsequent battles of Moodkee and Ferozeshah, such loss had been inflicted on the 20,000 men comprising the Indo-British Army under Sir Hugh Gough that with difficulty it maintained its ground in the Punjaub.

On January 24, 1846, despite its very recent arrival in India, our Battalion received orders to hold itself in readiness for immediate service in the field. On the 29th it accordingly marched out of Poona; embarked on February 6 at Panwel, and on the 11th landed at Karachi in Lower Scinde. Colonel Dundas having taken command of all the troops there collected, Lieut.-Colonel Bradshaw assumed that of the Battalion.

'The Army of the Indus,' consisting of 17,000 men and 100 guns under command of the celebrated Major-General Sir Charles Napier, a pupil of Sir John Moore and a most brilliant soldier, pushed forward in boats up the Indus at Mittencote, and our Battalion was on the point of entering the Sikh country at the territory of the Nawab of Mooltan, when news arrived that the victory of Sobraon gained by Sir Hugh Gough and Sir H. Hardinge on February 10 had terminated the war.[1] The Army of

[1] By the terms of the peace treaty the Sikh country south and west of the Sutlej was annexed to the British dominions.

the Indus was thereupon broken up, and the European portion returned to Karachi, whence it was the intention of Sir Charles Napier to recall it in the possible event of further operations.

In June a terrible outbreak of cholera made its appearance : the Battalion lost about 80 men, and of the European population of Karachi one-seventh part was carried off by this disease. As early as the month of May the Depôt left at Poona had marched to Bombay, but on receiving news of the cholera it remained there and did not rejoin Headquarters until October 10.

On January 5, 1847, the Battalion was inspected by Sir Charles Napier.[1] Any one who has studied the life of that very distinguished man must realise his intense affection for the British soldier, and anxiety for his welfare. At the end of the inspection the General expressed his entire approbation of the appearance of the Battalion on parade and its movements in the field ; and then, as is customary, demanded to know whether any N.C.O. or Rifleman had a complaint to lay before him. In the expressions which the General used for the purpose, Colonel Dundas thought that Sir Charles had gone a little beyond what was required by Regulation, and when on bidding him good-bye Napier asked whether he could do anything for the Colonel, Dundas replied by requesting him to forward to the C.-in-C. in India his complaint that the G.-O.-C. in Scinde had been inciting his men to insubordination !

Another incident at this inspection was the fact that

---

[1] Among the Officers present on parade was 2nd Lieutenant Bernard Ward, who, in a letter written nearly half a century afterwards, says, ' I can bring before me with the greatest distinctness the very remarkable appearance of Sir Charles as he rode at a gallop down the line—a splendid seat on horseback, white helmet, fiery eyes which the huge spectacles he always wore made more sparkling, eagle-beaked nose, and long beard escaped under his cravat where he usually kept it. He was looked upon by every soldier under his command with love and admiration.'

Sir Charles Napier refused to admit that the rifle was as good a weapon as the old 'Brown Bess' smooth-bore musket. This was the more remarkable, since Napier had himself been a Rifleman; not, however, of the 60th. On August 4 Sir Charles, by this time Lieut.-General, again inspected the Battalion, and spoke in very flattering terms of its good conduct. A few weeks afterwards the General resigned his appointment, and was succeeded by Colonel Dundas in command of the troops in Scinde. Dundas handed over the Brigade at Karrachi to Lieut. Colonel Bradshaw, whereupon the command of the Battalion devolved upon Major Dennis, who had exchanged from the 5th Regiment with Major Rumley shortly before the Battalion left England.

Since the end of the war with France the Regiment had seen no active service. A new generation had arisen, and the only officer of the Regiment able to recall its glories in the Peninsular War was Colonel Commandant Sir William Davy, who, it will be remembered, sailed out of Cork Harbour *en route* for Portugal as a Major in Command of the 5th Battalion. So far as the conditions of peace permitted, the Regiment appeared to have upheld those traditions which it had learned from previous generations of Riflemen; but it remained to be seen whether in the test of warfare the Riflemen of the day were still the Riflemen of Badajoz and Salamanca. The time was now at hand for the question to be decided.

Many Officers of authority had long been of opinion that the peace made in 1846 with the Sikh power was merely a truce which would be broken by the latter at the first favourable opportunity. The Punjaub was administered by Sir Henry Lawrence, a man whose strength of character and happy address gave him a great influence over the native Chiefs. The frontier formed by the Sutlej rivers was being strengthened, and it was resolved that in the event of an outbreak a British-Indo force adequate to meet in arms the whole Sikh nation should be at hand. By this time Lord Hardinge had, however, returned to England, and thus it happened that an experienced General Officer had been succeeded as Governor-General by Lord Dalhousie, an arrogant doctrinaire, the consequence being that the Directors of the East Indian Company, influenced by motives of misplaced economy, gave inadequate support to the British Officers on the frontier.

It was in a somewhat unexpected manner that the storm burst. The province of Mooltan had been under British rule for little more than two years, in fact since the end of the Sikh War in 1846 only. During the month of April 1848 Mr. Vans Agnew of the Civil Service and Lieutenant Anderson of the 1st Bombay Fusiliers were sent with a small escort to the city of Mooltan to support a new Sikh Governor, Sirdar Khan Singh. On the 19th, while riding with the retiring Governor, the Dewan Mulraj, at whose instance they had arrived, they were set upon and wounded by some of his soldiers. A day or two afterwards the two Englishmen were murdered, after being deserted by the escort. It unfortunately happened that Colonel Henry Lawrence, Resident at Lahore, was absent on sick leave in England. His deputy, and Lord Gough, Commander-in-Chief, instead of despatching a force on the instant to Mooltan, referred the matter to the Sikh authorities, who, in a very half-hearted way, sent a force which did not reach Mooltan until July, by which time the rebellion had spread far and wide. Lieutenant (afterwards General Sir Herbert) Edwardes, engaged in civil employment beyond the Indus, alone attempted to stem the torrent. With a very miscellaneous force he thrice defeated

Mulraj and succeeded in driving him back within the walls of Mooltan. It was not until the middle of August that a British army under General Whish arrived at the city. By this time it had become obvious that the western Punjaub was ripe for revolt; and backed up by Dost-Mahommed, Ameer of Afghanistan. The British force in the Northern Provinces was barely strong enough to hold its ground, and the Government realised the fact that it was essential to draw reinforcements from the south.

A Bombay Division, which included our 1st Battalion, was in consequence formed at Roree, under command of General Auchmuty, and pending its arrival the siege of Mooltan was suspended. Then it was discovered that as Auchmuty was senior to Whish he could not serve under him. This led to correspondence, and correspondence in India is proverbially lengthy. Delay ensued.

In the meantime the Rifle Battalion, consisting of 30 Officers and 979 other ranks, had marched out of Karrachee on October 7, leaving 1 Officer and 31 other ranks behind to form a Depôt. On the 11th the Battalion reached Tatta, where it embarked on steamers of the Indus flotilla, and by the end of the month had landed at Roree.

The following is the list of its Officers present :—

Colonel, Hon. H. Dundas, C.B.; Majors, M. G. Dennis and J. Gordon; Captains, H. Bigham, J. Douglas, H. J. Darell, W. J. Yonge, R. F. W. Sibthorp, H. F. Kennedy; Lieutenants, C. N. North, G. Clapcott, E. F. Camphill, W. Hutchinson, D. D. Muter, H. F. Williams, J. A. MacQueen, C. A. B. Gordon, J. Maguire, A. Fitzgerald, F. A. St. John, F. Andrews, L. C. Travers, B. Ward; 2nd Lieutenants, V. Tongue, R. W. Brooke, R. J. E. Robertson, G. Clarke; Paymaster, Captain E. Coxen; Quartermaster, T. Berry; Surgeons, R. Boyes, W. J. Macfarlane.

Lieut.-Colonel Bradshaw rejoined the Battalion at Mooltan.

Want of transport necessitated a delay at Roree. On November 23 Colonel Dundas was confirmed in the command of the Division and received the appointment of Brigadier-General. Four days later his Division began its march; and on December 14 crossed the Sutlej by a bridge of boats at Pholadpore. On the 21st it reached Soornee Khund, where it joined the army under General Whish. Two days later 5 Rifle Companies formed part of a force detailed to reconnoitre the fortress. On the 26th the whole army marched eastward, taking up a position nearly south of Mooltan astride the Jhelum River, and about 3 miles distant from the fortress.

'The town of Mooltan,' observes the biographer of Sir Alexander Taylor, ' lies in the midst of the desert like an emerald isle floating in a sea of dust. Its climate in summer is exceedingly hot; how hot is suggested by the local epigram: "Having Mooltan, why did God make Hell?" Though rain rarely falls the city and its environment, which are exceedingly wealthy, are richly provided with artificial canals of running water. Wealth, heat, and abundant irrigation naturally result in incomparable gardens: the city and the large houses in its vicinity are embowered in groves of graceful date trees; the hot air is heavy with the scent of roses, tuberoses, and jasmine; the gardens are rich in oranges, peaches, and pomegranates, and produce mangoes which are among the most delicious in India. Between these walled gardens—enclosing country houses—lie dirty villages, temples, tombs, mosques, brick-kilns, ravines and fragments of mere jungle; ground easy to defend, and most difficult to clear.'

In addition to the Division from the Bombay Presidency, General Whish had under his command a Bengal Division and a native contingent under Lieutenant Herbert Edwardes from Bunnoo beyond the Indus, a contingent which included a considerable number of loyal Sikhs under the immediate command of General Corlandt, a European foreigner in their service.

The town of Mooltan was, according to the ideas of that period, fortified in considerable strength; a fort at the north-eastern angle forming a citadel.

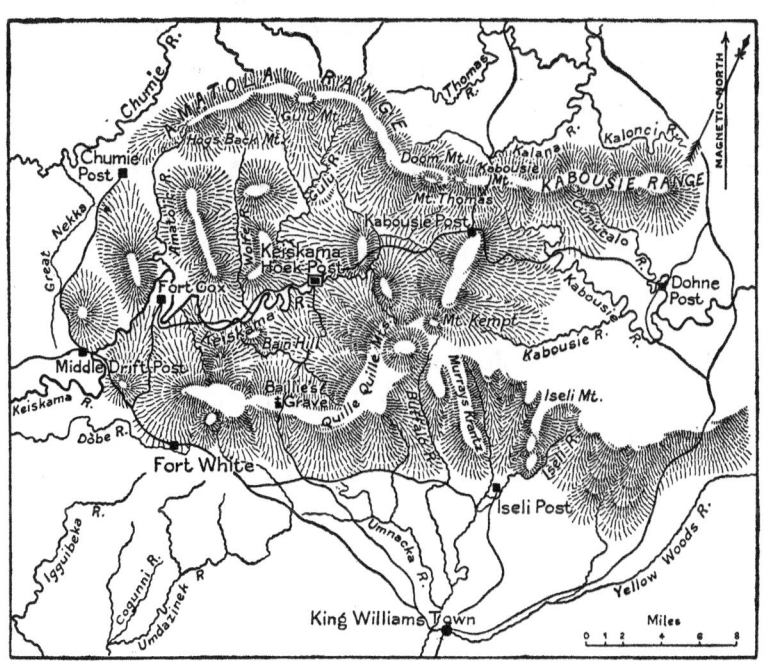

THEATRE OF OPERATIONS, KAFFIR WAR, 1851-3.

Early in the month of September General Whish had made an attempt to capture the city, but was foiled by the desertion of Shere Singh, our Sikh ally, who went over to the enemy with 4,300 of his men. Whish thereupon felt he had no alternative but to raise the siege and take up a defensive position pending the arrival of reinforcements. A species of three-cornered duel ensued; for Shere Singh never came to terms with Mulraj nor was allowed to enter the city, but lay to the north-west with his contingent.

Meanwhile what was known as the second Sikh War had broken out in the north, and the siege of Mooltan would have been of secondary importance but for the fact that the artillery engaged was badly needed in the Punjaub by Lord Gough, the Commander-in-Chief. Lord Dalhousie, whose contempt for military men is comprehensible only on the theory that he felt confident in his own person the qualities of a Solon and a Bonaparte, directed Lord Gough to give him a victory. The consequent engagement on January 13, 1849, resulted in the disaster of Chilianwallah, which for the time being paralysed the British arms.

3

We must now return to the siege of Mooltan. On December 27 General Whish, who, in accordance with the views of Colonel (afterwards Lord) Napier (of Magdala), had decided to attack the fort at the north-east angle of the city, directed Dundas to form a diversion and shorten the line of investment by capturing the enemy's entrenchments on the south side of the city. Dundas moved out of camp at 11 A.M. in two columns. That on the left, under his personal command, consisted of a Squadron, a Battery,

SIEGE OF MOOLTAN

and a Battalion and a half of infantry: the right, under Brigadier Capon,[1] was similarly composed, but included 5 Companies of the Royal Rifles. The remainder of the Division, under Command of Brigadier Stalker, was held in reserve.

Headed by the five Rifle Companies[2] in quarter-column, Capon moved directly to the front upon the prominent mound known as the Mundee Awa; and having advanced about a mile, directed Major Dennis to extend two Companies of Riflemen and cover the front. For another quarter of a mile the advance continued. Then the enemy guns opened with grape shot. The Brigadier directed his skirmishers to occupy a large building named the Ranteerut, some 600 yards to the front. This was quickly done with the loss of one Rifleman killed and another wounded. 'The excellent fire of the Riflemen in and about the building,' says Capon in his despatch, 'soon subdued that of the enemy's skirmishers.' Our guns then opened fire upon the Mundee Awa, some 700 yards distant, and after an interval of about 20 minutes Capon ordered his force to advance. With a cheer the troops carried the Mundee Awa at the double. It was found to have been evacuated. The greater part of the Riflemen followed the enemy into the suburbs, where Major John Gordon of our Regiment was killed by a bullet fired from one of the houses. This was the sole casualty at the moment, for the steadiness and skill of the Riflemen in taking cover were conspicuous. Brigadier Capon in his despatch remarks, 'nothing could exceed the gallantry and discipline of the 60th Royal Rifles.' The casualties of the Regiment during the operations of this

---

[1] Capon had as his A.D.C. Lieutenant Charles Boswell Gordon, the well-known Colonel of our 1st Battalion from 1871 to 1877.

[2] Strength of the Rifles: 2 Field Officers, 3 Captains, 10 Subalterns, 18 Sergeants, 10 Buglers, 420 Riflemen.

day amounted to 1 Officer and 2 Riflemen killed; Major Dennis, Lieutenant Brooke, and 10 Riflemen wounded. The result was the capture of the suburbs, which had been abandoned at the end of the earlier siege, and the extension of the British position in a north-easterly direction as far as Moolraj's garden palace, Am Khas, 500 yards from the north-east angle of the Fort. The enemy was driven in at the Delhi Gate on the east side, and it became possible to erect breaching batteries against the south-eastern walls and the Bloody Bastion of the Fort. Thenceforward three Companies of Riflemen were continuously employed in holding the position thus established; and Edwardes' force beyond the Chenab was brought across to the left bank.

On the 28th Lieut.-Colonel Bradshaw joined from leave of absence and took Command of the Battalion. On the 30th the great Mosque inside the citadel, containing the enemy's principal powder magazine, was pierced by a shell and blew up with a terrific explosion. The total casualties in the Regiment up to the end of the year amounted to 6 Officers and men killed, and 17 wounded.

On January 2, 1849, the breaches in the wall of the city—one in the Bloody Bastion, the other near the Delhi Gate—were reported practicable. The suburbs between the Delhi Gate and the left breach were occupied by piquets from the 1st Brigade under Major Dennis, the Rifle Company of Captain James Douglas being stationed in the houses opposite the breach in the Khoonee Boorj to cover the advance of the storming party. Two other Companies under Captains W. J. Yonge and R. N. Sibthorpe were destined to cover the advance of the Bengal Column from the north-eastern side. The assault on the Delhi Gate was led by the Engineer Robert Napier, afterwards Field-Marshal Lord Napier of Magdala;

that on the Bloody Bastion by Alexander Taylor, whom we shall meet a few years later at the Siege of Delhi.

'The steady and well-directed fire of Her Majesty's 60th Rifles,' said Brigadier Stalker, C.B., in his despatch, 'kept down that of the enemy very considerably while the troops were approaching the breach.'

The breach near the Delhi Gate was carried by the Regiment of the murdered Anderson, then known as the 1st Bombay Fusiliers, and later on as the Royal Dublin Fusiliers. Since those days they have often fought side by side with ourselves, and of them at our Regimental Dinner in 1907 Sir Redvers Buller, our Colonel Commandant, said—

'I give you the health of the Dublin Fusiliers who are dining in the next room, of whom I will only say this, that when we marched into Ladysmith I placed them at the head of the column.'

The Fusiliers planted their Regimental Colour on the crest of the breach and captured a retrenchment within.

'Then,' says Sir Herbert Edwardes, who was present, 'from every crowded height and battery whence the exciting struggle had been watched rose the shouts of applauding comrades; and through the deafening roar of the musketry which poured along the ramparts, and marked the hard-earned progress of the Columns through the streets, both friend and foe might distinctly hear that sound never to be forgotten—the hurrah of a British Army after battle.'

The citadel was now formally invested, yet for nearly three weeks Mulraj withstood the bombardment; but on the 21st the breach in the wall was so large that the enemy drove horses in and out, and Mulraj offered submission on condition that his life should be spared. General Whish refused any terms. The assault was ordered for the following day. The sun rose amid a storm of thunder and lightning. The British troops were formed up in readiness for the attack, when at the last moment Mulraj hoisted a white flag. Then the bodies of Vans Agnew and Anderson were carried through the breach and buried with military honors on the summit of the bastion. Their epitaph should be formed by the gallant words of defiance which they had spoken with their last breath, and which many other Englishmen under like circumstances have uttered and will, it is to be hoped, continue to utter so long as our Empire exists, '*They can kill us too if they like; but we are not the last of the English. Thousands of Englishmen will come down here when we are gone, and will annihilate Mulraj and his soldiers and his Fort.*'

The operations before Mooltan had cost our Regiment 11 Officers and men killed, and 30 wounded. It may be incidentally mentioned that Whish's guns had fired 42,387 rounds.

4

To Lord Gough, the Commander-in-Chief, the capture of Mooltan was of the first importance. The battle of Chilianwallah had left him in dire peril; for the Sikhs advancing turned his right flank, threatening his communications and forcing him back to the Chenab. It was even then doubtful whether he would be able to hold his ground; impossible for him to resume the offensive until reinforced from the south. Whish's own Division was the first to leave Mooltan, followed on February 2nd by Dundas; the march before them was one of 283 miles. Dundas halted *en route* for some Court Martial duty. Lord Gough—an old man in his 70th year—was in a state of fever, and directed him to send forward the 60th by forced marches. On the 18th the Battalion, which included all its officers who had fought at Mooltan, accordingly marched 30 miles, and having after a few hours' rest completed the remainder of the distance, joined

SIEGE OF MOOLTAN.   Col. Dundas

Lord Gough at Trikur. Next day the army advanced to Shadiwall, the Riflemen showing it is said some signs of the fatigues to which they had been exposed. This is hardly matter for surprise, since they had averaged about 17 miles a day, inclusive of halts. On the 21st at 7 A.M. began the decisive battle of Goojerat. The enemy's position, occupied by 50,000 men and 66 guns, could be plainly seen covering the eastern and southern sides of that town; his right was behind a nullah, his centre and left in an open plain, and the British attack was consequently to be concentrated thereon, while Dundas's Division on our extreme left, consisting (in addition to the Riflemen) of the 2nd European, and the 3rd and 19th Bombay Native Regiments, merely threatened the nullah. The rising sun threw light over the long lines of snowy mountains and on a wide intervening plain, revealing to the Riflemen the Sikh camp on their front, and behind them the British line of battle, 21,000 strong, containing pretty nearly the whole fighting strength of India, stretching for miles, and supported by a powerful artillery of 60 Field and 12 heavy guns, the latter drawn by elephants. The guns opened fire with terrific effect. General Dundas advanced with his Division, the battalion being in line of quarter-column covered by the Rifles under Bradshaw and a troop of Horse Artillery. As the attack on the right developed Dundas deployed into line and continued his advance. A huge body of Afghan horse threatened to charge his left flank, but our Horse Artillery made great lanes in their ranks and the enemy galloped away, hotly pursued by the newly raised Scinde Cavalry called up by General Dundas for the purpose.[1]

[1] Scinde had been added to British territory but five years previously, by the victories of Sir Charles Napier. The order for their advance was carried by Lieut. B. Ward, 60th Rifles, A.D.C. to Dundas.

The Division then kept on advancing, but without firing a shot; for so successful had been the attack on the enemy's left and centre that he made no stand, but moved off too rapidly to be within rifle range, although the Artillery lost no opportunity of harassing his retreat. On went Dundas through the enemy's camp, which had been left standing, and bringing up his left shoulder turned the city of Goojerat. At the outset the ground was studded with bushes and hedges of prickly pear, but when the open ground was again reached two abandoned guns were the sole remaining sign of the enemy. Referring to our regiment in his book on the campaign, Captain Thackwell remarks : 'It was a pity that the gallant Corps did not come within immediate contact with the enemy, for its ball practice would have startled them.'

The loss of our army in this action amounted to 767 killed and wounded; that of our regiment was confined to one bugler wounded. The battle had been decided by the skilful use of our Artillery. The enemy was routed, losing 53 guns and enormous numbers of men.

5

It may be that Lord Gough was still oppressed by the recollection of Chilianwallah or that he did not realise the decisive nature of his victory, for he took no immediate action in pursuit. But next day a force of 12,000 men and 40 guns under Sir Walter Gilbert was detached to follow up the fleeing enemy. This force included our First Battalion—now commanded by Major Dennis, for Bradshaw was given a Brigade—although surprise was expressed that, despite the fatigue of its long march to the field of battle, troops from the Bombay column should have been selected for the pursuit. During the first day (22nd) 25 miles were traversed in intense heat over a nearly waterless country. On the 23rd a heavy storm broke at 2 A.M., changing the heat to cold. A narrow gorge three miles long was threaded. The route continued, at times amid magnificent mountain scenery. One march in particular lingered long in the memory of those who took part in it, and was compared with the more famous one of the Light Division to Talavera in 1809. On March 3 Sir Walter Gilbert crossed the Jhelum river, and at Hoormuk on the Sohan near Rawul Pindee came up with the retreating enemy. Here on the 11th Shera Singh surrendered, the remainder of his army—16,000 strong with 41 guns—following his example three days later at Pindee, a distance of 115 miles from Goojerat.

The pursuit of Dost Mahommed and the Afghans was continued for 98 miles through Attock and Peshawur up to Jumrood at the mouth of the Khyber Pass, where on the 18th our army encamped. Here it remained, for the pursuit from Goojerat had been pressed for at least 213 miles, and there was no desire to follow the fugitive Afghans into the perilous passes of their own country. The Riflemen had fairly earned a rest. The whole distance marched by the Battalion—Mooltan to Jumrood—between February 3 and March 18 had been 496 miles.

On March 29, the day after our arrival at Jumrood, the whole of the Punjaub was annexed to the British dominions.

6

At the mouth of the Khyber Pass the Battalion remained until May 7, when it went into temporary barracks near Peshawur. On October 14th it was inspected by Brigadier-General Sir Colin Campbell, whom we last saw when a Captain in the 5th Battalion at Gibraltar during the year 1818. He was now commanding the Sinde Sogee Division.

The Sam Barzai tribe, dwelling in the hill country between Peshawur and the Swat River, which had just come under British rule, refused to pay our Government any revenue, despite the fact that it had done so regularly to the Sikh authorities. At the instance of the Deputy Commissioner at Peshawur a punitive expedition was organised and placed under Command of Colonel Bradshaw. The contingent furnished by the 60th consisted of 7 Officers (in addition to Bradshaw), viz. Captains Bingham and Sibthorpe; Lieutenants H. F. Williams, A. Fitzgerald, F. Andrews, B. Ward; and 2nd Lieutenant R. J. E. Robertson; 9 Sergeants, 3 Buglers, and 200 Riflemen. Lieutenant F. A. St. John also accompanied the column as Orderly Officer to the C.O. The remainder of the force comprised a Troop H.A., 61st Regiment 300 R. and F., the 15th Irregular Cavalry, 1 Company Bombay Sappers and Miners, and the 3rd Bombay Native Infantry. It was joined a day or two later by the celebrated Guide Corps and 100 men of the 1st Bombay N.I.

On December 3 the forces quitted Peshawur and marching westward crossed the Kabul river at Nowshera, 25 miles distant. Thence it turned northward, and on the 11th, after a march of 40 miles, reached the neighbourhood of Sunghao in the Euzuffzye country.[1] Sunghao is situated immediately beneath a precipitous rock 2,000 feet high, whence two spurs project for 900 yards into the plain. The village consequently formed a *cul de sac* and the position was strongly held by 2,500 men.

[1] Sometimes spelt Yussufzai.

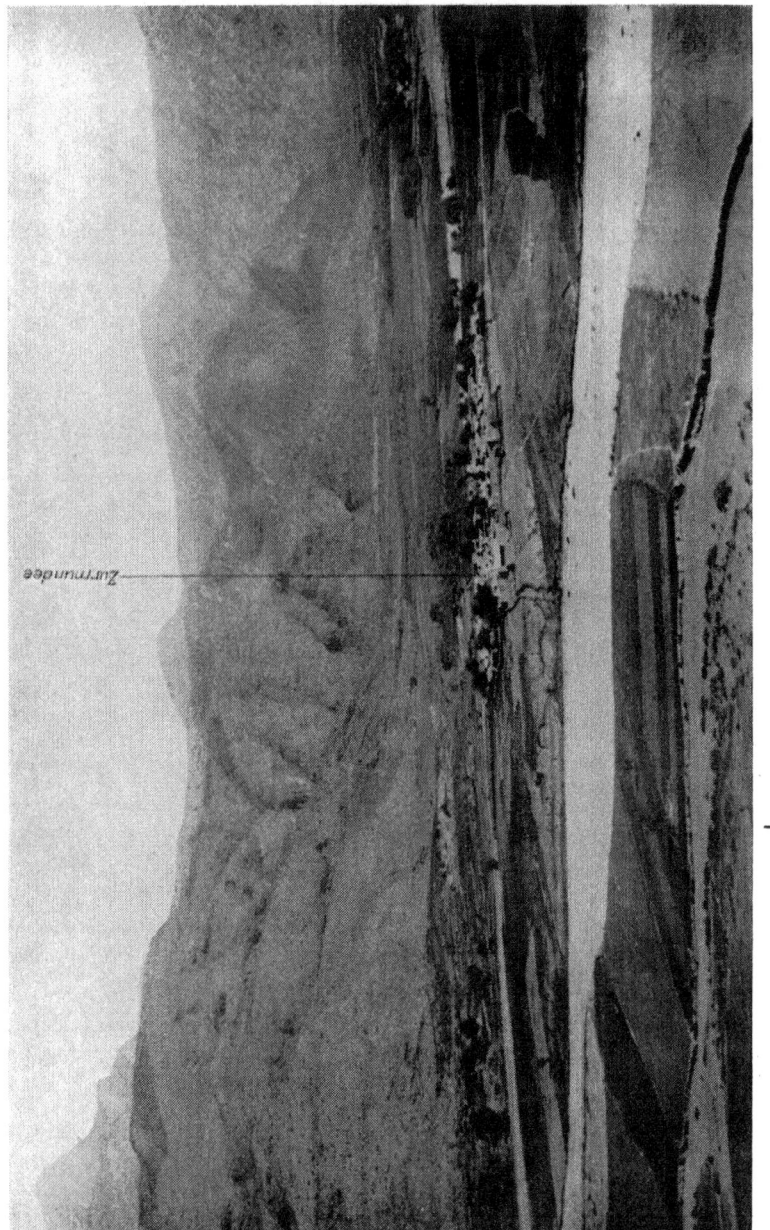

VILLAGES OF PULLEE AND ZURMUNDEE.

After reconnoitring the ground Colonel Bradshaw directed the Riflemen, supported by two Companies of the B.N.I. and 2 guns, to attack the spur on the left of the village, while the Guides assailed that on the right. The hill was steep and rocky. The attack was met with heavy fire and showers of stones from the defenders. But the work was well suited to Riflemen, and despite the difficulties ground was slowly but steadily gained. Although the operation occupied five hours, the village was eventually outflanked on both sides and captured. The loss of the British-Indo force was 4 killed and 18 wounded. Among the latter was Captain Bingham, who commanded the two Rifle Companies, Sergeant Rigney, and 6 Riflemen. There were probably many contusions in addition from the stones, but the small number of casualties must be attributed partly no doubt to the inferior weapons of the enemy, but largely also to the way in which the Riflemen utilised the ground for taking cover and avoidance of hurry.

On the 13th the force, marching eastward by hill tracks for some five miles, reached the mouth of the Buzdura Valley, approaching the villages of Pullee, Zoormundee, and Sher Khan. These villages were situated in echelon, Pullee, the most western, being that nearest to the British, with the other two on its left rear. On its eastern side Pullee was commanded by a height; so were the other two, with spurs thrown forward into the valley. Both high and low ground were occupied, for the villages had been reinforced from neighbouring tribes, and the position was garrisoned by more than 11,000 men.

On the 14th Colonel Bradshaw, having made his disposition, moved forward. The Riflemen, supported by 6 Companies of the Bombay Native Infantry and 4 H.A. guns, which opened fire with great effect, masked the hill commanding Pullee. On their right the Guides and a detachment of the 1st Punjaub Infantry supported by three Companies B.N.I. moved against and ultimately outflanked the enemy's left.

As soon as Bradshaw saw that the Riflemen were making progress and that the left of the enemy was being turned he advanced up the valley with the remainder of his disposable force, supported by the 4 guns hitherto attached to the Rifles. The hill adjoining Pullee was stormed by the Riflemen and the heights on their right by the Guides. The villages were taken in detail and destroyed. The tribes were driven at every point from their positions and a charge of the Irregular Cavalry completed their *déroute*. They fled, leaving their numerous dead on the field—an abandonment considered by themselves a great disgrace. Three thousand maunds (about 84 tons) of grain were captured.

The Deputy-Commissioner—Major George Lawrence—having informed Bradshaw that the object of the expedition had been accomplished, the Colonel withdrew his force through the valley unmolested. It was subsequently ascertained that the combination of the hill tribes had been very thorough, and that 15,000 were advancing in aid of the villages when they were met by the fugitives, and retired.

During the advance of the Riflemen (by files in extended order) against the Pullee Hill an episode of interest to our Regiment had taken place. A black flag was noticed protruding from behind a rock, towards which two Riflemen, Michael Burke and John Connell his rear-rank man, were pointing. Just as the rock was reached a Pathan fanatic on horseback dashed out from behind the rock and shot Connell dead. Without a moment's hesitation Burke sprang upon the man, seized him by the head, hurled him to the ground, and shot him as well as another Pathan who came to his friend's rescue, Burke himself being slightly wounded. Among the Rifle Officers present was Lieutenant Bernard Ward. His son writes:

' I shall never forget the dramatic action made by my father in describing Burke's exploit, which evidently made a deep impression on his mind. The Victoria Cross was not instituted until some years later, otherwise my father would have recommended Burke for it.'

The flag carried by the Pathan was of course captured, and the following memorandum was a few days later attached thereto :—

'Camp, Peshawur, 12th January, 1850.

' This standard was taken in a personal encounter by Private James Burke,[1] 1st Battalion 60th Royal Rifles, in which he killed two of the enemy and was himself slightly wounded at the storming of the Heights of Pullee in the Buz Dhurra on the 14th December, 1849.

' The above Private presented the standard to Lieut.-Colonel Bradshaw commanding the force, and was for his gallantry promoted Corporal on the Field by him.'

The subsequent history of this flag is rather curious. Colonel Bradshaw died very shortly afterwards, and by some means unknown the flag came into the hands of General Sir George Scovell, K.C.B., one of Wellington's most distinguished Staff Officers in the Peninsula, and at the period of which we are speaking Governor of the Royal Military College, Sandhurst. The General presented it to the College; but in 1897 H.R.H. The Duke of Cambridge, our Colonel-in-Chief, ordered it to be returned to our Regiment. It was accordingly entrusted to the 4th Battalion, to be retained pending the return of the 1st Battalion from foreign service. When the 4th

---

[1] Burke's Christian name was in reality not James but Michael.

Battalion went to Ireland in August 1898 the flag was sent for safe custody to the Rifle Depôt.

Burke's exploit is commemorated on the well-known centrepiece of the 1st Battalion, presented to the Officers by Major Thomas Maughan, R.A., the plinth being formed by part of the tusk of the elephant 'TULLALA employed at the Siege of Multan in placing the guns in position on the MUNDE AVA mound.' It would appear that Tullala was the gigantic elephant which on the march to Goojerat carried the pole of the marquee belonging to the Officers' mess.[1]

It will be remembered that in 1897, when the *Warren Hastings* was wrecked in conveying the Headquarters of the Battalion to Mauritius, the box containing the centrepiece was by a piece of extraordinarily good fortune rescued from the wreck.

It is pleasing to be able to record that Burke, the capturer of the standard, continued his distinguished career, and ultimately became Regimental Sergeant-Major of his Battalion.

In the action at Pullee-Zoormundee two Riflemen were killed and seven wounded.

On the 21st the Battalion returned to Peshawur. In his despatch Colonel Bradshaw mentioned Captain Bingham and Lieutenant St. John. His own name was brought forward by higher authority in praise of his 'zeal and abilities,' and the whole force received the thanks of the Governor-General of India.

7

In November Sir Colin Campbell was transferred to the command of the Peshawur District, and when in

---

[1] It is recorded that the sensible animal always declined any additional burden.

Wm. Norman, Montreal.

CENTRE-PIECE IN OFFICERS' MESS OF 1ST BATTALION, REPRESENTING THE CAPTURE OF A FLAG IN EUZUFFZYE COUNTRY.

February 1850 Sir Charles Napier, now C.-in-C. in India, came to Peshawur on a tour of inspection Sir Colin was able to show him on parade 3 Regiments of Cavalry, 3 Troops H.A., 2 Field Batteries, 3 European and 3 Native battalions of Infantry.

Just at this moment trouble arose with the neighbouring Afridee tribes. Peshawur and Kohat—a city southward—although in British territory were separated by a mountain road running through a large and dangerous gorge in Afridee country. The Afridees complained that they had not received the remuneration promised them for keeping the road in repair, and vented their wrath by the massacre of a party of Sappers and Miners working thereon. It was resolved to force the defile, and Sir C. Napier decided to accompany in person the column released by General Campbell for the purpose. That column, which was commanded by Campbell in person, included a detachment of Riflemen under Captain Douglas, who was accompanied by Captains Darell and Kennedy, Lieutenants Ward, Tongue, and Robertson, 2nd Lieutenant G. B. MacQueen—who survived this little campaign nearly three-quarters of a century—10 Sergeants, 4 Buglers, and 200 Riflemen. The remainder of the force included a Troop H.A., two $5\frac{1}{2}$-inch Mortars carried by elephants, two Companies of the 61st, two of the 98th Regiments, the 15th Irregular and 1st Punjaub Cavalry, the 23rd and 31st N.I. and 1st Punjaub Infantry. Command of all the European troops forming the advance guard was given to Colonel Bradshaw.

The object of the expedition was to force the pass and send the Punjaub regiments on to Kohat to punish the offending Afridees. Provisions for 14 days were carried.

The force quitting Peshawur on February 9 marched ten miles southward to Mutamin, at the foot of the pass.

Next day the force entered the defile, but although at Akhor some five miles further on strong opposition was encountered, the heights were cleared at night by the Native Infantry. The march was then continued for about the same distance to Zurgan Khel, where the enemy was again discovered in occupation of a strong hill position. The heights on the left were, however, captured by the Punjaub Infantry and those on the right by the Riflemen and 98th. The village was destroyed.

Beyond Zurgan Khal the pass became very narrow and difficult. The column along its whole length was harassed by stones and musketry. On the night of the 11th it encamped at the foot of the Kohat Kotal. Next morning at 8 A.M. the piquets of the 23rd and 31st N.I. were suddenly attacked and suffered loss. But the pass had now been successfully threaded. Bosti Khel to the west of it was taken and turned. The Punjaub regiments, accompanied by the Commander-in-Chief, advanced to Kohat, but early on the 13th the remainder of the force started on its return March to Peshawur. From Sheraki to Akhor, nearly the whole length of the defile, the tribesmen continued to harass the march. The casualties of the force from start to finish were 110, but the Riflemen were fortunate and had one man only wounded. Peshawur was re-entered on the 14th, a week later the Battalion marched thence to the hill station at Kassowlee. It was high time, for the heat of Peshawur, to say nothing of the innumerable multitude of itinerant snakes and scorpions, had been extremely trying and the cause of much sickness. Kassowlee was reached on April 10. Four Companies were then detached to Sabathoo.[1]

---

[1] At this period the Battalion had two Bands, one of them consisting of the Buglers only, all of whom could play other instruments. As these instruments were, however, now worn out, Colonel Bradshaw very generously presented the Buglers with an entirely new set.

For the recent campaigns Colonel Dundas received the K.C.B., Lieut.-Colonel Bradshaw the C.B., Major Dennis a Brevet Lieut.-Colonelcy.

In July Field Marshal H.R.H. the (1st) Duke of Cambridge, who had been our Colonel-in-Chief since 1827, died and was succeeded by H.R.H. Prince Albert, consort of Queen Victoria.

8

On October 18 the Battalion sustained a most severe loss in the death of Lieut.-Colonel Joseph Bradshaw, C.B., described as a great soldier, beloved by all ranks. There is reason to know that he had made his mark far beyond the limits of his own regiment, and must be accounted as one of the greatest of our Riflemen. In consequence of the continued absence of Sir Henry Dundas, who by this time had succeeded to the title of Viscount Melville, Brevet Lieut.-Colonel M. G. Dennis assumed command of the Battalion.

On November 1 the Battalion was inspected by the G.O.C. Sirhind Division, and in March 1852 by the G.O.C. at Jullundur. The reports elicited the following remarks from the Duke of Wellington, Commander-in-Chief of the British Army.

'It is gratifying to His Grace to find that this Battalion generally continues to maintain its high character for efficiency and discipline. The state of this Battalion seems in the highest degree satisfactory. The report of this Corps shows its perfect efficiency in all respects, and affords much satisfaction to His Grace.'

In a previous volume the Duke of Wellington's opinion of the Regiment was several times quoted. The remarks now made proved to be the great Duke's words of farewell, for his death occurred in the following September.

On March 6, 1853, Lord Melville rejoined the Battalion after his prolonged absence of six years and assumed command. Its period, however, was short, for on June 17 he was appointed to the command of the Sirhind Division, and Colonel Dennis once more took his place.

Early in 1853 a copy of the following letter was received :—

'Horse Guards, 30th December, 1852.

' SIR,—I have the honour by the direction of the General Commanding-in-Chief to acquaint you that Her Majesty has been graciously pleased to approve of the 1st Battalion of the 60th Regiment wearing on the Regimental appointments the word " Punjaub," in consideration of the services of the Battalion during the campaign of 1848-49 in that country, and that the words " Mooltan " and " Goojerat " be borne in addition thereto, in consideration of the Siege of Mooltan, which surrendered on the 22nd January 1849, and of the Battle of Goojerat, fought on the 21st February following.

' I have, etc.,
' (*Signed*) G. BROWNE,
' Adjutant-General.

' To Sir W. G. Davy, C.B., K.C.H.,
' Colonel, 1st Battalion 60th Regiment.'

Sir William Davy, to whom this letter was addressed, was the Officer who took the 5th Battalion out to the Peninsular War and commanded it at Vimieiro and Talavera.

On August 19, 1854, G.O. in India announced the promotion of Lord Melville to the rank of Major-General, and thus terminated his Lieut.-Colonelcy of the 1st Battalion, which had begun ten years previously, during less than three of which he had, however, exercised actual command. There can be no doubt that he was a good soldier and deserves the reputation of being one of the great men of the Regiment, which nevertheless in all probability owes less to him than to his deputy, Colonel

Bradshaw. We shall in due course meet him again as one of our Colonels Commandant.[1]

Lord Melville had evidently great independence of character and considerable influence with his superiors, who were perhaps just a little afraid of him. Captain F. S. Travers, happily still among us although a nonogenarian, remembers the fact of meeting Lord Melville at Simla, where the Commander-in-Chief, General Sir William Gomm, happened to be giving a ball. Lord Melville without further ado invited him and insisted on his attendance, notwithstanding the fact that Travers, being on his return from a shooting expedition, had brought with him no evening uniform.

Among other points it may be noted that Lord Melville was a great talker, so much so that although an abstemious man he remained at the dinner table until it was time to dress for the early parade! The officer of the day used to be detailed to keep him company, and the Colonel's conversational powers were good enough to make the time pass rapidly. The officer in attendance was always excused the approaching parade.

On being offered command of the Sinhind Division Lord Melville accepted it on the condition that his old Battalion should be included therein. This was found to be impossible; but a compromise was eventually agreed upon. The Battalion remained outside the Divisional Command, but the General was allowed to continue to reside with it.

It was said that to Lord Melville we owe the institution of our Annual Regimental Dinner, and that he took the idea from the Coldstream Guards, in which he had served as a subaltern. That regiment has the credit of originating those annual gatherings, which have long been general in the Service.

[1] Lord Melville had been made Lieut.-Colonel of the 83rd Regiment in December 1829, and in consequence was in nominal command of a battalion for nearly 25 years.

CHAPTER V

ON arrival at Portsmouth in June 1847 the 2nd Battalion, as already mentioned, was quartered at Chichester. Hardly had the battalion settled down when it was ordered to London for the purpose of being present at a Review to be held in honour of the Grand Duke Constantine of Russia. The Battalion, under command of Colonel Nesbitt, consisting of 2 Field Officers, 8 Captains, 18 Subalterns, 4 Staff, 39 Sergeants, 18 Buglers, and 686 Riflemen, proceeded accordingly to London 'by the London and Brighton Railroad,' as the Battalion Records inform us. It was quartered in the neighbourhood of Hammersmith, Headquarters being at the King's Arms, Kensington.

The other troops to be reviewed on June 17 consisted of five Battalions of the Guards and the 43rd Light Infantry, and were formed in Hyde Park 'in lines of contiguous columns' facing Grosvenor Gate. The whole force was under command of H.R.H. Prince George of Cambridge, in later years the well-known Commander-in-Chief of the Army, and Colonel-in-Chief of our Regiment. The Rifles, of course, took the left of the line.

Her Majesty Queen Victoria, H.R.H. Prince Albert, the Duke of Wellington, Lieut.-General Sir Harry Smith, and many other distinguished Officers were on the ground. Several foreign celebrities in addition to the Grand Duke

GENERAL LORD MELVILLE, G.C.B.

were present. The Records of the 2nd Battalion state that after the Royal Salute the troops marched past in open column in slow time and saluted the Queen, and afterwards by columns at quarter distance in quick time. Several manœuvres were then performed, the Battalion covering the movements of the 2nd Battalion Coldstream Guards.

On this interesting occasion the following Officers of the Battalion were present: Lieut.-General Sir W. E. Eustace, K.C.H., Colonel Commandant, Lieut.-Colonel Nesbitt, Major Crombie, Brevet Major Temple; Captains Robinson, Jones, McKenzie, Holbech, Hon. Adrian Hope, Mansel, and Sotheby; Lieutenants Mitchell, Jones, Rhodes, Blight, Rose, Warburton, Feilden, and Warren; 2nd Lieutenants Aldworth, Payne, Galton, Dawkins, R. H. Robinson, Greville, Freer, Fletcher, and Bowles; Lieutenant and Adjutant Kenny, Paymaster FitzGerald, Surgeon Cowen, Assistant-Surgeon Richardson. Of these Officers, Captain Jones subsequently commanded the 1st Battalion, Adrian Hope died in the Indian Mutiny as a Brigadier of distinction, Feilden also commanded the 1st Battalion, and Mitchell had been for ten years the celebrated Adjutant of the 1st Battalion who wrote a book, well known at the time, on Light Infantry drill and manœuvre.

The Battalion returned next day to Chichester—with 3 Companies under Major Crombie at Fort Cumberland—and a few days later proceeded to Winchester (where the Depôt and Service Companies were amalgamated), *en route* for Gosport, which was reached in the middle of July. The Battalion Records tell us that at the particular request of Lord Frederick FitzClarence, a distinguished General Officer commanding the South-Western District, the Sergeant-Major was sent to Parkhurst, Isle of Wight, for the purpose of instructing the Depôt Battalion in the principles of Squad and Company Drill as applied in the 2nd Battalion.

In December B.H.Q. moved from Gosport to Lancashire, where the companies were distributed as follows:—

>F, G, and I at Bolton.
>B and H at Blackburn.
>D at Liverpool.
>E at Manchester.
>Headquarters, A, C, K at Bury,

The Companies were frequently interchanged. On April 10, 1848, the famous Chartist movement came to a head, and on that date I Company proceeded to Macclesfield in aid of the Civil power. The demands of the Chartists were in those days considered revolutionary, and in London great preparations had been made for armed resistance. But the day passed off quietly with a great procession, and most if not all of the points of the Charter have in more recent times been sanctioned.

Towards the end of July the Battalion embarked for Ireland, and A, G, and H Companies (200 strong) were immediately despatched to suppress an insurrection in Tipperary. They proceeded to Thurles, and thence on August 7 to Limerick. There was happily no collision between the troops and the insurgents. The principal difficulty arose through the wet weather. The mobile Column under Major-General McDonald, to which these three Companies had been attached, was broken up on September 3, whereupon the detachment returned to Dublin.

The year 1848 was a most disturbed one throughout Continental Europe. Thrones were overturned almost like ninepins. Only the aftermath reached the British Isles; but in Ireland, owing to the failure of the potato crop, great distress prevailed, and a rising, of which Mr. Smith O'Brien was leader, took place. It was, however, quickly suppressed with little or no bloodshed. On September 13, at four hours' notice, six Companies, under the personal command of Colonel Nesbitt, proceeded on special service without baggage to Kilkenny, where they were encamped in the Barrack Square, and remained under canvas for six weeks. Four of them then returned to Dublin, and were followed by the remaining two in January of the following year.

In 1849 the Queen paid a visit to Ireland, and on the 19th held a Review in the Phœnix Park, at which the following troops were present: One Troop R.H.A., two Batteries R.A., 6th Dragoon Guards, 6th Dragoons, 8th Hussars, 17th Lancers, 2nd Battalion 1st Regiment, 2nd, 40th, 48th, 55th, 71st Regiments, and our own 2nd Battalion.

On October 5 Rifleman John Kelly of F Company was presented on Parade by Colonel Nesbitt with the Bronze Medal of the Royal Humane Society for gallant conduct in rescuing a man named James Hopkins from drowning in the Liffey.

On April 1st, 1850, the Battalion left Dublin for 'country quarters.' Headquarters with A, C, E, G, H, and I Companies was stationed at Templemore, and Company detachments were ordered respectively to Castlecomer, Fethard, Thurles, and Cashel.

These quarters were constantly being altered, until in June 1851 the Battalion was ordered to proceed to Cork, preparatory to embarkation for the Cape of Good Hope. On the 30th it was split up into six Service and four Depôt Companies.

On July 5 the six Service Companies embarked at Queenstown in H.M.S. *Retribution* and *Sidon*, Colonel Nesbitt with the Headquarters, consisting of eleven Officers and three hundred men, being in the *Retribution*, while the remainder, comprising fourteen Officers and three hundred and fifty-two O.R., under command of Major W. F. Bedford, sailed in the *Sidon*.

The nominal roll of Officers who embarked in addition to the two Field Officers already named is as follows: Captains J. F. McKenzie, Hon. A. Hope, C. W. H. Sotheby, A. Mosley, G. W. Bligh, G. Rigaud; Lieutenants W. P. Salmon, H. E. Warren, A. C. Greville; 2nd Lieutenants W. Brooke, C. W. Earle, W. Mure, J. Du Cane, J. Robertson, W. Cockburn, H. P. Montgomery, F. FitzPatrick, C. D. C. Ellis; Lieutenant and Adjutant S. Kenny, Paymaster W. H. FitzGerald, Quartermaster R. Power, Surgeon T. Alexander, Assistant-Surgeon B. Nicholson, M.D.

It was not until September 19 and 20 that the *Retribution* and *Sidon* arrived respectively at Simon's Bay, Cape of Good Hope. The women, children, and heavy baggage of the Battalion were disembarked and sent to Cape Town, while the Officers and men in the *Sidon* were transferred to the *Retribution*, which two days later sailed from Simon's Bay and arrived on the 27th off East London at the mouth of the Buffalo River. The surf was, however, so heavy that it was not until October 3 that the Battalion was able to disembark. Next day it started for King William's Town, which was reached on the 7th.

At this period the British dominion included the Cape Colony, the nucleus of which had been captured from the Dutch in 1806; Natal, which had been annexed in 1843; and the Orange River Colony in 1848, after the defeat of the Boers at Boemplatz by Sir Harry Smith.

Four times had the Kaffir tribes, a most warlike race, risen against British rule; and despite their want of success and acceptance of treaties—the most recent in 1848—the Chief Sandili took up arms a fifth time at Christmas 1850, ambushed a detachment of troops, murdered some settlers, and was joined by the Hottentots, hitherto our allies. It was only by degrees that disciplined troops and the weapons of civilisation began to get the upper hand.

The force in South Africa, under command of a very distinguished soldier, Lieut.-General Sir Harry Smith, G.C.B., Governor and Commander-in-Chief, consisted of about 7,400 Officers and men, of whom the 12th Lancers (400 strong), the 2nd Queens (650), the 6th (650), the 60th (650), the 73rd (630), were concentrated in British Kaffraria. The 74th, 91st, the Cape Mounted Rifles, and the 12th Reserve Battalion were on the frontier, and the 45th Regiment in Natal. Large forces of Kaffirs were in the field; and although ill-armed, their knowledge of guerilla warfare and the difficulties of the country itself made the task of quelling the revolt a hard one. Roads were almost non-existent; the rivers, liable to rapid floods, were unbridged. The only transport was that of large unwieldy waggons, slowly and painfully drawn by 16 oxen, who, despite all care, died in great quantities. The country was hilly and lent itself to the construction of ambushes, in the art of which the Kaffirs were past masters.

Sir Harry Smith lost no time in making use of his reinforcements. On October 14 Lieut.-Colonel Nesbitt was despatched with a strong patrol of 500 Officers and men, chiefly of his own Battalion, but also aided by detachments of soldiers with longer experience of the country, and was directed to move to Fort Hare, and by night attack the valley of the Chumie, which was reported to contain large numbers of cattle raided by the Kaffirs from the white settlers.

At this period the Army as a whole was still armed with the smooth-bore musket; and a principal reason for the selection of Nesbitt's battalion lay in the fact that the Kaffirs had a great dread of British rifles.

At the same time a force of the Cape Mounted Rifles, under command of Major-General H. Somerset, was operating in the neighbourhood of Fort Beaufort against the Kaffir Chief Macomo. Nesbitt's quest in search of cattle proved futile; but his position in the Southern Amatolas aided Somerset, by preventing Macomo receiving assistance from his colleague Sandilli.

Nesbitt now affected a junction with General Somerset, and on the 23rd the latter, with a force of R.A., Colonel Fordyce's Brigade, and the C.M.R., moved directly on the enemy's position at the head of the Water Kloof after directing Colonel Nesbitt to move at daylight up the Blinkwater and turn the right flank of the enemy's position on the Hog's Back Range.

At sunrise the fog lifted; and as Somerset advanced he detached the C.M.R. and two guns R.A. to his left to cover the movement of the 60th. From the western edge of Hog's Back Hill the guns opened fire. The Rifles were now observed to be hotly engaged with the enemy, 'moving up,' to use the words of the Despatch, 'in skirmishing order in fine style along the face of the ridge, receiving the enemy's fire and driving him up the hill.'

The direct and flanking attacks were carried out in successful combination. The enemy after gallant resistance at length evacuated his position, which was one of remarkable strength. The troops who had been marching and engaged with the enemy from 4 A.M. were halted at 11.30, and the immediate object having been gained with trifling loss, General Somerset directed the Rifle Battalion to return to King William's Town, which was reached on the 31st.

In his subsequent Despatch Sir Harry Smith describes the country of the Water Kloof and Blinkwater as being almost impracticable, and states that the position captured having been regarded by the Kaffirs as impregnable, the moral effect of the victory was great. He adds that the enemy fought with great bravery and skill.

Among the troops engaged were several regiments of local levies; and as those levies required strengthening, the Duke of Wellington, Commander-in-Chief at home, directed Sir Harry to allow volunteering for those Corps to the extent of 400 men from the regiments under his own command. The letter in which this sanction was conveyed mentioned that the vacancies caused by these volunteers would be filled up by drafts from home, and a certain melancholy interest is added by the intimation that the ship in which they were to embark was the ill-fated *Birkenhead*.

On November 4 another strong patrol, consisting of twelve Officers and three hundred and eighty O.R. under command of Major Bedford, proceeded to Fort Hare as escort to the Government Commissioners, who were on their way to the Orange River. On its return the patrol made a night march from Fort White to the junction of the Kiskama and Umdecina Rivers for the purpose of co-operating with one under command of Major Wilmot, R.A., for a joint attack upon the Kaffir Chief, Scyolo. But the elusive Scyolo having previously decamped, the patrol returned to King William's Town. The Battalion was constantly finding movable columns for the purpose either of escorting or carrying off Kaffir cattle, and had several men wounded during the course of these minor operations. But the Intelligence Department of the enemy was evidently on the alert, and the search for cattle seems to have frequently proved fruitless.

On November 29 an operation on a somewhat larger scale was attempted. Under command of Lieut.-Colonel Mackinnon was placed A Division, which was organised in two Brigades, the first under Lieut.-Colonel Michel commanding the 6th Regiment, and the second under Colonel Nesbitt.[1] A, B, and C Companies under Captains Bligh, Hope, and Rigaud took part in this expedition, A being attached to the 1st Brigade, B and C to the 2nd. The force also included a Brigade of Cavalry, consisting of the 12th Lancers and the Cape Mounted Rifles.

Near the Black Kei Mackinnon's Division was joined by General Somerset with a force of the Cape Mounted Rifles, Fingoes, etc. On December 9 Colonel Michel attacked a high and rocky mountain, on the summit of which were large quantities of cattle, which were, however, as usual successfully removed by the Kaffirs under cover of the heavy rain and fog.

On the 17th the force moved to the Somo River and encamped. On the 28th it moved to Butterworth, where it was joined by the 2nd Queen's Regiment.

Meanwhile D, E, and F Companies, under Captains McKenzie and Mosley and Lieutenant W. P. Salmon—the whole commanded by Major Bedford—had formed part of a force under Lieut.-Colonel Eyre of the 73rd Regiment, made up as follows : 12th Lancers, 99 R. and F. ; R.E., 2 ; 60th Rifles, 216 ; 73rd Regiment, 430 ; Cape Mounted Rifles, 63 ; Local Levies, 146 ; Total 956.

On December 2 Eyre bivouacked on the Konga. On

---

[1] Colonel (afterwards Field-Marshal Sir John) Michel was a remarkable man : an excellent soldier, of very independent character. He gained distinction in the Indian Mutiny, and commanded a Division in the Chinese War of 1860. Michel was for a very short time in the 60th.

the 4th he reached the heights above the Great Kei. Strict orders had been issued against any act of aggression on the part of the troops; but it was soon abundantly evident that the Kaffirs intended to dispute the passage of the wagon drift (or ford) over the river on the road to Butterworth. The enemy was well posted on the left bank commanding the Drift, and as Eyre reconnoitred the position a large body of Kaffirs (estimated from 3,000 to 4,000), many of them mounted, appeared in his rear. Four Companies, including one of the Rifles, were therefore left under cover to guard against any attack from this quarter. Hardly had these Companies been posted when a volley from the right shewed the presence of an enemy in another unexpected quarter. He was, however, soon driven away, although not without a sharp struggle and some loss on both sides. Colonel Eyre with his main body now marched down to the Drift, which had been rendered impracticable for wagons by the fact of the enemy having cleverly heaped together large stones in the river. The position of the Kaffirs on the further bank was also strengthened by a number of stone breastworks arranged in tiers. They were proof against musketry; and it being obvious that a frontal attack could not be made without great loss, the Grenadier Company of the 73rd, supported by Mosley's Company of the Rifles, was directed to move to its left and cross the river higher up under cover of the Krantz or mountain spur which concealed them from the enemy. These two Companies successfully crossed the river, outflanking the enemy's position. Colonel Eyre was now able to ford the river with his main body; but the enemy's resistance still continued on both banks, and the fighting in some cases was hand to hand. At length it ceased, and the whole force, including the four Companies which had been left to guard the rear and had been sharply engaged, established itself on the left bank. Eyre now advanced up the steep heights; and on reaching the final ridge, which on that side bounds the great valley of the Kei, encountered a fresh body of Kaffirs lining the crest Once more their position was turned; but it was not until 9 P.M. that the Springs were reached, the men having marched and been in action from daylight without any halt for refreshment. Eyre therefore directed the infantry and wagons to bivouack. He himself proceeded with the cavalry to Butterworth, with a view to ensuring the safety of the Europeans at the Missionary Station. Eyre's loss was slight, being only six killed and twelve wounded. The enemy acknowledged one hundred casualties.

In a subsequent Despatch to the Colonial Office Sir Harry Smith spoke in warm terms of Colonel Eyre's operations.

Next day the infantry were brought up to Butterworth and Eyre moved in the direction of the Bashee River, in the hope of rounding up a large head of cattle. The weather, however, proved adverse, and although the Colonel ultimately captured between 6,000 to 7,000 head, he was dissatisfied with the result.

Despite disappointments the cattle raiding was now made with greater success, and the number captured during the last few weeks was roughly calculated at 25,000. On January 6, 1852, General Somerset, leaving Colonel Eyre's force at Butterworth, advanced to the Great Kei and crossed it at Eyre's Drift on the following morning. After making a tour through the country of several Kaffir Chiefs Somerset returned to King William's Town, which he reached on January 12. During these minor operations one Rifleman was killed, several were wounded, and five died of sickness.

WRECK OF H.M.S. *BIRKENHEAD*

On January 27 the Rifle Battalion formed part of a column under Colonel Michel ordered to destroy the crops in Seyolo's country. This having been affected the column returned on February 29 to King William's Town.

2

The Records of the 2nd Battalion pursue the even tenor of their way until the early months of 1854. But at this point it seems to have occurred to some one that several matters of importance had been omitted, among others any allusion to the tragedy of the *Birkenhead*. The omission is accordingly atoned for somewhat casually in the following terms :—

'The draft of 2 Sergeants and 40 R. and F., which embarked at Cork on the 7th January, 1852, on board H.M.S. *Birkenhead*, was reduced to 2 Sergeants and 9 R. and F. by the melancholy loss of that vessel off Point Danger on the 26th February, 1852.'

The incident of the wreck of the *Birkenhead*—which had a celebrity almost world-wide—deserves something more than this curt statement, which—despite its brevity—contains three errors of detail.

H.M.S. *Birkenhead*, a paddle-wheel steamer of 1,400 tons, had been launched hardly more than two years, and was considered 'the latest thing in ships.' She was conveying drafts for the regiments in the Cape Colony, and after coaling at Capetown sailed at 6 P.M. on February 25, 1852, for East London, with—as nearly as possible—638 persons on board. Of these 130 comprised the ship's company, 478 were soldiers, 7 were women, and 13 children.[1] The troops were under command of Lieut.-

---

[1] The various returns made did not quite agree, but the figures given may be taken as substantially correct.

Colonel Alexander Seton, 74th Highlanders, and the several drafts were as follows :—

	Officers.	Sergeants.	R. and F.
12th Lancers	2	1	5
2nd (Queen's) Regiment	1	1	50
6th ,, ,,	1	1	60
12th ,, ,,	—	1	68
43rd ,, ,,	1	1	40
45th ,, ,,	—	—	4
73rd ,, ,,	3	1	70
74th ,, ,,	2	1	60
91st ,, ,,	1	1	60
Women	—	—	13
Children	—	—	7
60th Rifles	—	1	39

The draft of the 60th was attached to the 91st.

The names of the Riflemen were as follows :—

Saved : Sergeant David Andrews, W. Burlow, T. Nuttall, T. Smith, W. Sooter, A. Laskie, H. Voss, J. Hanlon, H. Maltier, J. Stanfield.

Lost : Corporal F. Curtis, J. Brown, J. Brookland, J. Callaghan, W. Chapman, E. Elliot, T. Frost, A. Hamilton, M. Kelcher, W. Kelly, C. Lucas, J. Maher, J. Moore, I. McAcy, D. McQuade, P. O'Brien, T. Peacock, J. Rees, W. Russell, H. Scutts, J. Story, P. Stokes, J. Thompson, W. Wilkins, W. Wilkinson, J. Wilson, W. Woolward, J. Wallis, S. Jacobs, J. Ladd.

The story of the *Birkenhead*, with the proceedings of the subsequent Court Martial, is told in full detail by Messrs. Addison and Matthews in their work, entitled ' A Deathless Story.' A summary only is needed here.

Between 10 and 11 P.M. on the day on which the vessel quitted Simon's Bay a military officer well acquainted with the coast told the Naval Officer of the watch that the ship was some miles out of her course. He proved to be right, for at 2 A.M. on the following morning she struck a sunken rock off Danger Point between one and two

WRECK OF H.M.S. *BIRKENHEAD*

miles distant. The night was dark, yet the sea calm, and all, or nearly all, on board would have been saved but for two fatal errors. The Captain running up on deck ordered the engines to be reversed, the consequence being that the ship at once filled with water.[1] He then ordered the boats to be launched; but it would appear that during the whole voyage boat drill had not been practised. Three boats were indeed successfully launched, and the thirteen women and seven children safely embarked; but in the case of the paddle-box boat the pin of the davits was rusted in and could not be extracted, and in two other instances the ropes or tackling broke while the boats were being lowered.

The forepart of the ship broke off within a few minutes of the ship striking. The troops had fallen in by order Colonel Seton, and the discipline was splendid. Even when the ship's captain called out that all survivors had better jump overboard and make for the boats the military officers had no difficulty in restraining the men, on the ground of endangering the lives of the women and children. At 2.25 A.M. the vessel, which had again broken in two parts, went down, but 40 or 50 men remained in the rigging, which was out of water. Some were gradually overcome by the cold and dropped into the water, but the majority were subsequently taken off by a schooner. The boats picked up as many as they could hold. A certain number on rafts or wreckage landed at Danger Point. Upwards of two hundred men with the aid of spars, etc., reached the shore east of Danger Point, but the surf was high and a species of weed, known as 'sea bamboo,' about a quarter of a mile from the shore proved an insurmountable

---

[1] It will be remembered that when—nearly half a century later—the *Warren Hastings* was wrecked, the Captain ordered 'full speed ahead,' and thereby kept the water from entering the hole made by the rocks, and saving the lives of all on board.

obstacle to men already exhausted by hours of immersion. Almost all consequently perished. Some were killed by sharks, which for the most part attacked those who were naked. Colonel Seton and the ship's captain were drowned, and of all on board not quite two hundred were saved.

The following is an extract from a letter written shortly afterwards by Sergeant Andrews of the 60th :—

'During the short time that elapsed from the striking to the sinking of the ship Colonel Seton was most calm and firm in all his orders, his first care being directed to putting in the boats the women, children, and sick; and then, on account of the heavy lurching of the vessel, which caused the horses to plunge, thereby endangering the lives of those on board, he ordered the horses to be thrown overboard.' (It is said that all safely reached the shore.) 'Colonel Seton was most kind, although at the same time he was most calm and firm in all his orders, and even at the most critical moments his instructions were carried out without a murmur from either side, for he was so much esteemed by all present. His last words to me were, "Sergeant-Major, keep the men steady and quiet, and I shall be the last man that leaves the ship." During the time the vessel was on the rocks it was pitch dark '—except for one or two lanterns, and the binnacle light—' and the commander of the ship was trying to capsize (*sic*) the paddle-box boats; but with all the confusion on board all listened most attentively to Colonel Seton's orders, and so great was the silence that a pin might be heard to drop.'

Of the ten Riflemen saved, four were picked up by the boats and six either clung to the rigging or swam ashore.

Such an instance of steady discipline and unflinching self-sacrifice created a sensation of appreciation far beyond the limits of the British Isles; and, by order of the King of Prussia, its story was read three times to his troops on parade. Nearly half a century elapsed before a similar incident on the *Warren Hastings* proved that the serene courage of British soldiers in a terrible emergency shone not less brightly than it had done in the *Birkenhead*.

3

Early in 1852 Sir Harry Smith assumed personal command of the forces in South Africa; and on March 5 concentrated his troops at Fort Beaufort, with a view to driving the enemy from the Eisener Krantz, or 'Iron Mountain,' a formidable stronghold held by a large body of Kaffirs. The force comprised a Cavalry Brigade made up of the 12th Lancers and Cape Mounted Rifles, and two Brigades of Infantry, one under Colonel Michel, composed of the 6th, 60th, and four Companies of the 45th, with two Guns R.A.; the other of the 43rd and 73rd, with two Guns R.A., under Colonel Eyre. Both Brigades contained detachments of Hottentot and Fingo Levies.

On the 10th the troops reached the Water Kloof, and on the 15th the base of the Iron Mountain, which was seen to be occupied in force by the enemy. An attempt to turn his right flank was frustrated by the clever tactics of the Kaffirs, advantageously posted in bush and scrub in rear of a rocky ravine. A frontal attack became therefore necessary, and was led by the 60th. The steep and difficult ground caused a momentary check; but Captain Hope's Company (B) fixing swords charged and, supported by the remainder of the battalion, carried the mountain with the loss only of a Rifleman killed and two wounded.

'The enemy,' says Sir Harry Smith in his despatch, 'was driven over Krantzes and rocks with great slaughter. Much cattle and many horses were captured, in the defence of which so stout a resistance had been made; and Major Bedford with two Companies of the 60th Rifles pursued the fugitives over declivities nearly impassable, many more cattle falling into his hands. . . . In this gallant and rapid affair Colonel Michel reports that he remarked the especial gallantry displayed by Captain Hope and Lieutenant Du Cane of the 60th Rifles.'

Michel did not linger, but continuing his operations, cleared the whole neighbourhood. Colonel Nesbitt was also mentioned in the C.-in-C.'s despatch.

The Brigade returned through the Blinkwater and Chumie, and on the 21st bivouacked in the Wolf's Den. Three days later it rejoined the Battalion in the Amatola Basin, and on the same day reached the Headquarter camp on the south side of Seven Kesof Mountain. Next day the Brigade was again detached by Sir Harry Smith and marched via Fort Cox to the foot of the Slenya Mountain, where a standing camp was established. On the 26th the 45th Regiment in bivouac at the Wolf's Den was contained by a body of Kaffirs and Hottentots, while the 60th arriving on the overlooking heights was attacked by another force and lost five men wounded, mostly belonging to E Company. The 45th then joined us, and the enemy was driven from his positions. On April 17 the Brigade, now commanded by Colonel Nesbitt, had a sharp skirmish with the enemy under the Amatola Rocks. An attempt had been made by B and F Companies to ambush him, but the wary Kaffir avoided the trap. On April 29 some wagons were for the first time successfully moved up the Slenya Mountain. The 60th with Cape Levies also moved up, reaching the summit on the following day, whence they constructed a road into the Basin.

Meanwhile a change had taken place in the command, Sir Harry Smith having been recalled and succeeded by Lieut.-General Hon. George Cathcart. Sir Harry had been considered dilatory by Lord Grey, Secretary of State for the Colonies, whose opinion was, however, flatly controverted by the Duke of Wellington, perhaps a more competent authority![1] On April 25 Sir Harry Smith

---

[1] Lord Grey was self-opinionated and eccentric to a degree not far removed from mental aberration.

had come to bid farewell to the Brigade, and a few days afterwards took leave of the troops in a charming and sympathetic General Order.

'Brother Officers and soldiers,' said he, 'nothing is more painful than to bid farewell to old and faithful friends. I have served my Queen and country many years; and attached as I have ever been to gallant soldiers, none were ever more endeared to me than those serving in the arduous campaign of 1851-52 in South Africa. The unceasing labours, the night marches, the burning sun, the torrents of rain, have been encountered with a cheerfulness as conspicuous as the intrepidity with which you have met the enemy in so many enterprising fights and skirmishes in his own mountain fastnesses and strongholds, and from which you have ever driven him victoriously.

'I leave you, my comrades, in the fervent hope of laying before your Queen, your country, and the Duke of Wellington, these services as they deserve, which reflect so much honour upon you.

'Farewell, my comrades, your honour and interests will be ever far more dear to me than my own.'

General Cathcart arrived at Slenya Camp on May 5, and wishing to reconnoitre the neighbouring country was on the next day escorted to Keiskama Hoek and back by Major Bedford with B, E, D, and F Companies, and next day by Captain Hope with A, B, and C Companies to Yellow Woods.

The Brunswick Rifle having been called in and the Minié served out in its place, the Companies began their practice therewith on the 10th. On the 29th the Battalion returned to King William's Town, whence from time to time it formed part of flying columns scouring the country.

On July 2 the Battalion, consisting of fifteen officers and 489 O.R., quitted King William's Town, reached Beaufort on the 4th, and on the 6th the standing camp at Paynter's Farm.

Here the Governor's Camp was also pitched; but next day the Battalion proceeded to the Krumoo Heights (where they were joined by the 1st Battalion of the Rifle Brigade from Bear's Farm), and bivouacked. The country was scoured and the troops occupied in escorting supply wagons, clearing the bush, and road making, etc.

From the 15th to the 17th operations were conducted on the Waterkloof and adjoining heights by four columns under superintendence of General Cathcart. The columns successfully converged on each other and cleared the Waterkloof.

On October 2 the Battalion was concentrated at the Headquarter camp, Fort Hare. On the 16th D Company, under command of Captain Sotheby, proceeded in charge of supply wagons and cattle to Fort White. At 1.30 A.M. next day the guard, consisting of a Corporal and six riflemen, was attacked by Kaffirs. The fighting, although on a small scale, must have been sharp, one Rifleman being killed and two wounded, all by assegai wounds. The Company returned next day to King William's Town.

The movement of flying columns was incessant. A vast quantity of the enemy's crops and many of his huts were destroyed. Several Kaffirs were killed and others taken prisoner. By degrees order was restored, and the Kaffir Revolt subdued.

'The result of these vigorous and unceasing movements,' observes General Cathcart in his despatch dated the 1st November, 'extending through the whole of the mountain range of the Amatolas from the Chumie Heights over the Hog's Back, the Gulu, the Doorn Mountain to the Kabousie Neck on one side of the Buffalo Range, from Mount Kempt to T'Slambie's Kop on the other, has been to drive the enemy completely out of all his favourite haunts.'

A few days later he mentioned among other Officers the name of his A.D.C., Lieut. Arthur Greville of the 60th.

So passed the year away, and on March 9, 1853,

KAFFIR WAR ENDED

General Cathcart was able to report that peace had been restored throughout South Africa.

The news that the long and wearisome campaign had come to an end must have been received with general satisfaction. Hostilities had been forced upon us by the action of the Kaffirs, for the lives of European settlers and even British dominion had been threatened. But there was little glory to be gained in defeating half-armed savages; and the necessary action of burning their Kraals, destroying their crops, and carrying off their cattle must have been most repugnant to all concerned; the more so, that the conspicuous gallantry of our foe, his commanding presence, and his many good qualities could not fail to excite admiration in the heart of the British soldier. The extremes of climate have been already described in Sir Harry Smith's farewell Order. The almost roadless country, the steep mountains, the unbridged rivers, passable only by drifts which could at one moment be forded dry shod and an hour afterwards be fifteen or twenty feet under water, all combined to make progress extremely difficult and terribly fatiguing; but on the other hand no better school for the training of Riflemen could easily be found.

During the progress of the war Colonel Nesbitt, Major Bedford, and other Officers of the Battalion had been repeatedly mentioned in despatches, and at its termination Major Bedford received the Brevet of Lieut.-Colonel, Captains Hope and Mackenzie that of Major. A Medal was subsequently issued to all ranks. The list of our officers engaged is as follows: Lieut.-Colonel C. L. Nesbitt; Major W. F. Bedford; Captains J. K. Mackenzie, Hon. A. Hope, C. W. H. Sotheby, G. W. Bligh, G. Rigaud, W. P. Salmon, S. Kenny; Lieutenants H. E. Warren, A. G. Greville, C. W. Earle, W. Mure, H. J. E. Robertson;

2nd Lieutenants H. Cockburn, H. P. Montgomery, F. Fitzpatrick, C. H. C. Ellis; Quartermasters Holmes, Storey, Fitzgibbon, Fitzhenry, Tilford; Assistant-Surgeon Nicholson.

4

On the termination of the war the Battalion was split up into detachments either in occupation of strategical points or for the purpose of road construction.

Early in September Lieut.-Colonel Nesbitt proceeded to King William's Town to take over command of the 2nd Division of the Army vice Major-General Yorke, who had gone to England, leaving Captain G. W. Bligh in command of the Battalion. On October 1 occurred a tragedy, for Colonel Nesbitt while visiting his outposts was drowned at Hobb's Drift on the Keiskama River. Every possible effort to save him was made by his A.D.C., 2nd Lieut. Ellis (son of the late Lieut.-Colonel Ellis), and two Orderlies of the 12th Lancers; but all in vain, and it was not until the 9th that his body was even recovered. Next day the whole garrison paraded in King William's Town for the funeral.

In General Orders the Commander-in-Chief stated that 'the Army has been deprived of the services of an able officer who upon every occasion of the arduous contest with the Kaffirs performed the duties entrusted to him with every credit to himself.' And Lord Hardinge, who on the recent death of the Duke of Wellington had become Commander-in-Chief of the British Army, wrote to express his deep regret at Colonel Nesbitt's death and his sense of the great loss sustained by the Service.

Colonel Nesbitt was succeeded by G. A. Spence, hitherto 2nd Lieut.-Colonel of the 1st Battalion. Colonel Spence did not, however, join his new battalion until July 1854.

5

During the year 1853 hostilities had broken out between Turkey and Russia. In March 1854 France and England formed an alliance with Turkey and declared war upon Russia. In what is generally, although inaccurately, termed the Crimean War our Regiment necessarily took no part, its two battalions being far away from the scene of action. The Home Government asked, however, that the 1st Battalion might be sent from India to the Crimea, but was informed by the Governor-General that it could not be spared.

Major Hon. A. Hope was, however, personally engaged in the Crimea. He had gone home soon after the conclusion of the Kaffir War, and on the outbreak of that with Russia was appointed Brigade-Major to the Highland Brigade under command of Sir Colin Campbell. In this capacity he gained distinction, and in December 1854 was given the Brevet rank of Lieut.-Colonel. Early in the following year Hope received the Regimental rank of Major, and was in consequence obliged to give up his Staff Appointment and return to England. Being, however, like a good soldier anxious for further active service, he succeeded in being appointed 2nd Lieut.-Colonel of the 93rd Highlanders, and again went out to the Crimea. Our own Regiment, therefore, saw him no more. His subsequent career was brilliant but lamentably brief. During the Indian Mutiny, being still only thirty-seven years of age, he was appointed to the command of a Brigade and took part in the Relief of Lucknow. In April 1858 he was killed. Lord Wolseley in his autobiography speaks of Hope in the highest terms, and evidently considered him one of the most rising soldiers in the Army.

6

In May 1854 the rank of 2nd Lieutenant hitherto borne by the junior Officers of Rifle Regiments was abolished and that of Ensign substituted.

On November 1 two new Companies were added to the 2nd Battalion, which now consisted of six in South Africa and six at the Depôt. The Establishment of the service companies was as follows:

F.O.	Cpts.	Lts.	Ens.	Staff.	Stf.-Sgts.	Sgts.	Bgls.	Cpls.	Rflmen.
2	6	8	4	5	7	30	13	30	579

In February 1855 the organisation was again altered to eight Service and four Depôt Companies. The Establishment of the former being:

F.O.	Cpts.	Lts.	Ens.	Staff.	Stf.-Sgts.	Sgts.	Bgls.	Cpls.	Rflmen.
2	8	10	6	5	7	40	17	40	760

During the following June a draft under Captain R. J. Feilden, consisting of six Officers and 193 O.R., joined the Battalion at King William's Town. In September the Battalion was armed with the Enfield-Pritchett rifle. In April 1856 the Officers' 'slung jacket' and the rifle coatee were replaced by the new tunic.

The remainder of the year passed away uneventfully. The Battalion was split up into various detachments and companies, which were constantly quitting and returning to Headquarters. In October two subalterns, both of whom at a later date commanded battalions, viz. Lieuts. J. S. Algar and K. G. Henderson, joined Headquarters at King William's Town.

7

Meanwhile the exigences of the war with Russia had shown the need of increasing the Infantry of our Army,

3RD BATTALION RAISED

and on April 1, 1855, a third Battalion was added to the Regiment, command of it being given to Brevet Lieut.-Colonel Bedford. The other Officers posted thereto were Majors Hon. H. L. Powys and Hon. A. Hope; Captains C. N. North, W. P. Salmon; Brevet Lieut.-Colonel E. Parker; and the following Lieutenants were given Companies: A. FitzGerald, F. St. John, F. Dawson, J. P. Battersby, J. L. Barnes, B. E. Ward, V. Tongue, R. Freer, F. C. Fletcher. The Subalterns included Lieut. C. D. C. Ellis, W. A. Dean Pitt, F. D. Farquharson, J. J. Phillips, H. G. Deedes, J. George; Ensigns F. Northey, W. F. Carleton, J. C. Shackle, R. M. Hazen, Hogge, and B. D. Forsyth. Lieut. J. Forbes was appointed Adjutant, and H. Campbell Quartermaster. Other ranks comprised 10 Sergeants, 16 Corporals, 6 Buglers, 508 Riflemen.

The Battalion was raised in Dublin, and during the first two years of its existence was quartered partly there, partly at the Curragh. It was dressed in a double-breasted tunic in place of the Rifle coatee hitherto worn by the two other Battalions. Its armament was the 'long' Enfield Rifle.

On the news of the outbreak of the Indian Mutiny two years later it was determined to re-raise the 4th Battalion, and this was accordingly done at Winchester on July 27, 1857.

In the case of the 3rd Battalion the commissioned ranks had been filled up by promotion within the Regiment, but for the 4th Battalion the Field Officers, Captains, and Lieutenants were brought in from outside regiments. This assembly of heterogeneous and strange Officers appeared rather unpromising for the future of the Battalion; but as it happened the effect was not detrimental. The Lieut.-Colonel, Edward Vesey Brown, retired the following year and was succeeded by the Senior Major,

William Pretyman, who had served regimentally with the 33rd Regiment and also on the Staff during the Crimean War. Pretyman left behind him a good reputation as a C.O., but his period of command lasted little over a year. On retirement his place was taken by Major Robert Beaufoy Hawley, a master of his art, whose practical instruction and influence permeated far beyond the limits of his own regiment. The 4th Battalion had the advantage of being under Hawley's command for nearly thirteen years with the best possible results; results which remained permanently in the Battalion even when subsequently commanded by Officers of a less distinguished type.

The advantage to the 4th Battalion of Colonel Hawley's long period of command can hardly be overestimated; but the 3rd Battalion was less fortunate in its Commanders, and not until many years had elapsed did it have the benefit of being commanded by an Officer of first-rate capacity, and that Officer had been Hawley's Adjutant.

Both Battalions have now been disbanded, and it is therefore admissible to comment on their respective careers. From 1879 to 1885 the 3rd Battalion experienced what may be termed one long period of active service. It fought in Zululand, in Natal, and in Egypt; and its fortitude and tenacity at the Ingogo River in 1881 is one of the brightest spots in the history of the Regiment. In the 2nd Boer War it was greatly distinguished in the actions preceding as well as following the relief of Ladysmith.

The 4th Battalion, on the other hand, prior to the outbreak of the Great War, saw service only in an Indian Frontier expedition, in two small frontier expeditions, and during the fag end of the Boer War.

In the Great War the two Battalions were brought home from India post haste in the same ship. They were brigaded together in the 27th Division and fought with equal distinction; both were almost destroyed in the 2nd Battle of Ypres. Not long afterwards the Battalions, reinforced by drafts, were sent to Salonika, where the 3rd remained until the Armistice. The 4th Battalion was brought back to France in 1918, after three years' respite from hard fighting. Having been filled up by drafts, a large proportion of which consisted of the sick and wounded in the earlier phases, it had claims to be still regarded as a Battalion of the Old Army and enhanced its reputation accordingly during the concluding actions of the War.

CHAPTER VI

WE left the 1st Battalion at Jullundur in 1854.

It had been customary in the battalion to devote a part of its annual course of musketry to 'skirmishing practices,' and this custom being brought to the notice of the Commander-in-Chief at the Horse Guards it commended itself to him, and proved the germ of the 'Field Firing' of the present day.

In General Orders of November 14, 1854, the following compliment was paid to the Battalion :—

'The half-yearly confidential report of the 1st Battalion 60th Royal Rifles (in which the Skirmishing Ball Practice introduced into that Corps is reported upon) having been laid before the General C.-in-C., his Lordship [1] has directed that steps may be taken to ensure the same system of instruction being practised at all stations in India where it may be practicable, as it cannot fail to prove most useful and advantageous. His Excellency the C.-in-C. in India is pleased accordingly to order that wherever it may be feasible from local circumstances the system above alluded to is to be carried out.

'In the 60th Rifles a sufficient number of targets are planted out to admit of the extension of a Company. All the usual Light Infantry practice is carried out within a distance of 500 yards, and the men become thereby accustomed to judging distances and consequent range of sight.'

It is needless to say that the principles of that system have ever since been maintained throughout the whole Army.

[1] *I.e.* General Viscount Hardinge, C.-in-C. at the Horse Guards.

The C.-in-C. in India at this period was General (afterwards F.-M.) Sir William Gomm, erstwhile a distinguished Staff Officer under Wellington in Spain and Portugal. He decided on forming a Camp of Exercises at Umballa, to which our Battalion proceeded in December, reaching its destination on the 29th. The force assembled consisted of one Cavalry, one Artillery, and three Infantry Brigades under Major-General M. Fane, commanding the Sirhind Division.[1] Colonel Dennis commanding the Battalion was appointed a Brigadier, his Brigade including his own Battalion, temporarily commanded by Major Bingham, with the 60th and 61st Native Infantry. During the continuance of the Camp of Exercises the Battalion was inspected by Sir W. Gomm, who made complimentary remarks on the appearance of the men, the steadiness and celerity of the Battalion, and on the order and regularity of the Camp arrangements.

2

On December 1, 1855, the 1st Battalion marched from Jullundur to Meerut, its strength being 18 Officers and 814 other ranks. Meerut was reached on the 28th, where a draft of 93 Riflemen from England awaited the Battalion. On August 1, 1856, cholera broke out and did not disappear until the 29th. The losses from this scourge amounted to 29 men, 7 women, and 12 children. On December 19 the Battalion was inspected by General the Hon. George Anson, who had recently succeeded Sir William Gomm as Commander-in-Chief in India. He expressed himself in

---

[1] *I.e.* Cavalry Brigade, the 9th Lancers, 4th and 9th Light Cavalry, under Colonel Hope Grant, C.B.; Artillery Brigade, three Troops Bengal Horse Artillery; Infantry: 1st Brigade, 32nd and 52nd Regiments, 28th N.I., Colonel Brooke, C.B.; 2nd Brigade, 53rd Regiment, 70th Regiment, N.I., Nusseret Battalion, Colonel Sibbald, C.B.

terms of high compliment, and made a special request for a copy of the printed Standing Orders of the Battalion and of the book written by its late Adjutant, Thomas Mitchell, on Light Drill and Field Exercises. On January 1, 1857, the Battalion was armed with the long Enfield Rifle. It had not been proposed to issue any ammunition with this Rifle, and only on strong protest from the Commanding Officer did the Military Authorities allow the Battalion ten rounds per man. When the Mutiny broke out five months later these ten rounds were the whole of the ammunition that had been served out.

3

Although Great Britain had had a footing in Hindustan, principally in the neighbourhood of Calcutta, for a much longer period, the rise of our Indian Empire may roughly be dated from the victory of Lord Clive at Plassey in 1757. It was governed by a large commercial concern known as the East India Company, which exercised almost full powers of government, and raised a military force composed partly of Europeans but as to the large majority of native troops. Successive Governor-Generals were sent out from England with the special object of maintaining the policy of no extension of territory; but despite of all instructions force of circumstances compelled gradual advance. As we have already seen, at the termination of the Sikh Wars the Punjaub was taken over by the East India Company, and in 1856 the very last act of Lord Dalhousie before his retirement was the annexation of Oude.

These various enlargements of territory were not affected without exciting considerable discontent among the natives. Other causes of dissatisfaction and alarm were not wanting. In some quarters, military not less than civil, the conversion of natives to Christianity was pursued with far more zeal than discretion. The introduction of railways, even on a small scale, had a disturbing effect, for to the Hindoo mind a steam-engine at full speed represented some horrible monster or angry deity rather than a mechanical contrivance. Then, again, there was the old prophecy which said that the rule of the East India Company would terminate at the end of a century after Plassey. Finally the losses and disasters of Great Britain in the recent war with Russia were greatly exaggerated; and the Native Indian troops, ridiculously flattered by their European commanders, came to the conclusion that they were strong enough to defeat the British forces in Bengal in open warfare. So far as numbers alone were concerned it may perhaps be thought that they had some reason for this opinion. For although for many years past the handful of European Regiments in the service of the East India Company had been reinforced by British Cavalry and Infantry Regiments of the Line, there were in Bengal at this period only some 22,000 white soldiers as against 150,000 of the native army. Long-headed soldiers of experience had for some years past foretold the outbreak; and seven or eight years previously Major Hodson, the well-known leader of Irregular Cavalry, had in conversation with Captain Muter of our Regiment expressed the opinion that the next war would be one between the British and Native Armies. In days gone by movements of a mutinous character, notably one at Vellore in 1824, had broken out, but had been rapidly quelled by firmness on the part of the Military Authorities concerned.

After the annexation of the Punjaub discipline in the Native Army became more and more relaxed, and General

Sir Charles Napier, Commander-in-Chief, determined to disband the worst of them. Unfortunately Lord Dalhousie, Governor-General, took the opposite view, and Napier in consequence resigned his command.

Speaking generally the people of India were satisfied with British rule, and though the expression 'Indian Mutiny' has been hallowed by time, the term Sepoy Revolt would perhaps be more accurate. Matters were eventually brought to a head by the issue of cartridges which in some instances at all events were really greased with animal fat, obnoxious both to Hindoo and Mussulman; to the former as tending to break his caste, to the latter as being the flesh of a possibly unclean animal. However small may have been the number of cases in which this fat was used, the news in a community such as that of India would spread like wildfire with no doubt every possible exaggeration. The traditional differences between Hindoo and Mussulman had been hitherto considered to constitute a bond of safety; for the former regarded the Mussulman as an unclean creature, while the Mussulman despised the Hindoo as an idolator. Common action between the two sects appeared therefore impossible; and it was either astonishing carelessness or bad fortune that the cartridge grease should have cemented a bond of union between them. But although this may have been the immediate cause, there were concurrently circumstances which gave strength to a belief in the easy-going and conservative native mind that the country was being ruined by such new-fangled ideas as the introduction of railways, the electric telegraph, etc.

The Native Army had in addition been pampered by its rulers, civil and military. Its exploits on the field of battle were ridiculously exaggerated in despatches, while those of the white troops, the real authors of victory, received little or no notice; and the consequence was a belief on the part of the Cipahi (corrupted into Sepoy) that not only was he himself invincible but that he was more than a match for the British soldier. Sir Colin Campbell, hastily summoned from England as Commander-in-Chief when the outbreak took place, remarked in conversation that the East India Company had been given a long trial and that its rulers, whether military or civilian, were directly responsible for the Mutiny.

When the revolt broke out the force of white troops throughout India consisted of about 26,000 men of the British Army, together with about 12,000 Europeans of the East India Company's own army; and of this force probably less than three-fifths were serving actually in the Provinces of Bengal and the Punjaub, the remainder being stationed in those of Madras or Bombay, which happily were not affected by the disturbances. At this period the Royal Artillery were never stationed in India, and the guns were manned either by the Company's Europeans or by Native gunners.

The Native Regular Army in Bengal was, as already stated, about 150,000 strong. There were also contingents in the pay of Native Princes, and of these many joined in the revolt. On the other hand there were a good many irregular regiments, both cavalry and infantry, recruited largely from the Punjaub after its anexation at the end of the Sikh War of 1849. Despite the fact that the soldiers of this force had so recently been our enemies, almost all remained strictly faithful to us throughout the crisis.

4

On May 5 a Brigade Parade was held at Meerut, and cartridges, in this case at all events, of the old kind, which had been used from time immemorial, were served out to the 3rd Native Cavalry Regiment. Eighty-five men refused to take them. The men were arrested and brought before a Court Martial composed of Native Officers, who condemned them to periods of imprisonment with hard labour from six to ten years. The sentences having been confirmed by the G.O.C. Meerut Division, the Mutineers were placed under a guard composed of two companies of the 60th and five-and-twenty men of the Carabineers, and a general parade for the promulgation of the sentences was ordered for the morning of Saturday, May 9. At daybreak all the troops in the Station were drawn up on the Rifle Parade Ground. They consisted of the Carabineers, the Rifles, a Troop of Horse Artillery, a Field Battery, and the 11th and 20th Native Infantry. The Carabineers, the Riflemen, and the Horse Artillery were then ordered to load, and were so disposed on the Parade Ground that the least movement of insubordination would have been followed by instant death.

The Mutineers of the Light Cavalry were then marched on to the ground, where they were stripped of their uniform and accoutrements and put into irons. The prisoners made a vain appeal for mercy, and then broke out into reproaches against their comrades for allowing the sentence to be carried out. So little apprehension was however felt of native interference that the prisoners were handed over to the Civil Authorities and placed in gaol under the charge of native warders.

The Parade was dismissed. The Native Regiments marched back to their lines, but in a state of suppressed excitement, and it is believed they at once planned an immediate outbreak, and sent word to that effect to the Native Regiments at Delhi. This incident caused the Mutiny to break out prematurely, for it had been intended to wait until the Queen's birthday on the 24th of the month, when they hoped to secrete ball ammunition in their own pouches and surprise the British Regiments, which would be provided only with blank for the purpose of a *feu de joie*.

Although for months past signs of conspiracy had been noticed, an outward form of which was the forwarding from town to town of small cakes called *Chupatties*, and rumours had been widely spread that the Government intended to force the natives to embrace Christianity, the civil authorities had taken but little alarm. On the present occasion Mr. Greathead, the Commissioner (*i.e.* representative of the Civil Authority at Meerut), was entirely unaware of what passed on the dismissal of the Parade on the 9th, and was consequently unable to give any warning to the General Officers.

CHAPTER VII

A LITTLE before 6 P.M. on the following day, May 10, 1857—4th Sunday after Easter—the Riflemen assembled for the Church of England Parade were standing about in their white summer uniforms waiting for the 'Fall-in' to be sounded, and Lieut. Ashburnham, the Acting-Adjutant,[1] who had inspected and dismissed the N.C.Os., was on the point of giving the Buglers the order to 'Sound-off,' when a Rifleman off duty ran up to him so breathless as to be unable to impart the evidently alarming message which he was struggling to utter. Before the man could find words Ashburnham heard behind him the sound of hurrying feet, and looking round saw to his surprise the Riflemen running to their bungalows, whence in an incredibly short time they emerged, armed with rifles, swords, and the only ten rounds of ammunition which had as yet been served out to the battalion since the issue of the Enfield Rifle. By this time Ashburnham had received the message of terrible import. The Sepoys had broken out, had murdered their officers, were massacring every white man, woman, and child they could find, and burning their houses, which were for the most part beyond the Cantonments. The senior officer on Parade at the moment was Captain Douglas Dunbar Muter. Muter instantly grasped the situation; and, as the men formed up

[1] The late Major-General Sir Cromer Ashburnham, K.C.B., Colonel Commandant of the 3rd Battalion.

1857] OUTBREAK OF THE MUTINY 95

in quarter-column, without loss of a moment despatched the first fifty—who happened to belong to A, his own Company—under command of Lieut. Austin to seize the Treasury, some mile and a half distant.[1]

The number of men available that evening for Church Parade had been small; but, these being joined by casuals of every description, Nonconformists and Roman Catholics, the number which emerged from the Barrack rooms and fell in on Parade was large, possibly some 700 or 800 men. Then a delay occurred, for the news was still indefinite; no orders had arrived, and no Staff Officer was at hand. But presently the second Lieutenant-Colonel of the Battalion, John Jones—soon to be known throughout the length and breadth of the land as 'Jones the Avenger'—who was commanding the Battalion during the absence in England of Colonel Dennis, came up and took charge of the Parade.[2] To him Lieut. Ashburnham reported that only ten rounds per man were available. A party was thereupon sent to seize the Regimental Magazine, which had been left in the sole charge of a native guard. This guard at once fled. The ammunition was taken over by the riflemen, and a fresh supply served out. When this had been done, Jones ordered an advance upon the Native Lines. Just then up came at a gallop

---

[1] Muter was always under the impression that the Riflemen—who had certainly realised the imminence of an outbreak more clearly than their officers had done—guessed the purport of the unspoken message, and ran of their own accord for their arms. But the fact is established that, unknown to Muter, Captain H. F. Williams had come up on horseback—no doubt at the other end of the parade ground—and given the necessary orders. Thence Williams appears to have ridden to the Quarter-Guard, and to have ordered the Bugler to sound the Alarm and the Assembly. By the time he returned to the Parade the men had fallen in, and Muter, who was his junior in the regiment, was in the act of despatching the half-Company to the Treasury.

[2] It is remarkable that two officers present on this parade, viz., Jones and Ashburnham, received the honour of K.C.B. when Lieutenant-Colonels in command of Battalions. So rare is this distinction that at the moment we can recall only six other instances since its institution in 1814. They were those of John Colborne of the 52nd, Andrew Barnard and Robert Walpole of the Rifle Brigade, William Williams, John Keare and Lord Melville of our own Regiment.

the Brigadier-General, Archdale Wilson of the Bengal Artillery, pursued by the bullets of the men of his own command, from whom he had barely escaped with his life.

Flanked on the left by some troops of the Carabineers and on the right by a Battery H.A., the Riflemen moved forward in the direction of the Native Lines, Muter with the remainder of his Company forming the advance guard. And then burst upon them a sight as thrilling as it was terrible—a city for the length of over a mile in flames. A large body of insurgents, some being the Budmashes (or Hooligans) of the place, but the greater number Sepoys, were soon encountered. The arrival of the troops was evidently a source of consternation, for the Sepoys were unaware that the time for Parade had been altered by half-an-hour, and had counted on surprising the British soldiers inside the Church and unarmed.

By this time the sun had set; but the moon rose upon the lurid scene and the darkness was illuminated by the burning roofs of thatched bungalows, amid which the forms of mounted Sowars riding furiously about with brandished swords could clearly be discerned. Captain Muter turned to Brigadier Wilson, who was riding close behind him, 'Are we to load with bullets and shoot straight?' 'Yes,' was the reply, 'shoot them like dogs.' A volley followed—the first fired by British troops in the Indian Mutiny. The rebels turned and fled, their flight accelerated by the Horse Artillery, which, coming up at a gallop, unlimbered and poured in three rounds of case. The Battalion then marched through the Bazaar and picked up the bodies of some of the murdered, after which it returned and, forming a ring of piquets round a throng of English women and children who had taken refuge in our lines, bivouacked that night on the Mall.

2

Meanwhile Lieut. Austin, on receiving his orders, had set off at the double, and on reaching the Treasury found the native guard drawn up in a state of evident irresolution. In a voice of thunder he ordered the Sepoys to ground arms, a command which, though numerically double the strength of his party, they dared not disobey. Austin then took possession of the Treasury; and the consequence of Captain Muter's prompt and well-judged action was that, whereas in all other places the first act of the Sepoys was to seize the Treasury, at Meerut it remained in our hands; and during the events of the following months every soldier received his pay as regularly as in times of peace. The incident is even now quoted at the India Office as an instance of ready thought and prompt decision. Some people might think that out of the vast sum saved a small provision might have been made in her old age for the widow of the officer who rescued it. But the admiration and sympathy of the India Office did not extend as far as its breeches pocket.

Austin now occupied the Treasury building and the surrounding Compound. At the time when he had been despatched from the parade ground the actual state of affairs was evidently not realised, for strict orders were given to the men on no account to fire upon the mutineers. But one of the sentries in the Compound, a veteran Rifleman named Brownlow, seeing a number of white people fleeing from the rebels, was unable to restrain himself, and shot the foremost of their pursuers. For this act of disobedience he was made a prisoner, but quickly released. During the night a mob attempted to rush the enclosure, but was repulsed. In the small hours of the morning sounds of riot and rapine were heard from a large bungalow about 500 yards distant in the direction of the gaol. A party of men was despatched thither under command of a Sergeant with orders to ascertain what was taking place, but not to fire. They had, however, been absent only about ten minutes when the Guard left in the Treasury heard shots, and a second party was sent to reinforce the first. Volley after volley ensued. Then both parties returned, and Lieut. Austin demanded the reason why his orders had been disobeyed. Both Sergeants replied that they had come upon the insurgents engaged in pillage but had fired only in self-defence, and the matter dropped.

3

The Subaltern Officer of the day left in Barracks when the Battalion marched on the Native Lines was Ensign Alfred Spencer Heathcote, an officer who had entered the Army late in life after an already adventurous career. At about 8 P.M. Heathcote, armed only with his sword, started on his pony to visit the sentries. Suddenly he found himself in the midst of a party of the Sepoys, through whom he cut his way with desperate energy, and after a hand-to-hand encounter galloped back to Barracks, his sword crimsoned with blood. On reaching the lines he was greeted with the piteous cries of the women within, imploring him to say whether their husbands were dead or alive. The report of musketry at no great distance was continuous. Heathcote was directed to take a piquet and disarm the native guard at the Arsenal. Should the guard resist it was to be shot down. It did resist, but a volley from the piquet killed almost the entire number.

The terrible day was over, but bad as it had been things might have gone very much worse. It was only at the last moment that the hour for Church Parade had been altered, and this fact spoiled the plans of the mutineers, who had reckoned on surprising the British troops in Church and unarmed; for the regulations under which rifles are taken to Church came into force only at a later date.

4

The night was passed on the Mall without further attack, the Riflemen lying down beside their arms, the Artillery horses harnessed to their guns. In the morning the Riflemen moved out to make a reconnaissance, for no one knew whither the revolted regiments had disappeared. The first objects which met their view were the bodies of two Riflemen of A Company, so hacked to pieces that it was with difficulty that their own comrades could recognise them. Then they came upon the corpse of Mrs. Chambers, who had recently arrived from England, and was a general favourite in society, lying in a ditch and literally cut to pieces. Horror-stricken at the sight, officers and men raised their weapons in the air and vowed to avenge her death.[1] They kept their oath; in a few weeks' time the Battalion had produced such an impression upon the natives that it was commonly known among them as 'Shaitan-ke-Pultan'—the Regiment from Hell.

Sights of horror abounded on every side. The Civil Commissioner and his family, taken absolutely by surprise, owed their lives to the fidelity of their servants. Others were less fortunate; and the corpses of men, women and children, hacked and mutilated, were collected and carried to our lines on gun-carriages. At the house near the Treasury where the firing had taken place over-night the

[1] Her murder was traced to a butcher a day or two later. An officer rode single-handed into the Bazaar and brought the scoundrel into our lines, where he was promptly hanged.

scene was horrible. A social gathering had evidently been surrounded and surprised. None was left to tell the tale. Piled up among broken furniture were the bodies of these unhappy people, slashed and hewed by knife and tulwar. A futile attempt had been made to burn the house, and a sickening odour of blood and burnt flesh pervading the place almost overwhelmed those who entered the bungalow.

Such sights were enough to nerve the arm of officer and man for the coming struggle. More difficult—far more difficult—was it for the Civil or Military authority to discriminate between guilt and innocence, to give to the loyal Indians the protection due to them, and benefit of the doubt to those against whom no crime was actually proved. Be it remembered that the native servants showed magnificent examples of fidelity, that the civil population was, as a rule, at least neutral, and that even among the Sepoys a large proportion mutinied, not by choice but by compulsion.

During the course of this day it was ascertained that the native regiments put to flight on the previous evening were marching on Delhi, forty miles distant. Captain Rosser of the Carabineers volunteered to take a squadron in pursuit, but the offer was declined. This inaction has been severely criticised. People say that a force of all arms should have been desptached the night before towards Delhi; and it seems to have been the fact that, in expectation of the immediate arrival of British troops, the King of Delhi kept his Sepoys to some extent in restraint until late on the 11th. It is therefore not entirely impossible that without endangering his men the very fact of Rosser's presence might have been the means of saving life; yet, although present at Meerut were men distinguished in after life for dash and initiative,[1] no one but

---

[1] *Inter alios* Sir Hugh Gough and Sir Baker Russell.

Rosser thought it advisable to follow in pursuit. They were no doubt influenced by the horrors around them. Their primary duty was to guard the crowd of defenceless women and children at Meerut. The Carabineers were a young regiment and mounted on untrained horses. They were too late to overtake the mutineers, and it was at all events possible that the latter would find the gates of Delhi closed in their faces, for some one in authority had at the first alarm despatched a Sowar (native trooper) on horseback with an urgent note to Mr. Fraser, the Commissioner at Delhi.

The event proved unfortunately far otherwise. At 7 A.M. on Monday the 11th the garrison of the magazine at Delhi, commanded by Lieut. Willoughby of the Bengal Artillery, noticed an advance party of the 3rd Light Cavalry approaching from the Meerut Road, and presently crossing the bridge of boats which led into the city. In due course followed the main body of the regiment, and later still the mutinous infantry battalions, wearied indeed with their long night march—about 37 miles—albeit aided by native conveyances, and straggling on the road, yet resolute to attain their goal. Willoughby at once grasped the situation, closed and barricaded the gates of his magazine, and made every preparation for defence.

Meanwhile the Sowar despatched from Meerut on the previous day had reached Delhi late at night. Simon Fraser, the Commissioner,[1] was asleep in his chair after dinner, when his Bearer—native servant—handed him the letter, which he mentioned was urgent. Fraser in dudgeon threw it aside unopened, and in due course went to bed. Next morning a British magistrate came to report what was happening. Fraser bethought him of the despatch,

---

[1] The Commissioner is the representative of British Civil Authority.

tore it open, and, horror-stricken, read the contents. Calling for his carriage, in vain he drove through the streets at full gallop, in the hope of closing the City gates. The mutinous Sowars had already entered; and, joined by the refuse of the population, were riding through the streets, putting to death every European whom they met on the road. Among the first to fall was the Commissioner himself.

5

The present city of Delhi was the capital of the Mogul Empire; and although the sceptre had in reality long departed, Delhi still represented to the Mussulman's imagination the glories of the fallen dynasty. To the present Emperor, Mahomed Suraj-oo-Deen Bahadur, the degenerate descendant of the great Aurangzebe, both conquering Mussulman and conquered Hindoo naturally turned as the fitting head of a movement to expel the hated Feringhee.

The city itself was of considerable strength, with its eastern front washed by the Jumna which at that point flows in a southerly direction through a channel about a thousand yards wide, and all its sides strongly walled, bastioned, and strengthened by a dry moat. The ramparts were penetrated at seven gates, of which the principal were the Cashmere Gate on the north, within half a mile of the right bank of the Jumna, the Kabul and the Lahore Gates on the west, and the Delhi Gate, some 600 yards from the river, on the south. The old fortifications of the city had been re-modelled by Colonel Napier, afterwards Lord Napier of Magdala.

The walls and river enclosed a space of some seven miles, within which the population of 100,000 carried on a large and varied commerce. In the centre was the vast mosque named the Jumma Musjid, situated on an elevation and ascended by a flight of stone stairs, with an entrance through a gateway of red stone. Overlooking the Jumna was the King's Palace, composed of a group of buildings, some of inexpressible beauty, extending over an area upwards of half a mile from north to south, and for some 500 yards from east to west. The palace also was, comparatively speaking, strongly fortified. It commanded the bridge of boats crossing the Jumna, and was intended as a citadel in the whole scheme of defence. Beyond the outer walls of the city were several suburbs forming outworks, and capable of offering considerable resistance to a besieging army. To the north, a feature unusual in Indian scenery, is a distinct ridge, which from a point near the Jumna runs in a south-westerly direction for about three miles, until it terminates at about 1,000 yards from and westward of the Kabul Gate. On the further side of that ridge were the European Cantonments.

Inside the walls of Delhi confusion now reigned supreme. To a very large proportion of the inhabitants the news of the outbreak at Meerut and the arrival of the advance guard of the mutineer Cavalry had come as a surprise and shock. But the hooligans of the city opened the gates, which had been closed, and let in the troopers. The Royal family as a whole prepared to take their part, but the King said he had no cause to quarrel with the English; and there seems reason to believe that, had immediate steps been taken to rouse the leading men of the city, the situation might have been saved. There were also on a visit to Delhi native noblemen whose personal retinue might have been quite sufficient to expel the new arrivals and preserve order. But the moment for action was unfortunately lost; within the next few minutes nearly all the British officials were murdered. The convicts were released from gaol, and amid the undesirable element, termed the 'budmashes,' the rebellion spread like wildfire. The King found himself unable to stem the tide, and had really no option but to put himself at the head of the revolt. His principal councillors, finding their lives in danger, followed his example, but unwillingly; and there is evidence to show that the massacre of the Europeans was not due to their instigation.

There were at Delhi no British troops. The garrison consisted of three native infantry regiments, the 38th, 54th, and 74th, and a native battery. Of these, the first-named instantly joined in the mutiny and murdered its officers, the other two regiments also joined the mutineers, but less willingly; and aided their officers to escape. Although they refused to fire upon the 38th they abstained from committing murder.

A large portion of the inhabitants was horrified at the scenes of slaughter, and not only refrained from joining in the rebellion, but fervently longed for the arrival of the English and the restoration of order. The fact of the loyalty of these citizens was unfortunately not recognised in the British camp; and when the city fell at length into our hands, a large number of loyalists were put to death, either in the street fighting or on the gallows a day or two afterwards. False accusations on the part of private enemies sealed the fate of many; and to use the words of Mainodin, 'the slaughter of innocent helpless women and children was revenged in a manner that no one ever anticipated.'

The King, being forced to take an active part, appointed first his son Mirza Arbu Bakr, and afterwards Mahomed Bakht Khan, Commander-in-Chief. The latter had fought in the British Army during the Sikh War; he survived not only the siege of Delhi, but the whole Mutiny, and at its end succeeded in disappearing. Hakim Ahsanullah

Khan acted as the principal councillor. The King's sons were a terrible trial to their father; they took part in all the excesses, and thoroughly deserved the fate which at length overtook them when the city was captured.

Those Europeans whose business or occupations had taken them inside the city quickly realised the situation. Their natural course was to join their compatriots in the cantonments. Some succeeded in doing so: the greater part were either murdered in the attempt or carried prisoners to the Palace. During this time the King had made no sign; his eyes were fixed on the Meerut road, whence he expected every moment the cloud of dust that would usher in the arrival of a strong and uncompromising British force. But hours went by; it became evident that the Meerut garrison was not on its way. The importunity of his officers increased every moment; impatience broadened into discontent, muttered disappointment into words of rebellious anger. Somewhat before 3 P.M. the King gave way and assented to an attack on the magazine. Willoughby, deserted at once by his native garrison and aided by a mere handful of Europeans, whose names should live in English history as long as the name of England survives, held his post with desperate gallantry until defence was no longer possible. Then with stern and measured resolution he blew up the magazine, and buried under its ruins 400 of the Sepoy mutineers who were swarming over the walls.[1] No man could have done more; it would be the pride and duty of any Rifleman in such a case to do no less.

It is said that the Sepoys, seeing the explosion, remarked, 'What a bad man the General is to kill our people in this way!'

[1] It is remarkable that out of about a dozen who composed the defenders at least nine escaped with their lives. Among them was Willoughby himself; but he was murdered either on the same or the following day.

The destruction of the magazine broke the last shreds of restraint on the part of the Royal Family. As already mentioned, a large number of Europeans, principally women and children, had been captured and conducted to the Palace. It was rumoured that the children, in the presence of their mothers and despite their heart-rending entreaties, were hacked limb from limb; that the ladies, stripped of every vestige of clothing, were paraded through the streets amid the execrations of the mob; and that, after this torture, they were brought back to the Palace and beheaded. No wonder that when the avenging force of British troops attacked the guilty city their blood was fired and their arms were nerved by the cry repeatedly heard in battle, 'Remember the ladies and the children.'[1]

While these scenes of bloodshed were taking place inside the town, the Europeans in the Cantonments, reinforced by their fugitive countrymen from the city, crowded on the Ridge at the point called the Flagstaff Tower, whence, after a march of infinite toil and pain, the greater part eventually succeeded in reaching Meerut.

We must now return to that city. After the departure of the revolting regiments no further disturbances took place among the civil population. But the position of the Europeans was, to say the least, one of the most intense anxiety. The wildest rumours prevailed. It was even stated that the British residents at Calcutta had been driven to take refuge on board the ships in the river. This was, of course, quite untrue; but other tales of astonishment and alarm proved to be well founded. The position was one of the most complete isolation. It looked as if the

---

[1] Some attribute the massacre to the instigation of the King's favourite wife. Neither of the two native narratives of the Siege of Delhi confirm or deny this rumour. Both writers speak with the utmost horror of the deeds of blood, but they do not mention the details given above, which it is possible may have been exaggerated. Of the murders there can, however, be no doubt whatever.

garrison, although comparatively strong, might in the long run be overwhelmed by weight of numbers; but a firm front was shown, and such measures as could be taken to punish crime were not omitted. The butchers who had been prominent in the recent scenes of murder were paraded before the Riflemen, and any man recognised as a participator was hanged. The postal authorities of the neighbouring village having been murdered a detachment was sent to inflict summary punishment, a mission which was possibly executed with less discrimination than zeal; but which at any rate had the effect of striking terror into the minds of the inhabitants. At the moment such action seemed to be of supreme importance. After the lapse of more than half a century one can regret the failure to realise that the great mass of the civil population was at least not unfriendly to us, and had taken no part in the deeds of blood. Those who were servants to Europeans were as a rule conspicuously faithful.

Fugitives from Delhi came in and were given a share of such accommodation as could be offered; but the heat was almost insupportable and all suffered; the women and children intensely. Duty was very heavy; the officers with the regiment were few in number. On May 15 a battalion of native sappers and miners marched in from Roorkee. Their arrival was welcomed as a reinforcement; but next day they mutinied and murdered their Colonel. The Riflemen and Dragoons promptly turned out and shot 50 of them.

Orders now arrived directing Brigadier-General Wilson to march with as large a proportion as possible of the Meerut garrison to join the Field Force which was being collected, in order to march on Delhi, under the Commander-in-Chief in person. In accordance with these orders, B and G Companies, under Captain Muter, having been left behind in garrison headquarters of the battalion, with six Companies, consisting of 16 officers and 450 men under the command of Lieut.-Colonel Jones,[1] quitted Meerut at 6 P.M. on the 27th. With them marched two Squadrons of the Carabineers, Tombs' Battery H.A., Scott's Battery B.A., and two 18-pounder guns. The force marched by night and halted shortly after sunrise. On the 30th it encamped at Ghazeeooddeen-nuggur, on the left bank of the Hindun River, some nine miles from Delhi. At 4 P.M. a vedette rode in to report that the enemy was marching to the attack. Bugles rang out, and the battalion had hardly fallen in when an 18-pounder shot carried off a leg from each of two Palkee bearers. The Hindun, a mere rivulet in May, was spanned at this point by a causeway (600 yards in length), upon which two Companies of Riflemen at once advanced. The enemy, commanded by Mirza Abu Bakr, a son of the King of Delhi, was discovered in position at the further end of the defile, which was enfiladed by five heavy guns taken from the Delhi arsenal. The Riflemen, under immediate command of the Colonel and supported by the four remaining Companies, crossed the bridge in column of sections. The enemy's muzzle-loading guns opened fire, but their elevation was too high. Observing their error the mutineers depressed the muzzles: the word of command 'Numbers 1 and 2 fire' was distinctly heard, and it seemed inevitable that the column should be blown

---

[1] The following are the names of the officers: Lieut.-Colonel J. Jones; Captains H. F. Williams, J. R. Wilton, F. Andrews, C. Jones; Lieutenant and Adjutant G. C. Kelly; Lieutenants G. C. Waters, H. P. Eaton, J. D. McGill, H. S. Deedes, P. J. Curtis, C. Ashburnham; Ensigns R. Jennings, W. G. Turle, W. H. Napier, A. S. Heathcoe, Phillips, N.L. (attached).

Captain Sir E. Campbell, Lieutenants R. W. Hinxman, J. D. Dundas, and J. Hare, joined the column a few days later. Dundas came in disguise through a disaffected region.

The battalion was largely composed of veterans, and the C.O., although infirm on his feet and unwieldy in appearance, had a fighting spirit second to none.

to pieces. The matches flashed, but, in their hurry, the gunners had put in the shot before the powder![1]

On clearing the defile the Riflemen extended and continued to advance. When within eighty yards of the guns the Colonel gave the order to charge. With a ringing cheer the battery was captured at the point of the sword by D Company, gallantly led by Captain Francis Andrews. At the last moment a Sepoy fired his musket into a tumbril, which instantly blew up. Andrews and several of his men were killed. The body of the Captain was found in the road devoid of every stitch of clothing, and rifles were picked up twisted into knots. Ensign Heathcote, galloper to the Colonel, was hurled into the air; but though his horse was killed, he himself remained unhurt. The enemy's infantry was strongly posted and entrenched in a village hard by. Our skirmishers drove it out, but the resistance was not very great. Fifty Sepoys took refuge in a ditch: they were shortly observed by the Riflemen, and none survived. The action was soon at an end; and although the British force was not strong enough to clear the village thoroughly, the bulk of the enemy retreated into Delhi with heavy loss. The success of the day's operations was largely due to the skill with which our two batteries had flanked and supported the Riflemen. Speaking of the action, the Rev. J. E. Rotton[2] observes that '700 Englishmen put to flight a disciplined army of more than seven times their number, and entrenched within so strong a native village that, if you would only garrison it with two Companies of the Rifles, no British regiment would be able to drive the occupants from their hold, or scarcely any man of the attacking regiment leave the

---

[1] 'On remarking the unsteadiness of their fire,' said General Wilson in his despatch, 'I ordered Lieut.-Colonel Jones to advance his Rifles and attack. This was done in a most splendid manner. They drove the enemy from the heavy guns.'

[2] 'The Chaplain's Narrative of the Siege of Delhi,' p. 26.

place with his life.' The loss of the Regiment on this day appears to have been eleven killed and nine wounded.

On the following day, Whit-Sunday, the British troops, who had returned to their camp on the left bank of the Hindun, observed the enemy again posted about a mile distant on the further side. The battalion once more crossed the bridge; and two Companies of Riflemen wheeling to the left attacked a village, which they took and occupied. This relieved the pressure on the left flank; and the remainder of the battalion, in extended order, compelled the withdrawal of the guns which were playing on the front line. Then, changing front to the right, the rifles recaptured the village occupied the previous day, and this time set it on fire. The fighting lasted for some hours, but the enemy's shelling was more easily endured than the burning rays of the sun and the suffering caused by thirst. Twelve Riflemen received sunstroke: four died. The other losses of the battalion this day were two killed and six wounded; among the latter was Ensign William Napier, who lost a leg and died a few days afterwards. To his gallant spirit the agony of the wound was as nothing; but his bitter grief was vented in the repeated exclamation, ' I shall never lead the Rifles again ! '

Towards evening news of the action reached the citizens of Delhi.

'It transpired,' says the Munshi Jeewan Lal, 'that the artillery of the mutineers had been taken and the gunners had fled. The firing of the English had been so good that many of the rebels, covered with dust, had gone to hell : many, like birds borne on the wing, had fled back to the city ! . . . The Delhi Hindoos, who had suffered much at the hands of the mutineers since their arrival in the city, expressed their joy that these wicked men, like decapitated fowls with bloody wounds, had now themselves been tossed hither and thither.'

6

Wilson's column was obviously too weak to advance upon Delhi single-handed. Reinforced next day by the 2nd Goorkhas (600 strong), a regiment second to none, and with whom it is our pride to have been linked ever since by ties of the warmest friendship, the column occupied its position on the Hindun for a few more days, and then on June 5 moved by a flank march, not without peril but unmolested, in a northerly direction.[1] On the 6th it crossed the Jumna at Baghput, and reaching Aleepore [2] at 9 A.M. on the following day, joined the main body of the field force assembled for the capture of Delhi. It was now commanded by Major-General Sir Harry Barnard, for General the Hon. G. Anson, Commander-in-Chief in India, had just died of cholera.

Writing under date June 7 Colonel Keith Young remarks:

'Brigadier Wilson's force marched in this morning and I can't tell you how well they all looked. . . . Colonel Jones of the Rifles, as fat and rosy as ever. . . . The Rifles in particular, though they had had a long march, came along stepping out merrily and singing in chorus.'[3]

But black indeed was the outlook.

'Far and wide, the whole continent seemed hostile. No news arrived except of disaster. Fort Agra besieged; Lucknow beleaguered; the trained armies of native princes in open hostility. The whole British force in India was but a handful to oppose to an army

---

[1] The delay had been partly caused by a difference of opinion between the civil and military authorities, the former wishing to withdraw the column for the defence of Meerut, while the latter insisted on its forming part of the Delhi Field Force.

[2] One of these marches lasted from 6.30 P.M. to 1 P.M. the next day; water was scarce, and the feat will be appreciated by those who have had experience of June heat in India.

[3] 'Delhi, 1857,' by Colonel Keith Young.

ten times as great, trained under British officers ; and as the British were cantoned in stations hundreds of miles apart—thousands spread over the country in hourly peril of their lives—the circumstances, as may well be conceived, were appalling.

'All that could be done was to collect all available British soldiers with a view to a dash on Delhi ere the enemy attempted further destruction. But it took time to collect troops by long marches through a country where all means of transport and supplies were hidden away.'[1]

[1] 'The Siege of Delhi,' by General F. R. Maunsell, *Nineteenth Century Magazine*, October, 1911.

CHAPTER VIII

DESPITE the forced marches, no halt was made at Aleepore. At 1 A.M. on June 8 the camp was struck, and the army advanced to the attack of the enemy's entrenched position at Budlee-ka-Serai, some seven miles north of Delhi. The troops were organised in one mounted and two infantry brigades; the former, commanded by Colonel Hope-Grant, consisted of three squadrons 9th Lancers and ten guns H.A. The 1st Infantry Brigade, under Brigadier-General Showers, was made up of a squadron of the Carabineers, four guns of position, four guns of Scott's Battery, the 75th Regiment, and the 1st European Fusiliers. The 2nd Infantry Brigade, commanded by Brigadier-General Graves,[1] comprised the 60th, the 2nd European Fusiliers, the Sirmoor Battalion—now known as the 2nd P.W.O. Goorkhas,—a squadron of the 9th, and a Battery H.A. Escorting the small siege train was a rearguard, composed of a squadron of Carabineers, a Company of Fusiliers, and the remaining two guns of Scott's Battery. The units comprising the entire force were far below their normal strength, and included only between three and four thousand of all ranks.

General Showers moved straight upon the entrenchments, and Hope-Grant, supported by the 2nd Brigade,

---

[1] Graves had been the General commanding at Delhi when he was deserted, but happily not murdered, by his men.

made a flanking movement with a view to descending upon the mutineers' left. At 4.30 A.M., with the first streak of dawn, the enemy's guns opened fire with great accuracy : his heavy battery being cleverly posted under cover amid enclosures. The advance was not, however, checked : the 75th with the utmost gallantry charged and carried the guns of position at the point of the bayonet ; the 9th Lancers, arriving at an opportune moment, charged and captured the enemy's field guns. The 2nd Infantry Brigade came up on the enemy's right, and the whole force advanced to the bank of the Nugufgurh canal. The Rifles moving to the left extended, and having crossed the canal, either by the bridges or by fording with the water up to their waists, attacked the heights on the further side. Continuing to advance, the Riflemen, by bugle call, brought up their left shoulders and outflanked the enemy on the second line of heights. The main body of the force on the right co-operated ; the guns on the heights were captured, and the enemy, composed entirely of Mussulmans, driven into Delhi with a loss of some 400 men. Our casualties were about 200. The British troops then occupied the Ridge previously mentioned, and encamped : but Mainodin Hassan Khan and Munshi Jeewan Lal agree that, so great was the panic of the mutineers, the British force could easily have entered the city [1] with the fugitives.

From the Flagstaff Tower the observer looking southward could see the King's Palace, flanked on the east by the old Pathan fort of Salimgarh and on the west by the Jumma Musjid : while nearer to him was the northern part of the city containing the Water Bastion abutting on the river Jumna, the Cashmere Gate and Bastion, the Morree Bastion at the N.W. angle of the ramparts, and

---

[1] 'Two Native Narratives of the Mutiny in Delhi,' A. Constable & Co., 1898.

the Kabul Gate through which runs the Grand Trunk road from Peshawar to Calcutta. To the left of the observer flows the Jumna. The space between the Ridge and the City was wooded near the river, and intersected throughout by walls, roads, and nullahs. Near the city it was studded with houses, Mosques, and gardens. Half a mile north of the Cashmere Gate stood Ludlow Castle, the residence of the British Commissioner, enclosed by walls and occupied by the enemy.

The city of Delhi was occupied by an armed force of unknown strength, perhaps ten or twenty thousand men; and the extent of its area protected it from investment by Barnard's small field force. The consequence was that the garrison could be, and frequently was, reinforced from outside till its numbers were at length some 60,000 men of regular and irregular troops. Sir Harry Barnard therefore contented himself with the occupation of the Ridge from the Flagstaff Tower on the left to Hindoo Rao's house on the right, a position extending in a S.S.W. direction over about a mile and a half of ground, with a command averaging about 40 feet above the interior level of the city. In order to command the approaches from the city some light guns were placed along the Ridge, at the Mosque, at the Observatory—some 600 yards beyond the Mosque—and at Hindoo Rao's house, 180 yards further on. The distance from the nearest battery (that at Hindoo Rao's) to the walls of the city was about 1200 yards, and whereas the left of our position was fairly secure, the right, from its proximity to the ramparts, positively invited attack.

Piquets were posted to protect the guns. A line of posts was established from the Observatory to the Subzee-Mundee (the main piquet at Hindoo Rao's house, commanded by Major—afterwards Sir Charles—Reid of the Sirmoor Battalion, being the most important). This was held exclusively by Reid's own Corps the 2nd Goorkhas, and the Rifles. The latter furnished at first a Company at the Observatory and one at Hindoo Rao's, which were relieved weekly; but before many days had passed four Companies were required, and it often happened that the whole battalion was brought up. The British encampment was formed behind the Ridge, between the latter and the Nugufgurh canal. Hardly had the position been taken up when the Sepoys made an attempt to retake it; but before the firing ceased a welcome reinforcement appeared in the shape of the Guides, a distinguished Frontier Corps composed partly of cavalry and partly of infantry, which, under command of Captain (afterwards Sir Henry) Daly, arrived in camp after a wonderful march of nearly 600 miles in twenty-two days, and came straight into action, subsequently forming the support to Reid's line of posts.

On the same day cholera broke out and made great havoc. The riflemen were, however, exempt from this scourge, an immunity due partly perhaps to the fact of being old and seasoned campaigners, partly to the foresight of Reid, who kept a sentry on the well at Hindoo Rao's house; but partly also to the regimental surgeon, J. H. Kerr-Innes, by whose advice Officers and Men wore their green serge jackets instead of the fancy linen garments in which most of the other regiments delighted.

On the following day, the 10th, the piquet at Hindoo Rao's was again attacked, and fighting took place in the Subzee-Mundee, a village with a large vegetable garden about a quarter of a mile south of the road along the Ridge. Lieutenant J. Hare, with some 20 riflemen who failed to hear the 'Retire' sounded, found themselves isolated among the enclosures, but eventually made good their retreat. Hare, walking alongside the last man, had a narrow escape. A round shot struck the man's rifle, and took the flesh off his hands and thighs.

The 11th passed without incident, but a general attack of a formidable character took place next morning. Before daylight the enemy surprised the piquets beneath the Flagstaff Tower, and as nearly as possible captured the guns. Two companies of Riflemen, hastily ordered up from camp, arrived just in time to save the situation. The attack was then repulsed all along the line.

With a view to strengthening the position on the left flank, a piquet was now established close by the river, at the ruined house of Sir T. Metcalfe. On the following night, in pursuance of a plan of attack proposed it is said by a young Engineer Officer, the battalion advanced to within 300 yards of the city walls; but other and more prudent counsels prevailing, Brigadier Graves very properly refused to bring in his piquets without a written order; and apart from them our force was too small to make the attempt. The troops were consequently recalled.

Few days passed without a skirmish of some sort. On the 13th the Sepoys, to the number of 5,000, made a sortie, headed curiously enough by the 60th N.I., which, by the way, had been brigaded with us two years previously at the Umballa camp of exercise. Reid reserved fire until the enemy was within twenty yards, then crashed into his columns with a volley, followed with a charge by a company from each of the three regiments. The Rifle Company came upon forty-nine Sepoys in a ditch. It is said to have sprung upon them 'like tigers.' None escaped. On this occasion Lieutenant J. D. Dundas, who twenty years later became Colonel of the Battalion, distinguished himself by saving the life of a Rifleman. After this fight the force under Major Reid was strengthened to four Companies of

Riflemen, 300 Guides, 350 Goorkhas, 10 heavy and 2 light guns in battery.

It was now discovered that the enemy was erecting a battery at Kissen-Gunge, a Serai some 600 yards south of the Ridge, whence artillery would rake our entire position. On the 17th two Companies of Riflemen, two of Goorkhas, with Tombs' guns, broke down gates and other obstacles, got in rear of the enemy's post and burst open the doors of the Serai. The Goorkhas, with their 'Kookries,' killed 40 to 50 Sepoys who were found inside; for the latter had so strongly fortified the place that they left no means of exit for escape in case of emergency. Their total loss during the skirmish amounted to some 300 killed and wounded. Their new batteries and magazine were destroyed. Of the Rifles Ensign Heathcote and three Riflemen were wounded. Sir Harry Barnard came that evening to the regimental mess to thank the battalion for what it had done. After this, our position being too extensive, the Subzee-Mundee was temporarily evacuated. On the 19th the enemy made a demonstration against Hindoo Rao's House, while the main body worked its way round and attacked the British camp in rear. The moment was critical; two and a half Companies of Riflemen stood their ground against at least 2,000 Sepoys. Ensign Heathcote described the affair in a letter as follows :—

'Only fancy, they sent 150 of us to attack 3,000 men. We got so far in advance of our guns that they actually fired two rounds of grape into us, fortunately doing no damage. We were only 10 yards from the enemy's guns, behind a small mound. . . . We had formed a square against cavalry.'

Supported by the 75th, the Riflemen drove the enemy however from one position to another, till at length darkness put an end to the contest, during which Captain Williams and Lieutenant Dundas of the Rifles had been wounded, and Lieutenant Humphries of the 20th N.I., a gallant officer attached to the regiment, killed. Field-Marshal Lord Roberts in his 'Forty-one Years in India' writes of this attack as follows, Vol. I, p. 170 :—

'As long as it was light the steady fire of the Artillery and the dashing charging of the Cavalry kept the rebels in check, but in the dusk of the evening their superior numbers told. They very nearly succeeded in turning our flank, and for some time the guns were in great jeopardy. The 9th Lancers and Guides, bent on saving them at all hazards, charged the enemy; but with a ditch and houses on each side their action was paralysed and their loss severe. All was now in confusion, the disorder increasing as night advanced, when a small body of Infantry (about 300 of the 60th Rifles) came up, dashed forward and cutting a lane through the rebels, rescued the guns.'

It was a fine piece of work on our part, but the boldest on the Ridge could not fail to see that the little force was by degrees dwindling away. Yet, with the impatience begotten of crude ignorance, people in England were beginning to ask, 'Why don't they go into Delhi?' Writing on the 26th, Heathcote summarises the situation very clearly :—

'We have now been twenty days besieging Delhi and are no nearer than when first we came. We (*i.e.* the Rifles) have had 11 officers wounded out of 14—three of them killed—and in men we have had nearly 200 killed and wounded. To-morrow we are to be attacked again, and 12,000 of the Gwalior contingent have risen against us: the whole country is in arms; but, never fear, we shall lick them.'

But despite these bold words 'a nightmare shape' brooded continually in the background of the besiegers' thoughts.

'There were 10,000 English women and children in the Punjaub alone. What would be their fate if Delhi should not fall soon? Every man in the force was fighting, not for glory or personal honour, or even only for racial predominance, but for the lives and honour of British women. The issues at stake were the deepest that life holds. The appeal made was to the chivalry of northern manhood. Every soldier on the Ridge was a Knight, and bore the glove of womanhood on his heart. "For us men the worst that can happen is easy," writes Colonel Neville Chamberlain;[1] "but the blood runs cold when one thinks of the defenceless women and children." It was the danger overshadowing these helpless creatures that spurred our soldiers to exertions which were almost superhuman. Time might mean so much. If Delhi did not fall soon the Punjaub might rise, and then would be the opportunity of its counterparts of the ruffians of Meerut and the Princes of Delhi. This torturing thought made the waiting policy enforced by circumstances well-nigh unendurable' ('Life of Sir A. Taylor').

A few of the enemy lingered near our camp all night. In the morning they were reinforced, and round shot came rolling into the General's kitchen tent, but the Sepoys were soon forced to retire.

It was well known that an ancient prophecy had foretold that the rule of the East India Company would last but a hundred years. The decisive Battle of Plassey had been fought on June 23, 1757, and the natives were convinced that a determined attack on the centenary would inevitably drive the British from their position. For such an attack we were quite prepared.[2] At 5 A.M. on that day the Sepoys concentrated their attack upon the Hindoo Rao piquet: the Rifles, Guides, and Goorkhas held their position for hours against overwhelming numbers. The enemy then extended through the Subzee-Mundee Gate in rear of the Ridge, and threatened our camp. At 11 A.M. a reinforcement of Europeans and Sikhs made its appearance from the north and was at once thrown into the fighting line, while the contest continued with unrelenting fury. At 4 P.M., despite 11 hours of

[1] Afterwards Field-Marshal.
[2] The Munshi Jeewan Lal states that Brahmans and astronomers were consulted as to the prospects of victory. They replied that great disturbance would last for a year, but that from 19th Sambat peace and security would spread over the land.

hard fighting and tropical sun, the Rifles and their gallant comrades were ordered to assume the offensive and re-occupy the Subzee-Mundee. This was effected 'with their customary dash, and the enemy were driven from wall to bank, from bank to wall. Now the Sepoys ascended the tops of houses, of which there were many in the immediate neighbourhood, but their tenure of these only lasted for the few moments which it took our brave troops to reach them.' At sunset the mutineers, who, to do them justice, had fought with courage and resolution, retired within the walls of Delhi, leaving on the ground, however, one-fourth of their whole strength. The Subzee-Mundee was henceforward occupied by a piquet and formed the extreme right of our position. During the course of the day Captain Fagan—a hero among heroes—commanding the right battery in front of Hindoo Rao's House, asked Lieutenant Hare to drive the enemy from a temple—the Swansi (or idol), but corrupted by the British soldier into the 'Sammy' House—which the mutineers had occupied as a post of vantage, and whence a well-directed fire upon our embrasures was being maintained. This fire could not be returned; for, although the distance was only about 250 yards, the temple stood on ground so much below Fagan that he could not sufficiently depress his guns. The men of Hare's Company were by this time lying on the ground utterly exhausted: the task appeared desperate; but at Hare's call for volunteers the whole Company at once rose and rushed down upon the Sammy House, which was soon in its possession. Sergeant Stephen Garvin set an example of distinguished valour, for which, in due course, he received the Victoria Cross. The Sammy House thus taken was never again occupied by the enemy.

About 6 P.M. the mutineers retired into Delhi. The

British losses seem to have been about 120 ; those of the regiment are a little difficult to specify. Captain C. Jones was shot through the thigh, and according to the 'History of Services of the 1st Battalion,' 6 men were killed and 12 wounded. Some perhaps did not return themselves as wounded, for the Rev. J. E. Rotton places our casualties at 27, while Colonel Hare says that 23 men—including himself—were killed and wounded in his company alone.

During the next few days nothing of importance occurred, but from 6 A.M. till 2 P.M. on the 27th the mutineers made a resolute attack on both flanks. At 2 P.M. on the 30th our piquet at Hindoo Rao's House was violently assailed but repulsed the assailants. Heavy as was the loss inflicted on the enemy, our own, in this and other combats, though numerically small, was large in proportion to the force. From May 30 to June 30 the Rifles had lost at least 3 officers, 40 N.C.Os. and riflemen killed ; 12 officers and 108 men wounded ; while 2 had died of disease. The casualties in our regiment therefore were already nearly 40 per cent. of their strength. Nor did the political conditions improve. The base of the Delhi Field Force—so far as it could be said to have a base—was the Punjaub. From Calcutta it was isolated by a broad belt of rebellion, and from the few British troops in Oude and Agra nothing was to be expected. They were fighting for their own lives.

Even from the Punjaub matters looked pretty dark. Sepoy regiments had been disarmed ; but re-arming themselves, had committed murder, mutiny, and massacre. The loyalty of the native Chiefs was strained. The capture of Delhi became more and more essential. But how was it to be done ? The answer is given in a letter written on June 28 by Sir H. Barnard, 'The thing is too gigantic for the force brought against it.'

But the grim determination to hang on to the Ridge till the last never failed, and the confidence of the regimental officers and men increased with every repulse of the enemy.

Writing on June 29 Alfred Heathcote says :—

'Our men are thought a great deal of, and certainly they are beautiful shots; the enemy funk us more than any other regiment, so much so that the King of Delhi has offered a reward for every Rifleman's jacket brought into Delhi.'

The historian of the 2nd Prince of Wales' Own Goorkha Rifles most kindly says, 'It is pleasant to read in the letters written by Major Reid during the siege his admiration for the 60th Rifles and their discipline, so different to that of any other Corps.' The point which seems to have been especially noticed by all present was the invariable practice of those minutiæ of military duty, such as the inspection of companies going on and off piquet, which in time of war are sometimes neglected.

Meanwhile reinforcements were arriving on both sides : to ourselves by half-battalions, to the enemy in large numbers. It was reported that General Wheeler, with four European regiments, was marching to Delhi. In due course the truth came out. Cawnpore had surrendered ; Wheeler and the garrison had been massacred.

On July 5 Sir Harry Barnard died of cholera and was succeeded by General Reed.[1] On the 9th another fight took place at Hindoo Rao's House, during which 15 men were lost. The 8th Irregular Cavalry penetrated temporarily to the centre of the British camp. Wilmot's Company of the Rifles was sent down with four guns to clear the Subzee-Mundee, which had been occupied by the enemy. A party of fanatics dashing out from a Serai surrounded

---

[1] Reed, who had fought at Waterloo, was temporarily Commander-in-Chief in India after the death of General Anson, who also had been at Waterloo. His name must not be confused with that of Reid, the Goorkha C.O.

Captain Wilmot. The day was wet and his pistol missed fire. Rifleman James Thompson rushed forward, bayoneted two of the assailants and saved his Captain's life. For this action Thompson received the first of seven Victoria Crosses awarded to the Battalion after the siege.

The heat all this time was terrific. The temperature 120°: the plague of flies awful. Cholera increased, but was principally confined to the 8th and 61st Regiments, which had just arrived.

At 7 A.M. on the 10th a force of 3,000 Sepoys attacked our positions with great violence, and maintained the fight in pouring rain until 4 P.M., when, by arrangement with the Adjutant-General, Neville Chamberlain, that officer counter-attacked the enemy's left; and Reid, with two companies of Riflemen, five of Goorkhas, and 180 Guides, his right flank. The mutineers were driven full tilt down the Great Trunk Road to within 400 yards of the city walls. The arrival of Scott's Battery enabled Reid to advance for another 150 yards; but the Sepoys having retreated through the Ajmeer Gate, he retired once more to the Ridge.

On July 14 the enemy attacked our right flank, and though they were easily repulsed the British loss was 16 killed and 150 wounded, including Lieutenant Tulloch of the 20th N.I., who was doing duty with the Rifles.

On the 16th General Reed's health gave way and he was succeeded by Brigadier-General Archdale Wilson. At 9 A.M. on the 18th the 'Alarm' sounded; the main piquet at Hindoo Rao's House was reinforced with 100 Riflemen; and Colonel Jones was directed by General Wilson to take command of a brigade, including detachments of the 8th, 61st, and 75th Foot, the 2nd Bengal Fusiliers and some others, with 4 guns, and to drive the enemy out of the Subzee-Mundee. Jones carried out his orders with great skill : the operation took place under the eyes of Wilson, who congratulated him on his success and the small cost at which it had been obtained, a circumstance which he attributed to the admirable way in which the troops were handled.

'Colonel Jones,' observed the militant Chaplain, Mr. Rotton, 'is without question an able Brigadier; his powers of perception in military matters are singularly acute, and his knowledge of strategy has been strikingly displayed on every occasion on which he has had the opportunity of exercising independent command. One of the greatest proofs of his capacity as a soldier is the high state of efficiency and discipline which distinguish his regiment; another is afforded by the universal confidence reposed in him alike by his own officers and men without a single exception. If he does but lead, they are ready to follow wherever he shall direct, not doubting but that in following him implicitly they will assuredly be led to glory and victory. This is a confidence which very few Commanding Officers enjoy.'

The rains continued. The camp was a sink of malaria ; the stench of unburied bodies of men and animals added to the plague of flies made life a positive burden, and officers and men of other regiments died every day of cholera.

So passed away the month of July, and with it the rains abated and cholera disappeared. August 1 was the great Mohammedan Festival of the Bukhra-Eed, commemorating Abraham's readiness to sacrifice his son. Except for a heavy cannonade the morning passed quietly ; but in the afternoon an attack, fiercer than any preceding it, was made by some 10,000 men with two batteries upon the right flank of our position and upon the Hindoo Rao piquet. This lasted till the middle of the following day. At 10.30 P.M. Sir Edward Campbell's Company and that to which Heathcote belonged were detached to reinforce the companies in the breastwork at the Crow's Nest. The gardens in front were lit up by the incessant fire of the enemy's musketry, but the breastwork was gained with little loss. The enemy's fire was continuous; he was in great force, and again and again assailed the breastwork, only to be driven back to his own entrenchments 150 yards distant. At length a Rifle bugler, on his own initiative, sounded as a ruse the Regimental Call, followed by the 'Retire' and the 'Double.' Out came the enemy, only to be received with a salvo of grape and canister, whereupon the Sepoys, having received a practical example of a Rifleman's stratagem, ran back again with heavy loss. No further attack seems to have been made, and an hour after dawn the Riflemen charged the enemy's works and drove them from their position.

About midnight Campbell's Company had been directed to go to the left to reinforce the party holding the temple called the Sammy House: the movement was executed under fire, and the party, which had been hard pressed, was relieved. Later on the Company returned to Hindoo Rao's, and Lieutenant Deedes was looking over the crest of Brind's battery when Rifleman J. Jackson, suddenly pushing his head in front of his officer, was shot through the cheek. What had happened to the bullet could not be discovered, and the Surgeon thought it must have been swallowed! Five years afterwards at Aldershot Jackson complained of a headache, and said he believed it was caused by the bullet. Next morning he was found dead in his bed, and the bullet was discovered in his brain.

The following extract from the journal of Sir C. Reid describes the action generally:—

'The engagement commenced at sunset on the 1st, lasted the whole night, and until 4 P.M. yesterday. The mutineers tried hard to get in our rear. They managed to erect a bridge across the canal at Bussie, but it was carried away by the flood; their guns were for

ACTION OF AUGUST 1

some time left on one side, and their Infantry and Cavalry on the other. This report was sent me by the General about 4 P.M. on the 1st. About half an hour later I saw the whole force returning—guns, mortars, etc.; it was joined by about 3,000 or 4,000 from the city, and the whole force, in all about 20,000, came straight at my position. I was prepared for them. The General sent up my supports sharp, as he always does, and we commenced work. The Sammy House was attacked first by about 5,000. At this time I had only 150 of Coke's men in it, under Travers, and 50 of the Guides. I at once sent them reinforcements from the Rifles, and the 61st. At dusk the enemy brought up their guns, supported by a very large force, and these commenced the sharpest fire I have ever heard on the whole of my position. They were very desperate indeed. Before midnight we had driven them back a dozen times. The firing then ceased for about a quarter of an hour, and I began to think I had got rid of my friends; but, shortly after, the moon rose, for which they apparently had been waiting, and up came fresh troops from the city, bugling and shouting on all sides. I passed the word from right to left to allow the enemy to come up close, and to keep a dead silence in the ranks. On came the enemy with their light guns, up the Grand Trunk Road, as also up the Kissengunj Road. My three light guns which were in Battery across the road were all loaded with grape, and when the enemy were close up, they opened. Round after round, with volleys of musketry from the Sammy House, had the effect of driving them back again. Still, there they were, within four hundred yards of me, making preparations for another attack, whilst their light guns kept up a continuous blaze, as also their heavy guns from the Moree and Burn Bastions. This sort of thing went on the whole night: 900 men against at least 20,000! My troops behaved admirably; all were steady and well in hand; and I never for one moment had any doubt about the result.

'At daybreak more troops were seen in the Kissengunj buildings, and on they came again at the Sammy House. I accordingly sent Sir E. Campbell with a Company of the 60th Rifles to reinforce the troops at that post. At 8 A.M. they gave us time to get a little breakfast, but before 9 o'clock on they came again, and it was not before 5 P.M. last evening that I had the satisfaction of seeing them in full retreat, guns and all. Thus ended the great attack, being number twenty-four on my position! . . . I have had no return as yet of killed and wounded, and I dread looking at the reports; the enemy's losses must have been very severe.'

During the forenoon of the following day Colour-Sergeant A. Williamson fell shot through the head, and Rifleman T. Chivers, a young soldier, had his hand taken off by a round shot and died from the shock. Sergeant J. Wallace and six other Riflemen were also wounded. Bugler W. Sutton, who for another feat afterwards received the Victoria Cross, distinguished himself by dashing forward and killing a Sepoy bugler in the act of sounding.

By this time the rains had abated and August 4, a fine day, was celebrated by a cricket match and a pony race in the Rifle Lines. On the 5th an unsuccessful attempt was made by our Engineers to destroy the bridge of boats on the Jumna. English newspapers up to June 27 were received and eagerly scanned. The disappointment was great, for the gravity of the situation was evidently not appreciated at home, and it was not realised that anything out of the common was taking place in India. This lethargy was no doubt partly due to the mis-statement (it is difficult to avoid the word falsehood) uttered by a Cabinet Minister in reply to a question on the subject.

But within the city walls matters were also going badly. The Sepoys clamoured for pay; they were unruly and the terror of the inhabitants. The King felt sure that the place would be captured and bewailed his impending fate. On the 7th the gunpowder factory blew up, killing nearly five hundred persons. It was in all probability the work of our spies; but they must have lost their lives, for they never returned to claim the promised reward.

Although during the next few days the fire never ceased, our regiment had comparative rest. On the 14th came a welcome reinforcement, consisting of the 52nd Light Infantry, the second wing of the 61st, a battery and 200 Mooltanee Horse: the 52nd was, however, not more than 600 strong. A few days previously had arrived the celebrated Brigadier, John Nicholson, a man of overbearing manner and crude notions of generalship, but strong in character, full of energy, and a magnificent fighter.

During all this time one lady, the wife of Captain Tytler, had been present with the besieging force. It so happened that she presented her husband with a baby, which was baptised under the not inappropriate, if somewhat unconventional, name of 'Delhi Field Force.'

By this time a siege train was on the way. In the hope of intercepting it the enemy sent out a force which was, however, attacked and overthrown by a detachment under Nicholson. An assault on the city was now evidently at hand. A plan of attack based on the observations taken in his personal and very hazardous reconnaissances had been prepared by Captain Alexander Taylor, a most able and gallant officer of the Bengal Engineers.

'This plan was designed to meet three all-important considerations : 1, The necessity of keeping the mutineers ignorant as long as possible of our intentions to attack from the left ; 2, that of getting so decided a command of the approaches to the field of operations as could make it impossible for the enemy to attack our works in force ; 3, the necessity of making our first battery strong enough to overwhelm the mutineers' artillery fire from the Northern Bastions, and thus to force them, if they attempted to mount new guns, to do so under our fire ' (' Life of Sir A. Taylor ').

General Wilson realised more clearly than any one the difficulties of his position and the hazardous nature of the enterprise. His force was obviously too small for an assault : and failure would entail the annhilation of his force and a general rising throughout Northern India. Writing to Colonel Baird Smith the chief engineer on the 20th, he says :—

'A letter has been received from the Governor-General urging, our immediately taking Delhi, and he seems angry that this was not done long ago. I wish to explain to him the true state of affairs

—that Delhi is seven miles in circumference, filled with an immense fanatical Mussulman population, garrisoned by fully 40,000 soldiers armed and disciplined by ourselves, with 114 pieces of artillery mounted on the walls; with the largest magazine of shot, shell, and ammunition in the Upper Provinces at their disposal, besides some sixty pieces of field artillery, all of our own manufacture, and manned by artillerymen drilled and taught by ourselves; that the fort itself has been made so strong by perfect flanking defences erected by our own engineers,[1] and a glacis which prevents our guns breaking the walls lower than eight feet from the top without the labour of a regular siege and sap, for which the force and artillery sent against it has been quite inadequate; that an attempt to blow in the gates, and escalade the walls, was twice contemplated, but it was considered, from the state of preparation against such an attack, . . . would inevitably have failed, and caused the most irreparable disaster to our cause; and that, even if we had succeeded in forcing our way into the place, the small force disposable for the attack would have been most certainly lost in the numerous streets of so large a city, and have been cut to pieces. It was, therefore, considered advisable to confine our efforts to holding the position we now occupy—which is naturally strong, and has been daily rendered more so by our Engineers—until the force coming up from below could join and co-operate in the attack.'

2

The British force was now organised as follows:

Brigadier-General Archdale Wilson, commanding Delhi Field Force.
    Brigadier Neville Chamberlain, Acting Adjt.-Genl.
    Lieut. Henry Norman, A.A.G.
    Colonel Arthur Becher, Q.M.G.
    Captain Garstin, D.A.Q.M.G.
    Lieut. Frederick S. Roberts, D.A.Q.M.G.

Brigadier Garbett, commanding Artillery.
5 Troops H.A. (one with 4 guns only: one with none).
6 Batteries F.A., Major Brind.

Lieut.-Colonel Baird Smith, commanding Engineers, 3 Coys., and 300 Sikh Sappers and Miners.

---

[1] The City had been fortified by Colonel Hare and Colonel—afterwards Field-Marshal Lord Napier of Magdala, at that time an officer in the Bengal Engineers.

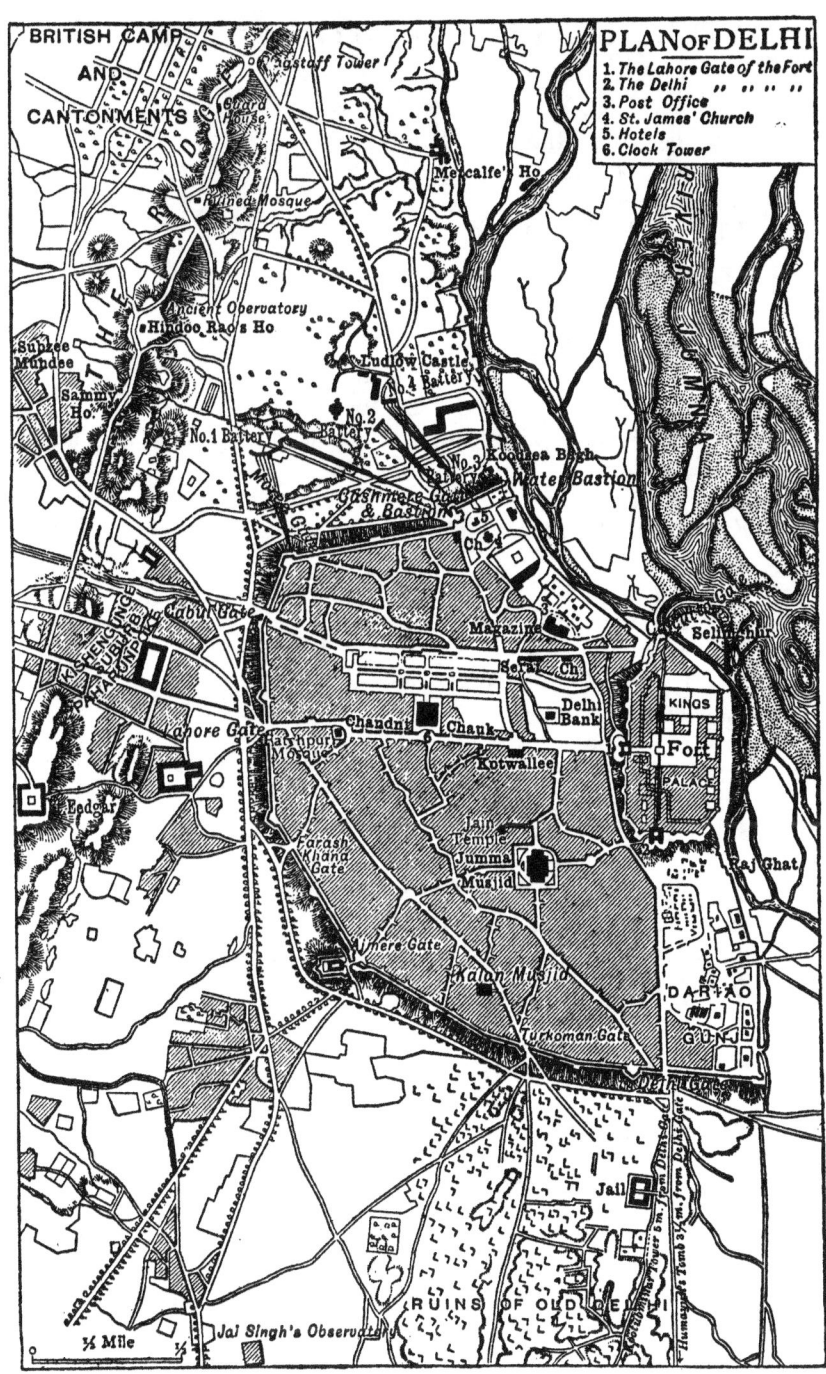

Cavalry Brigade

Brigadier Hope Grant, 9th Lancers.
4 Troops 6th D.G.
9th Lancers.
2 Troops, 1st Punjaub Cavalry.
,, ,, 2nd ,, ,,
,, ,, 5th ,, ,,
Lind's Mooltan Horse.
Hodson's Sikh Horse.

1st Infantry Brigade

Brigadier Showers, 2nd European Fusiliers.
75th Regiment.
2nd Fusiliers.
Kumaon Battalion.

2nd Infantry Brigade

Brigadier Longfield, 8th Regiment.
52nd Light Infantry.
1st Bn. 60th Rifles (6 companies).
Sirmoor Battalion.

3rd Infantry Brigade

Brigadier Jones, 61st Regiment.
8th Regiment (5 companies), 61st, Rothney's Sikhs.

4th Infantry Brigade

Brigadier J. Nicholson, 1st Fusiliers.
Coke's Sikhs.
Green's Sikhs.

Not Brigaded

Corps of Guides.

Meanwhile the sorties never ceased.

'On the 26th,' writes Heathcote, 'they again came out of Delhi and attacked the batteries in full force. One very plucky though foolish thing they did, namely, that their heavy cavalry charged our batteries. We were there and our rifles took well. They went down to a man: they charged again, but just as they were forming, three of our heavy guns opened on them with grape over our heads. We were, of course, in advance of the batteries, and sweetly they got it, I can tell you. A cheer, and we charged in our turn ; over they went pell mell . . . away they scampered, but not before we fellows let them have three volleys. Our guns threw shells and shrapnel among them.'

August passed away and September was ushered in with intense heat, the thermometer being 99° in the tents. Cholera returned but did not attack the Rifles. On the 3rd the long-expected siege train arrived, escorted by a detachment of the 8th Regiment and a wing of the Beloochee battalion. The roads had been inundated by the rains; and the progress of the train had in consequence been delayed. It consisted of four 10-inch mortars, six 8-inch howitzers, six 24-pounders, and eight 18-pounders. The train arrived at a fortunate moment, for the situation was critical. Gwalior had risen ; at Agra the mutineers had gained a success ; and in the Punjaub the natives had begun to wonder whether the British force was really strong enough for the work it had to do. To the maintenance of our prestige in India, the capture of Delhi, and that at an early date, was essential.

3

It had now become necessary to occupy the ground between the Ridge and the north-eastern corner of the city, which was to receive the weight of the impending assault. A personal reconnaissance on the part of the Engineer Officer, Alexander Taylor, had shown him that the Sepoy guards were often slack in their duties, and that an interval occurred between the departure of the old and the arrival of the new guard.

On September 6 Sir Edward Campbell was directed

to occupy with his Company after dark the whole of the ground lying between the Metcalfe piquet and the Cashmere Gate.

Campbell impressed on his men the need of perfect silence and noiseless footsteps. Lieutenant Hare with the advanced guard searched every house and compound on the way; and the Riflemen, gliding over the ground with the noiseless step of Red Indians like their Regimental forbears of a past century, reached undiscovered a point within 200 yards of the city walls.

Fortune favoured them, for the buildings searched, although as a rule full of men, were on that night empty; and by 1 A.M. Sir Edward found himself in possession of a beautiful old palace surrounded by a garden called the Khoodsia Bagh. The scene of romantic beauty was indelibly graven upon the minds of those present. The beams of the great oriental moon illuminated the terrace overlooking the Jumna, and turned into silver the waters of the river beneath; while the balmy air was laden with the fragrant perfume of cypress and orange trees whose long dark shadows concealed the forms of the advancing Riflemen.

On a sudden Hare's advance guard came upon a piquet of Mutineers. Their arms were piled; some were peacefully smoking their hubble-bubbles, others were lying fast asleep. It would have been easy to put them to the sword as they lay; but avoidance of an alarm was the paramount object, and our men passed by within a few yards unnoticed.

Working parties were quickly sent down and batteries thrown up. It was a fine piece of work on Campbell's part, and the consternation of the enemy when he woke in the morning to find what had been done may be easily imagined. A hot fire was at once opened from the ramparts of the city, but by this time the Riflemen were well posted under cover; and not only did all attempts to dislodge them prove ineffectual, but British guns were speedily brought up and armed the Battery.

On the 6th also the Regiment was reinforced from Meerut by Captain Muter and 200 Riflemen. The detachment included some Gunners, and was received by the band of the 52nd playing 'Auld Lang Syne,' and escorted into camp with loud 'cheering and hurrahing' (Keith Young). That very evening the bombardment of the city began.[1]

On the day following General Wilson issued a spirited General Order. He had appreciated, he said, the fatigue and hardships to which his forces had been subjected ever since their arrival at Delhi, and he thanked the officers and men for the patience and endurance which had never failed. Largely had he been obliged to draw on the services of his troops, and cheerfully had those services ever been rendered; yet now he had no option but to demand even greater sacrifices; the culminating point had arrived; the assault of Delhi was at hand. Vengeance was invoked on the murderous miscreants in the city, but the General appealed to his men for the maintenance of their honour as Britons to allow no slaughter of women and children. The troops were instructed to keep together, and sternly warned against straying in pursuit of plunder. The Order terminated with the General's assurance that, whatever property might be captured, would be fairly divided in accordance with established rule.

The General did not overstate the case : rest was thenceforward unknown. Day after day, night after night, the toil continued until Delhi had fallen. A half-battalion

[1] With Muter came Lieutenants A. Morgan, J. O. Young, S. Mortimer. Captains North and MacQueen, Lieutenants Pemberton and Carlisle were attached to Sir C. Campbell's force marching to the relief of Lucknow.

of the Rifles advanced to within 600 yards of the walls, covering the working parties.

On this day, the 7th, the army was reinforced by the 4th Punjaub Infantry. Next day arrived the Jummoo contingent with 2,200 men and 4 guns. In the afternoon George Kelly, the celebrated Adjutant to whom the efficiency of our battalion was largely due, had a narrow escape from the accidental explosion of a shell.

On the night of the 7th and 8th No. 1 siege battery was thrown up with marvellous speed. On the latter evening it was completed and armed. This battery, commanded by Major Brind, of the Bengal Artillery, was divided into two parts. The first, consisting of five 18-pounders and one 8-inch howitzer, was trained upon the Moree Bastion, with a view to silencing its guns, destroying its defences, and shielding the assaulting columns from the flank fire during their advance. The range was only 700 yards. The second part, armed with four 24-pounders, on the left of the first, was intended to destroy the Cashmere Bastion and divert the attention of the enemy from the working parties engaged on the No. 2 siege battery.

The attack was directed upon the northern face, for it was known that, from the front, between the Water and the Cashmere Bastions, not more than 30 guns could be brought to bear upon our approaches. No. 2 siege battery was erected close to Ludlow Castle, the Residency house, and only 500 yards from the Cashmere Bastion. Like No. 1 battery, it was divided into two portions, the first of which, armed with seven 8-inch howitzers and two 18-pounders, was intended to destroy the masonry of the left portion of the Cashmere Bastion for 200 yards. The second portion of the battery, mounting nine 24-pounders, silenced the guns of the Cashmere Bastion and a parapet of the curtain on the right flank. The 3rd Battery was erected at the

Custom House within 160 yards of the city walls. The 4th—a Mortar—Battery was placed at the Khoodsia Bagh.[1]

The working parties were quite 1,200 strong—a large proportion from a force of 7,000 or 8,000 men. On the 10th Lieutenant Henry Eaton of the Rifles received at the advance batteries what was believed to be a mortal wound: the skull was fractured by a bullet, and his subsequent recovery was a marvel to all. On the same day Bugler Sutton and Rifleman Divane won the Victoria Cross; the former by volunteering to reconnoitre the breach, the latter for leading a party of Sikhs and Beloochees. Leaping out of the trenches Divane dashed at the enemy's breastworks, on the top of which he was shot down.

In the forenoon of the 12th the batteries opened fire, and a large part of the Cashmere Bastion was carried away by the first salvo.[2]

From that day, Saturday, until Monday morning the roar of cannon was incessant.

'Nothing,' says an eye-witness, 'could be grander, nothing more fearfully imposing than the circumstances attending upon a bombardment; and yet among them none is more so than the sight of living shells traversing the air with more than the brilliancy of many meteors falling simultaneously, and in brightness rivalling the glare of continuous flashes of lightning during a stormy night.'

On the night of the 13th the breaches at the Cashmere and Water Bastions—the latter having been battered from the Custom House, only 160 yards distant—were examined by four Engineer Officers, and pronounced practicable.[3]

---

[1] The following siege materials had been prepared—platform, scaling ladders, 100,000 sandbags, 10,000 fascines, as many gabions, etc. The loading and unloading of bullock-carts, mules, and camels (1,500) had been carefully practised.

[2] The Munshi Jeewan Lal says that many men, women, and children were this day killed by the shot, and the Cashmere Gate much injured.

[3] The first reconnaissance of one of the breaches was made by Lieutenant H. Lang, an Engineer, attended by four Riflemen. The second later in the day by the same officer, and another escorted by Alfred Heathcote, who gives the following account of it: 'I had command of 20 men to go with the Engineer officer and

In accordance with this report five Columns of assault paraded on the following morning at 3 o'clock, awaiting the order to storm.

The first Column, commanded by Nicholson, consisted of 300 men of the 75th, 200 of the 1st European Bengal Fusiliers, and 540 of the 2nd Punjaub Infantry. Part of the Column was directed to carry the breach east of the Cashmere Bastion, and part to escalade its left face.

The second Column on our extreme left, commanded by Brigadier-General Jones of the 61st,[1] was directed to storm the breach in the Water Bastion. It comprised 250 men of the 8th Regiment, the same number of the 2nd European Bengal Fusiliers, and 35 of the 4th Sikhs.

The third Column, under Colonel Campbell of the 52nd, included 200 of his own regiment, 250 of the Kumaon Regiment, and 500 of the 1st Punjaub Infantry. This Column was destined to enter the Cashmere Gate as soon as it had been blown open, (or—should the explosion party fail in its task—when the Gate had been taken in rear by Column 1), and advance upon the Jumma Musjid and the King's Palace.

On entering the city the first and second Columns were intended to move westwards along the ramparts, crossing the route of the third Column; and after capturing respectively the Lahore and Kabul Gates, to advance up

---

see if the breach was practicable. I left all but four in rear of us, and then we managed to slip cautiously through their men in the advanced trenches of the enemy. We succeeded in getting into the ditch and some way up the breach when we heard them talking on the top and had to retire. We were then between the enemy on the breach and his advanced piquets in the trench, who kept up a fire on our batteries which were quite done. We crawled along gradually on our hands and knees and got quite safely back to our party. Had we been observed of course it was certain death.'

[1] The number of senior officers named Jones may cause confusion. Not only were there Colonel Jones of the 60th, and Brigadier-General Jones of the 61st, but there was also a Cavalry Colonel Jones. The last-named seems to have had no great military reputation. He was unexpectedly called upon to command a Brigade. 'Bearer,' cried he to his servant, 'Brandy sharab, belatee panee lao, jeldi.' Thus equipped he forthwith commenced his new duties.

the main street toward the Chandnee Chowk, in support of Campbell.

The fourth Column, commanded by Major (afterwards Sir Charles) Reid [1] of the 2nd Goorhkas, was principally made up of men of his own regiment and of the Guides. It was directed to take the Kissen Gunge, and afterwards to enter the city through the Lahore Gate, and reinforce the other Columns by way of the Chandnee Chowk.

The fifth Column, the Reserve, was the strongest of all, including, as it did, 250 of the 61st, 450 of the 4th Punjaub Infantry, 300 of the Beloochee Battalion, and the same number of the Jheend Auxiliaries.[2]

As to our own Regiment, about 200 men were being employed in covering the advance of the assaulting Columns; but one Company was in the Reserve, and that of Captain Muter accompanied Major Reid in the fourth Column.

The Parade State of September 11 had shown the effective strength of the Delhi Field Force as 9,866 officers and men. The Infantry Regiments which alone could take part in the actual assault totalled 6,089, of whom 3,417 were natives, including men and recruits, and only 2,672 were Europeans. The strength of the British Regiments was as follows: 8th Regiment, 322; 52nd, 302; 60th, 390; 61st, 402; 75th, 459; 1st and 2nd Bengal Fusiliers (the present Dublin Fusiliers), 797. The actual numbers of the assaulting Columns seemed to have been about 4,000 officers and men, and of the Reserve 1,500. This handful was about to storm a fortress garrisoned by about 10 times its number. In hospital were 2070 men.

---

[1] A splendid soldier. 'No braver nor abler ever held a commission in any service in the world,' says the Chaplain.

[2] 'In addition to these troops,' says the author of 'The Chaplain's Narrative,' 'there was one Company of that Corps concerning which the public judgment agrees in placing it relatively as A1 among all the European Corps, whether Queen's or Company's, who had the good fortune to see service on this memorable occasion.'

CHAPTER IX

THE force, as already stated, paraded at about 3 A.M. on September 14. An officer present mentions that Colonel Jones inspected his Battalion as minutely as if it had been on the parade ground at Meerut. Then took place a touching episode which could not fail to appeal to all present. Father Bertrand, the Roman Catholic Chaplain, appeared on parade in his vestments. 'Although,' said he, ' we may differ in matters of religion, the blessing of an old man and a clergyman can do no harm.' Thereupon, raising his hands he solemnly blessed the soldiers and offered a prayer for their success and for the mercy of Heaven upon those destined to fall in the struggle. Then the troops marched off and concentrated under cover close to Ludlow Castle. But the breaches had been retrenched and the breaching batteries had to reopen fire. Day had consequently dawned before all was ready.

Sir Edward Campbell, commanding the leading Company of Riflemen, had orders to extend and cover the attack upon the Cashmere Gate; Lieutenant Hare with 'D' Company was directed to prolong the line of skirmishers to the left, covering the assault on the main breach which had been entrusted to John Nicholson, who happened to be standing in the battery engaged in conversation with General Wilson. After a time the latter asked, 'How soon can you be ready?' 'In less than five minutes,' was the reply. Wilson then said, ' You will advance whenever you hear the Rifles open fire.' Nicholson darted off to his Column, and a minute or two afterwards General Wilson leaned over the epaulment of the battery and said in a quiet tone to our C.O., ' Now, Colonel Jones.'

Then, with a ringing cheer, the Riflemen advanced at the double across a bridge and rapidly extending on the further side covered the heads of the advancing Columns, reached the glacis and opened fire on the defenders. It was not long before the heads of Columns Nos. 1 and 2 appeared, and at that moment our batteries ceased fire. Despite a storm of musketry from the parapets of the City, the ditch was reached. Ladders were quickly planted, and Hare's men were in an instant across the ditch and climbing the ramparts ; but elsewhere the ladder parties were not equally successful. Then came a pause ; and the assailants, confronted with the showers of grape and volleys of musketry, fell in crowds either dead or badly hit. The earth reeked with their blood. Nevertheless it was not long before the troops all along the line found their way into the ditch and various breaches were immediately stormed.

' Carried away entirely with the excitement of the occasion,' says the Chaplain, ' the Rifles, whose duty it was to cover, and who discharged that duty to the admiration of every beholder, could not withstand the temptation that now met them. Forgetting that being light infantry they were as such essentially skirmishers, they were among the very foremost to mount the walls of the city. Theirs were the first caps waved in token of victory ; and theirs among the first human voices proudly raised to proclaim what we had gained and the enemy had lost.'

Once inside the ramparts, Everard Phillips, an officer formerly of the Indian Army, who had been attached to our Regiment since the departure from Meerut and received the vacancy created by Ensign Napier's death, carried the Water Bastion at the head of some Riflemen, and turned the guns against the retreating enemy.

So much for the attack of the first and second Columns. The third had in the meanwhile been advancing against the Cashmere Gate. Covered by the Riflemen, a party of Engineers under Captain Home, detailed to blow in the Gate, advanced at the double in the teeth of a heavy musketry fire. The men carrying powder-bags reached and crossed the broken drawbridge in safety. Home laid the bags at the foot of the Gate and jumped into the ditch, followed by Bugler Hawthorne of the 52nd. Sergeant Carmichael was killed and Havildar Madhoo wounded. Lieutenant Salkeld seized the slow match, but was struck by a bullet and fell badly wounded into the ditch, yet in falling threw the match to Sergeant Burgess, who the next instant fell dead. Sergeant Smith picked up the match and fired the train. Bugler Hawthorne at the same moment sounded the 'charge,' and the Column, headed by the 52nd, passed slowly over the beams of the drawbridge and through the Gate just at the time when Columns 1 and 2 followed by the Reserve were entering the City.

Colonel Jones succeeded in collecting his battalion, and occupied a large building which had been allotted to him; but inside the walls the main bodies of the Columns fell into some confusion. For Nos. 1 and 2 crossed the front of Number 3 and became intermingled, but advancing westward along the line of the walls captured in succession the Moree Bastion and the Kabul Gate.

The two Column leaders were for the moment not at hand. Nicholson for some reason had quitted his men, and in their victorious career the troops outstripped Brigadier Jones of the 61st, who, coming up, found that they had reached and been checked at the Lahore Gate. This Gate might no doubt have been taken on the crest of the surging wave; but Jones, recollecting that it had been assigned to No. 1 Column, and failing apparently to realize that the two Columns were intermingled, unfortunately broke off the attack. Reaction followed, and the men fell back in confusion to the Kabul Gate. There Brigadier Nicholson came up. An altercation arose between him and Jones. Then Nicholson attempted to resume the advance. But barrier after barrier had been thrown up. The Mutineers, to do them justice, fought with the valour of desperation, and Nicholson fell mortally wounded in an ineffectual attempt to capture the Lahore Gate.

During this time Colonel Campbell of the 52nd was clearing the walls in a southerly direction, and penetrated through the Begum's garden up to the great mosque called the Jumma Musjid, which was too strongly fortified to be carried by a *coup de main*. Nicholson's failure prevented the arrival of support, and Campbell, who had received a severe wound, fell back to the Church and Skinner's House, immediately south of the Cashmere Gate. It was somewhere about 2 P.M.

2

We must now return to No. 4 Column under Charles Reid, which included 50 Riflemen, 200 Goorkhas, and the same number of Guides, with a detachment of the 61st and 1st European Fusiliers, and was supported by the Jummoo troops—200 Horse, 1,200 Foot, and 4 guns. This Column had duly paraded at 4.30 A.M., but misfortune dogged it from the outset. Three field-guns detailed to accompany the Column did not make their appearance before 5.30 A.M., and when they did come the officer in command reported that he had gunners for only one. By this time the day had dawned, and Reid waited in vain for the signal to advance, namely, the explosion of the Cashmere Gate. Just then the Jummoo contingent, drawn up a certain distance on Reid's right, and which, as already noticed, had been intended to support him, unfortunately engaged the enemy on its own account. Reid found it necessary to advance to its assistance. The enemy was encountered in occupation of a breastwork, but being charged by Captain Muter with a Company of Riflemen and the Goorkhas, was driven from his entrenchments. But now the want of guns to clinch the victory made itself felt. The enemy retired unscathed to his main position on the Kissen Gunge; and as Major Reid was preparing a feint on the Sepoys' front and an attack on their flank and rear, he was most unfortunately wounded in the head. The fall of Reid proved fatal to all chance of success. There was no cohesion between the firing line and its supports. Captain Muter took command of the former: Captain Richard Lawrence (brother to Sir Henry and Sir John) of the latter. But the enemy was strongly posted in a narrow lane; the Goorkhas and Riflemen in possession of the breastwork were left isolated, and found themselves unable to maintain the position. Their losses were heavy. Lieutenant Mortimer of our regiment was slightly hurt, and every man of his section was killed or wounded. Muter retired, covered by the artillery on the ridge.

So ended the 14th. Initial success had been gallantly won and our position hastily loopholed and barricaded, but our losses had been 1,170 officers and men killed and wounded—not far short of 30 per cent. of the assailants' strength—and a small fraction only of the city was in our hands. We had but penetrated a quarter of a mile from the walls. Our numbers had been too few, and the enemy's resistance too desperate, to allow of our driving the victory home. Yet although Columns 1 and 2 were in no condition for further immediate advance, Columns 3 and 5 were in good order and morale. But the failure at Kissen Gunge left the enemy in a favourable position for making a flank attack on our troops within the walls, and the question was mooted whether it were possible to retain possession of what had been won. On this day our own Regiment lost 27 killed; Captain Waters, Lieutenant Curtis, and 53 N.C.Os. and Riflemen wounded, of whom four, including Colour-Sergeant Hackett, died of their wounds.[1]

During the assault the Cavalry remained mounted within musket shot of the walls, in the hope of drawing off a portion of the defenders' fire from the columns of assault. Its losses were heavy.

The 15th was spent in bringing up guns and consolidating our position, but no great progress was made. A Sepoy gun well posted played upon our Regiment: Colonel Jones, who had been placed in command of the advanced posts, attempted to capture it, but failed and lost some men.[2] Sir E. Campbell took possession, however, of a large house in our front, and Heathcote, his subaltern, occupied a gateway still further in advance. The latter post was handed over to another regiment. It was attacked and abandoned, but Campbell held his ground at the house. Meanwhile another attack on the Lahore Gate failed, and the failure of Reid's Column rendered our camp on the Ridge liable to attack from Kissen Gunge, an attack the more to be feared that, until

---

[1] During the assault on Badajoz our loss had been 5 killed and 30 wounded; at Ciudad Rodrigo and Mooltan our loss was slight.

[2] The Riflemen were partly employed in destroying the barrels of beer and spirits left by the retreating sepoys as a bait. In some cases it succeeded only too well, and the intoxication of a part of his force, which rendered it defenceless against a counter-attack, was one of the factors with which General Wilson had to reckon. An officer of our regiment writing at the time says he saw no Riflemen the worse for drink.

the return of a portion of the cavalry and some H.A. guns, the camp was defended by few except convalescents from the hospitals.

All these circumstances, added to the losses of the previous day, raised a doubt in the mind of General Wilson as to whether it would be better to evacuate our position in the town and retire to the Ridge. Second thoughts, however, rightly decided him to hold on to the ground he had gained.

Next day, the 16th, the left—or Reserve—Column under John Jones, made up of the Rifles, the 61st, and two native Corps, gained ground. Heathcote re-occupied his gateway; and the Riflemen on the tops of the houses, aided by some small mortars, forced the gun which had annoyed them the previous day to retire. Men's blood was up: every native was thought to be a rebel; it was difficult to discriminate, and many loyal subjects of the Queen were unfortunately put to the sword.

On this day, too, the Reserve Column captured the enemy's magazine, containing 171 guns—the scene of Willoughby's heroism; and not less important was the fact that the Sepoys evacuated the suburb of Kissen Gunge, leaving behind them 5 guns.

On the 17th Colonel Jones pushed still further forward and occupied the Delhi Bank, into which mortars were brought, and bombarded the King's Palace. Heathcote with surpassing gallantry successfully defended his gateway against a severe counter-attack. On this day our Regiment sustained a severe loss by the death of Ensign E. A. Phillips. Phillips had been with us from the outset, and had acted as galloper to Colonel Jones: he was shot while superintending the erection of a breastwork.[1] He

---

[1] Phillips was brought into the regiment in place of Napier, and his commission dated June 5, the day after that officer's death. The intimation did not, however, appear in the *London Gazette* until September 15.

was a general favourite, and 'his name,' says Sir E. T. Thackeray, 'was proverbial in the Delhi Field Force for the number of gallant deeds performed by him during the siege.'[1]

On the 18th connection was established between the two lines of advance; our flank and rear were cleared of the enemy, and the bombardment of the Palace was unceasingly kept up. On the other hand, the right Column was again repulsed from the Lahore Gate and Burn Bastion.

A heavy storm of rain on the 19th ushered in the cold weather. Two houses immediately below the Palace were occupied, and Colonel Jones, whose operations had been marked with great skill, worked his way nearer and nearer to the Palace, and entrenched himself on the ground he had won. He was now in a position to command the enemy's guns at the Palace Gate, while the Riflemen, perched on the tops of the houses, picked off the enemy's marksmen inside. On this day, too, the right column captured the Burn Bastion.

Early on the 20th the Lahore Gate fell into Wilson's hands and the Jumma Musjid,[2] whose garrison was contained in front by the 52nd, was captured by the flank attack of a force of Riflemen. The Sepoy guns protecting the road to the Palace were next taken. Then the Engineers blew in the Palace Gate, and in a few minutes Jones was in possession of the building. Colonel Jones' first thought was to propose and drink the Queen's health. Peels of cheering greeted his act, which he followed up by sending to General Wilson the message, 'Blown up the Gate and got possession of the Palace.' In reply General Wilson sent a most complimentary note appointing Jones its Commandant.

[1] *Cornhill Magazine*, 1913, 'Recollections of the Siege of Delhi.'
[2] This beautiful Mosque is situated on an elevation scarped for the purpose and ascended by a flight of stone steps. Its form is oblong, and its length 261 feet.

Writing a few days later, Lieutenant Heathcote says :—

'Here we are living in the most gorgeous palace of the East and our troops quartered in the Jumma Musjid, where a few months ago not a European was allowed to enter unless he took off his shoes. . . . The scene of desolation that reigns through the place is fearful to contemplate. When we first came in it was awful : pools of blood, dead and dying men—the streets in some places actually choked with them—broken guns, houses in ruins from the effects of shot, . . . in some you may go into the drawing-rooms and see 18-pound shot that had crashed through and stuck in the wall opposite ; large mirrors broken. Everything seems desolate and fearful ; fine and lovely gardens ploughed up with round shot, shells lying here and there, or great pieces of them ; walls bespattered with blood. Every single native has been turned out of the city, and the silence seems almost overpowering after the incessant din of the last few months.'

A Royal salute at sunrise on September 21 proclaimed the fact that Delhi had been recovered. General Wilson established his headquarters in the Palace and paid the Riflemen and Goorkhas the compliment of forming his body-guard exclusively from the two regiments. During this day Captain Hodson, a celebrated leader of Irregular Cavalry, captured the Mogul Emperor and brought him into the city as a prisoner.[1]

On Wednesday September 23 the gallant General Nicholson died of his wounds. He was a really great Englishman, and the Army felt that it had lost a tower of strength.

3

Meanwhile the old camp behind the Ridge was being rapidly cleared. Not a day too soon, for the air was

---

[1] The next day Hodson captured the Emperor's two sons, and fearing a rescue on the part of the mob, shot them with his own hand. His action has been the subject of criticism, but it is not generally known that Wilson had expressed some impatience when he brought in the Emperor alive. On that very ground where four months previously British men, women, and children had been slaughtered in cold blood the bodies of these persons were exposed to the scorn and indignation of the victorious army.

contaminated by the putrifying carcasses of camels and bullocks. On the 24th a column left Delhi in pursuit of the mutineers. On Sunday the 27th an impressive Thanksgiving Service was held within the walls of the Palace.

The losses of the Army during the assault and subsequent street fighting had been 1,347, and from first to last during the siege, 3,854 killed and wounded. The casualties of our regiment, from May 30 to September 20, are stated in the 'History of Services of the 1st Battalion' at 137 officers and men killed and 252 wounded.[1] This is also the official statement, although in at least two cases men who died of wounds are included as also among the wounded. On the other hand, Mr. Rotton, in ' The Chaplain's Narrative of the Siege of Delhi,' places the casualties at 401. The truth seems to be that many men who were not much hurt never returned themselves as wounded. Of the original six Companies which had left Meerut in May, about three-fourths of the officers and men had been killed or hurt ; and including even the 200 men who arrived at Delhi early in September, the casualties—by the official account—amounted to nearly 60 per cent. During the 7 days occupied in storming the city the Rifle casualties amounted to 92 killed and wounded. Among the latter were Captain Waters and Lieutenant Curtis, both for the second time.

In a General Order issued on the conclusion of the siege General Wilson said : ' The 60th Royal Rifles have shown a glorious example in its splendid gallantry and its perfect discipline to the whole force.'

Lieut.-Colonel Jones received the brevet rank of Colonel and the C.B. Brevet Majorities were awarded to

[1] The wounded included Captains H. F. Williams, C. Jones, G. C. Waters ; Lieutenants P. J. Curtis, H. G. Deedes, J. D. Dundas, J. S. McGill, H. F. Eaton ; Ensigns A. S. Heathcote, W. G. Turle, E. A. Phillips.

Sir Edward Campbell, Captain H. F. Williams, Captain D. D. Muter and Captain J. R. Wilton.

In addition to those who received brevet promotion the following officers were mentioned in despatches: Captain C. Jones; Lieutenants R. W. Hinxman, H. P. Eaton, J. D. Dundas, H. G. Deedes, C. Ashburnham, G. C. Kelly, and Ensign E. A. Phillips.

The Victoria Cross was given to seven members of the Battalion in accordance with the following extract from the *London Gazette* :—

'War Office, January 20th, 1860.

The Queen has been graciously pleased to signify her intention to confer the decoration of the Victoria Cross on the under-mentioned officers and soldiers of Her Majesty's Army, whose claims to the same have been submitted for Her Majesty's approval on account of acts of bravery performed by them in India, as recorded against their several names, viz :—

'60th Rifles. Lieutenant Alfred Spencer Heathcote, for highly daring conduct at Delhi throughout the siege, from June to September, 1857, during which he was wounded. He volunteered for services of extreme danger, especially during the six days of severe fighting in the streets after the assault. Elected by the officers of the regiment.

60th Rifles (1st Battalion). Colour-Sergeant George Waller, for conspicuous bravery at Delhi on the 14th September, 1857, in charging and capturing four of the enemy's guns near the Cabul Gate; and again on the 18th September, 1857, in the repulse of a sudden attack made by the enemy on a gun near the Chandney Chouk. Elected by the non-commissioned officers of the regiment.

60th Rifles (1st Battalion). Colour-Sergeant Stephen Garvin, for daring and gallant conduct before Delhi on 23rd June, 1857, in volunteering to lead a small party of men under a heavy fire to the Sammy House for the purpose of dislodging a number of the enemy in position there, who kept up a destructive fire on the advanced battery of heavy guns, in which after a sharp contest he succeeded. Also recommended for gallant conduct in the operations before Delhi.

60th Rifles (1st Battalion). Bugler William Sutton, for gallant conduct at Delhi on the 13th September, 1857, the night previous to the assault, in volunteering to reconnoitre the breach. This soldier's conduct was conspicuous throughout the operations, especially on the 2nd August, 1857, on which occasion, during an attack of the enemy in force, he rushed forward over the trenches and killed one of the enemy's buglers who was in the act of sounding. Elected by the privates of the regiment.

60th Rifles (1st Battalion). Private John Divane, for distinguished gallantry in heading a successful charge made by the Beloochee and Sikh troops on one of the enemy's trenches before Delhi, on the 10th September, 1857. He leaped out of one of the trenches closely followed by the native troops, and was shot down from the top of the enemy's breastwork. Elected by the privates of the regiment.

60th Rifles (1st Battalion). Private James Thompson, for gallant conduct in saving the life of his Captain—Captain Wilton—on the 9th July, 1857, by dashing forward to his relief, when that officer was surrounded by a party of Ghazis who made a sudden rush on him from a serai, and killing two of them before further assistance could reach him. Also recommended for conspicuous conduct throughout the siege. Wounded. Elected by the privates of the regiment.

60th Rifles (1st Battalion). Private Samuel Turner, for having, at Delhi, on the night of the 19th June, 1857, during a severe conflict with the enemy, who attacked the rear of the camp, carried off on his shoulders under a heavy fire a mortally wounded officer, Lieutenant Humphreys, of the Indian Service ; during this service Private Turner was wounded by a sabre cut in the right arm. His gallant conduct saved the above-named officer from the fate of others whose mangled remains were not recovered until the following day.'

It was intimated that Ensign E. A. Phillips would also have received the Victoria Cross had he survived.

Through its conduct during these operations D Company, commanded by Captain Wilson, whose subalterns were Lieutenants Hare and C. Ashburnham, gained in the battalion the sobriquet of ' The Immortal D.'

Sergeant-Major Robert Duncan was awarded the medal for distinguished service in the Field.

The testimony of his brother officers awards a large

share of credit to Lieutenant G. C. Kelly for his conduct as Adjutant to the Battalion. Kelly had enlisted in about the year 1841, and promotion to commissioned rank had been the reward of his education and ability. It may be doubted whether Colonel Jones did not owe part of his reputation to Kelly's zeal and judgment.

'All,' declared Lord Canning, the Governor-General, in his despatch dated November 9, 1857, 'behaved nobly, but I may be permitted to allude somewhat to those Corps most constantly engaged from the beginning : the 60th Rifles, the Sirmoor Battalion, and the Guides. Probably not one day throughout the siege passed without a casualty in one of these Corps ; placed in the very front of our position, they were ever under fire. Their courage, their high qualifications as skirmishers, their cheerfulness, their steadiness were beyond commendations. Their losses in action show the nature of the service. The Rifles commenced with 440 of all ranks ; a few days before the storm they received a reinforcement of nearly 200 men ; their total casualties were 389.'

It must, however, be remembered that we were fighting for our own race, our own faith. With our comrades on the Ridge the case was different ; and posterity will therefore say that, however great our exertions, they yield to those of the Goorkhas and the Guides, whose unparalleled loyalty will shine as a beacon in history, and the record of whose splendid heroism will be handed down to future ages, until the British Empire be no more.

4

After the capture of the city martial law of necessity for a time prevailed. Drum-head Courts-martial could hardly fail, under the circumstances, to act with more zeal than discretion.

'Many well-known men of the city,' says Mainodin ('Two Native Narratives of the Mutiny in Delhi'), 'were killed, being mistaken for rebels. In this way God showed His anger . . . the guiltless shared the same fate as the guilty. As innocent Christians fell victims on the 11th May, so the same evil fate befell Mahomedans on the 20th September, 1857. The gallows slew those who had escaped the sword. . . . Many died in jail. Numbers perished. Until Sir John Lawrence re-established order and courts were once more opened for the trial of the guilty, every man who had an enemy was denounced. False witnesses abounded on every side. . . . The slaughter of innocent, helpless women and children was avenged in a way no one anticipated.'

Ere long a dramatic scene occurred. Under an escort of Riflemen and borne on a palanquin, the Mogul Emperor was brought into the Dewan Khass to be tried by a Court-martial of British officers. The descendant of Genghis Khan and Tamerlaine bore little semblance to his famous ancestors—a feeble old man, short and slight, and of refined features, which wore an expression of alarm at the presence of the dreaded Commission and of the green jackets which had so often struck terror into the hearts of his soldiery. But it is noteworthy to find that the demeanour of the natives called to give evidence was very different. Taking no notice of the Judges or of the escort, they bowed to the ground on coming into the presence of the prisoner squatting in Indian fashion on a pile of cushions.

The evidence showed that the King had condemned outrage and had striven to repress the excesses of his soldiers; even on the occasions when he sanctioned murder, he seems to have done so under compulsion. The Commission had no power to pass sentence; that was reserved for the Civil Authority at Calcutta, which spared his life, and sent him to pass his few remaining days in exile, at Pegu in Burmah.

5

So ends our tale of the siege and capture of the Imperial City, which may, we hope, be ranked without exaggeration among the finest feats of arms in the military history of our Army. In India the paramount importance of that feat has ever been realised; in England it has not been so; partly from the fact that there were no newspaper correspondents present, partly because the massacre of Cawnpore and the defence of Lucknow appealed to the imagination of the British public, whose ideas of military operations are usually crude, in a way the siege of Delhi never did. Yet the facts of the case are worth recording. Delhi was essentially the Imperial City, the focus of the whole revolt. Here was the titular monarch; here and here only could the issue lead to permanent success. Delhi was in short the heart of the rebellion. So long as Delhi held out the upshot of the struggle was doubtful. The loss of Cawnpore was a most terrible incident; had Lucknow fallen another chapter would have been added to the tale of blood; yet it would not have affected the ultimate result. But until Delhi fell the fate of our Indian Empire hung in the balance.

The march on that city was consequently made in accordance with the soundest maxims of strategy; but having driven the enemy within its walls, what was the position of the British force? A small army—some 4,000 or 5,000 men—attacking, without any power of investment, a fortified city held in strength by a garrison continuously reinforced from outside. All that the British force could do was to establish itself on the Ridge north of the town, hold on to it like limpets and contain there the large masses of mutinous troops. These masses employed elsewhere might have turned the scale against us. There was no possibility of retreat; a retrograde movement would have set the Punjaub on fire in our rear. Those Indian chiefs who were halting between two opinions would have fallen upon it, and our army would have been destroyed.

Of the British position, Hindoo Rao's House was certainly the key, and its loss would have meant the destruction of the Delhi Field Force. This fact the enemy fully realised. Upon Hindoo Rao's House he concentrated the converging fire of all the heavy guns of the Moree, Burn, Cashmere, and Water Bastions, and the Kissen Gunge battery; and the piquet posted there from first to last had no rest from these guns, nor from the musketry fire of marksmen occupying the enemy's entrenchments.

Upon Hindoo Rao's House the enemy made no less than 26 attacks, all of which were repulsed by the piquet, which at times was outnumbered by ten, and at others by fifty to one; and, be it remembered, the fighting was no child's play; under cover the enemy was always formidable and in the open he fought at times with desperation. In the defence of Hindoo Rao's House the Riflemen and Goorkhas lost one-half of their effective strength.

Near that Ridge Durbars and State functions of surpassing magnificence have often of late years been held; but what impresses the British spectator is not the splendour of the scene nor the gilded trappings of Empire, but the view from Hindoo Rao's House of the breached city walls, never rebuilt since they were battered down by the guns of Brind and Maunsell, and the thought that the spot on which he stands—aye, and every inch around—is hallowed by the blood of Briton or Asiatic who on one side or the other gave his life in what he believed to be the cause of his Country.

'Any hope of succour from the south or from England in time to affect the issue had long been seen to be vain,' remarks General Sir Frederick Maunsell ('Siege of Delhi,' *Nineteenth Century*, October, 1911). 'In fact it was over six months after the fall of Delhi that the force from England captured Lucknow, and that with the aid of a Brigade from Delhi which had relieved Fort Agra, beleaguered by the enemy; and many a long day would elapse ere help could arrive from Upper India, when perhaps few would remain to be rescued! The part taken by the Delhi force in the salvation of India by the capture of Delhi and in the capture of Lucknow, etc., was never acknowledged at the time; all thoughts were concentrated on the great force arrived from England and its able chief, Lord Clyde. Nevertheless it was the fall of Delhi which retained British dominion.'

And when the arrival of reinforcements and of the siege train enabled General Wilson to take the offensive —an offensive essential at all hazards, since John Lawrence felt that he could no longer keep down the Punjaub— not San Sebastian, not even Badajoz itself witnessed an assault more desperate than that of our still numerically insignificant army upon a city whose every house formed a citadel for defence.[1]

---

[1] No better judge of military prowess could be found than the late Field Marshal Lord Wolseley, who, in his 'Story of a Soldier's Life,' Vol. I. p. 290, says, 'This siege of Delhi was the most memorable event in the history of the great Mutiny, and never did the pluck and endurance of the British and of our Punjaub soldiers of all ranks, from the general to the private, shine forth more brilliantly. . . . Its assault and capture marked the turning point in the Mutiny, and we all breathed more freely when it fell. It was a splendid military achievement, and our subsequent proceedings in Oudh and elsewhere, though most creditable to all concerned, were not in importance to be compared to it. When I subsequently learned the details of its events from Sir Hope Grant and his A.D.C. Augustus Anson, I realised how much I had missed. The story of that siege told to me by them sounded to my ears like an epic. It is not to be surpassed either in the mighty consequences that hung upon its issue, in the brilliancy of its daily incidents, nor in examples of heroic daring on the part of the besiegers, by any siege I know of in ancient or modern history.'

6

It is remarkable that throughout these operations the 'red tape' for which the Government of India, both civil and military, has been so justly celebrated was conspicuous. On the military side it was ordered that no mention of gallant or distinguished conduct was to be considered official if written in pencil. During the long defence of Hindoo Rao's House Sir Charles Reid, again and again, despatched pencilled notes to the Commander-in-Chief detailing the exploits of his command.

According to the Indian Regulations he should have sent for pen and ink before inditing these letters; but since they were written in pencil, no notice was taken of them by those with whom lay the power of reward. Among those whose services were consequently ignored were many officers of our own regiment.

The civil department no less distinguished itself. While the Delhi Field Force was straining every nerve to save India, the officials at Calcutta were striving with equal enthusiasm to save a few pice. It was the custom to credit a month's pay to the accounts of British soldiers dying in India. This sum was intended partly for funeral expenses, partly as a bonus for the surviving relatives. In the case of Riflemen killed before Delhi the sum was disallowed, on the ground that there was no certificate for the construction of a coffin!!!

In accordance with the practice from time immemorial, the spoil of the city taken by storm was the property of the victorious army. Previous to the assault of Delhi prize agents were appointed for the fairer distribution of the plunder—two out of the three elected being, as it happened, officers of our regiment. But when the city had been taken the Indian Government announced that it intended to appropriate the spoil for itself, and in its place substituted a beggarly six months' batta. No wonder that the soldiers, in biting scorn, inscribed upon the walls of the city the words : ' Delhi taken and India reconquered for 36 rupees and 10 annas ! ' The sarcasm may have struck the mark, for prize money was by degrees distributed, the last instalment being paid in 1868

7

A striking feature of the siege of Delhi was the astonishingly large number of able men assembled on the Ridge. General—shortly afterwards Sir Archdale—Wilson was at the time subjected to severe criticism, and the censure, sometimes in virulent terms, has often been more recently repeated. But the evidence of those best qualified to judge seems to show that, although able to appreciate the difficulties of a problem from all points of view and to ascertain the opinions of others thereon, he was a man of strong character, and endued not only with a high degree of generalship, but with the capacity of dealing tactfully with such difficult men as Baird Smith and Nicholson. Yet there were others ready to claim for themselves the glory which was deservedly his own.

Among the Engineer officers the names of Baird Smith, Maunsell, Thackeray, and above all, Alexander Taylor, stand pre-eminent.[1] The Artillery was represented by such men as Henry Tombs, Fagan, and Brind ; the Cavalry by Hope-Grant ; the irregular horse by Hodson ; the Staff by Nicholson, Donald Stewart, Henry Norman,

---

[1] The first C.R.E. appointed to the force arrived with his Persian wife, whose baggage occupied a dozen carts and five-and-twenty camels. This officer was shortly afterwards superseded by Colonel Baird Smith.

Neville Chamberlain. Amid such a galaxy of talent the lesser lights of Probyn, Gough, Roberts—the late Field-Marshal and peer—and Baker Russell, so well known to our Regiment in later days, pass almost unnoticed. In the Infantry special honour was gained by Sir Charles Reid of the Goorkhas, Colonel Campbell of the 52nd, and Colonel John Jones of our own regiment. Of these three the two first-named were rendered *hors de combat* on September 14. To the wise leading and able tactics of Jones during the street fighting the ultimate success was perhaps more due than has usually been stated.

The army under Sir Colin Campbell, which relieved and eventually captured Lucknow, was granted a year's service in recognition of its exertions, which were, however, trifling as compared with those of the Delhi force. No such reward was given to Archdale Wilson and his men. As already shown, they were for years deprived even of the prize money which from time immemorial has been held to be the right of those who take a city. Yet the members of the Delhi Field Force had their consolation, for throughout the length and breadth of the land it was realised that they, and they alone, had saved India.

CHAPTER X

AFTER Colonel Jones and his half battalion had marched away from Meerut in May, two Corps were organised at that station : one termed the Volunteer Horse, the other the Elephant Corps. Both performed good service. The former was composed of officers of all ranks who had belonged to the Sepoy Regiments which had mutinied, and of civilians who had been magistrates, etc., but whose occupation was for the time being at an end.

The Elephant Corps was made up entirely of N.C.Os. and men of the Rifles and commanded by Lieutenant Stanley Mortimer. They were provided with some of the best commissariat elephants, at the rate of one for every four men; and as the elephants could carry a good supply of ammunition as well as rations for three or four days, the Corps was able to perform marches of 30 and 40 miles a day without undue fatigue.

The Police had been driven out of Purreechutgur, and Kuddum Sing had been proclaimed Rajah by the Goojurs, who numbered some 10,000 men. But the rebel who was giving the most trouble was Sah Mull, who, at the head of about 5,000 men, was slaughtering all the loyal natives in his district. Owing to the well-organised Intelligence Department of the Goojurs, several attempts to catch him had failed. About the end of July, therefore, the Volunteer Horse and the Elephant Corps, with two small 3-pounder guns, half a dozen Artillerymen and the same number of Sikh Sowards, the whole under command of Colonel Williams of the Volunteer Horse, left Meerut in search of Sah Mull. The expedition was well and secretly planned and took a route which entirely misled the enemy. About six carts laden with boxes accompanied our force, purporting to be hospital stores under escort to Delhi.

At 2 A.M. on the third day after leaving Meerut Colonel Williams ordered the carts to be quietly abandoned. The native drivers were brought on in charge of the Riflemen and all speed was made across country to Baraut. So cleverly and quietly had the details been thought out that at 7 A.M. on arrival of the force at Baraut Sah Mul and his troops were discovered outside the walls preparing to move to the attack of the supposed convoy.

The enemy—taken completely by surprise—found himself on a sudden confronted by the Riflemen, who had been dismounted about an hour previously and formed the advance guard to the column. The rebels fired a volley and then bolted helter skelter to their fort. The Riflemen, following in hot pursuit, entered the fort simultaneously. They gained the ramparts at the point of the sword, and then, firing down on the rebels below, forced them to abandon not only the fort but the village outside, where they were met by the Volunteer Horse, which did considerable execution. Sah Mull was killed.

But by this time the enemy had discovered how small was our force, and made a determined attack on the two small guns, which were in charge of only 10 Riflemen, the remainder of our force being at some little distance. The steady fire of these 10 men kept the mutineers, however, at bay, until the Volunteer Cavalry arriving on their flank was able to disperse them.

The rebels were driven away, but news arrived almost immediately afterwards that a large force had marched out from Delhi to assist Sah Mull, and would probably arrive at Baraut about 10 P.M. Colonel Williams consequently decided to retire on Surdhana, viz. Hurnawa. It was well that he did so, for subsequent information showed that the force sent out from Delhi consisted of a regiment of calvalry, two of infantry, and a battery of horse artillery, which would have been supplemented by perhaps 10,000 Goojurs from the Baraut district.

The night march proved very fatiguing: the horses were quite done up and even the elephants were tired. The enemy's cavalry and horse artillery were close behind, and it was a relief when at daybreak on the following morning Williams and his men reached and crossed the Hindun River. Here Colonel Williams entrenched himself, and in the afternoon received from Meerut a reinforcement of two troops of Carabineers, two guns H.A., and 40 Riflemen, who had started in all haste on receiving from the Colonel intelligence of his peril. The reinforcement had, however, been sent off without provisions, and arrived in a condition even more exhausted than that of the force it had come to relieve.

In the evening the column started again for Surdhana, on reaching which it bivouacked in the Begum's Palace. During the night a bugler, suffering from nightmare, uttered piercing yells. For the moment there was an alarm, which however quickly subsided. Curiously enough it was subsequently discovered that the rebels were at that moment advancing to attack, but that on hearing the cries they believed thay had been discovered, and in consequence retreated.

Two days later the column returned to Meerut, having captured the walled village of Ukulpoora on the way and killed the rebel Chief, Nirput Sing. Its success had been conspicuous. Two powerful rebels had been killed and their forces broken up, while confidence had been given to many towns and villages whose inhabitants were loyal. The force was duly thanked in General Orders by Major-General Penny, Commanding the Meerut district.

2

To return to Delhi. After the capture of the city a Brigade was despatched, partly in the hope of overtaking the mutineer bands who had evacuated the city, partly with a view to reinforcing the Commander-in-Chief, who was making preparations to operate in Oude.

But for those regiments, such as the Goorkhas and our own, which had suffered the most severe losses and had sustained the most prolonged fatigues, a period of rest was obviously indispensable, and the Battalion was accordingly one of those selected to garrison the City and, as a special mark of honour, quartered in the Palace.

With the fall of Delhi the back of the Mutiny was broken, but the province of Bengal was overrun with insurgent bands, the garrison of Lucknow was *in extremis*, and disaster had occurred at Agra, where our forces had been driven into the shelter of the Fort. We had still a stiff task before us, and Sir Colin Campbell, the new Commander-in-Chief, who had arrived at Calcutta from England on August 13, 1857, found himself confronted with the duty of restoring order in a country as large as France and Germany combined, with a force of less than the ordinary strength of a Division, and a portion only of which consisted of British troops.

With the fall of Delhi the tide had nevertheless turned, and on September 24 General Havelock, who had with him on his Staff Major Charles North of our Regiment, relieved, or (to be more accurate) *reinforced* the Residency at Lucknow; for hardly had he effected an entry before his force, together with the original garrison, was surrounded and beleaguered.

On October 10 Agra was relieved by Colonel Greathead. On November 12 Sir Colin Campbell was ready to take the field, and advanced to the relief of Havelock's force, now commanded by Sir James Outram. With him went three Officers of our 1st Battalion, Captain G. Bliss MacQueen, and Lieutenants W. L. Pemberton [1] and W. F. Carleton. But none of them got further than Cawnpore, where a detachment was left to guard the line of communications.

On the 18th Sir Colin relieved Lucknow, but not being in sufficient force to hold it, withdrew the garrison and evacuated the city. Six hundred women and children and a thousand wounded men were carried away in safety. Retiring upon Cawnpore the Commander-in-Chief found that the force left there under General Windham had met with a reverse in an action, during the course of which Lieutenant Pemberton was severely wounded, and MacQueen, in command of a Company of the 34th on the left of the line, distinguished himself by wheeling his Company back and repelling a charge of Native Cavalry.

The winter was passed by Sir Colin Campbell in making preparations for the recovery of Lucknow.[2] This object was achieved on March 20, 1858, and Campbell

---

[1] Afterwards Major-General Sir Wykeham Leigh Pemberton, K.C.B., Colonel Commandant of the 4th Battalion.
[2] At the capture of Lucknow Lieutenant H. G. Deedes of the 1st Battalion served as extra A.D.C. to Sir Archduke Wilson, who was commanding the Artillery.

immediately planned the invasion of Rohilcund, in accordance with a scheme under which various columns were to take the field and converge upon its capital town of Bareilly.

3

We left our 1st Battalion garrisoning the City of Delhi with 'their brothers' the Goorkhas. The time came for the two Corps to bid farewell to one another, but not before the Goorkhas had paid us the high compliment of asking leave to bear the designation of Riflemen, and to wear our uniform. Like the Royal Americans they had earned the title of Riflemen, not by performances in the barrack square, but in the field, by their proficiency in the duties of light infantry in general and of scouts in particular. Their feats of arms on the Ridge sealed their right to the designation.[1]

On January 31 our Battalion marched out of Delhi, and three days later reached Meerut, which it had quitted more than eight months previously.

The country in the neighbourhood of Delhi and

---

[1] 'The 60th and the Goorkhas,' writes a Rifle Officer present, 'were immense chums, and they left Delhi before us; but when they marched away we all turned out to give them a send-off, and our band played them out, a thing that was never done for natives by an English band.

'Afterwards, when returning from an expedition from Meerut to Kashgunge, we saw a camp in the distance. The band was playing at the time, and on approaching the white tents a big crowd of men rushed out from them and never stopped till they reached us. They were our little Goorkha friends. We were marching at ease, and there was wild enthusiasm as they dashed into our ranks, shaking hands with the men, seizing their rifles, and carrying them to show their love for the 60th.

'To prove what handy little fellows they were, I may mention an incident that occurred at Delhi. A rebel had ensconced himself in a house, and was taking a pot shot now and again at, I believe, our piquets. He was rather a nuisance, but a Goorkha spotted him and began a stalk. After a short time the rebel put his head through the window to look round. The little Goorkha crawled along like a snake until pretty close, and waiting till the rebel put his musket out, jumped up and ran like the wind to throw himself flat under the window, at the same time drawing his khookeri. Bang went the musket over his head, and out came the rebel's head for the last time, when the heavy Goorkha knife cut through the neck like a carrot!'

Meerut—termed the Doab—having been quieted, on March 8 a wing of the Battalion, consisting of 12 officers and 306 men, under Major F. R. Palmer, proceeded on service in the direction of Kashgunge, to form part of the field force under Major-General Penny (Commanding the Meerut District) destined to co-operate in the converging movement on Bareilly. The Battalion was, however, more urgently required for another object; and in pursuance of new orders Palmer marched to Roorkee, which he reached on the 31st, and a fortnight later was joined by the Headquarter wing commanded by Brevet-Major Muter, for Colonel Jones had gone on ahead.

During the march of the Headquarter wing a rather curious incident took place. The force had reached a point within about 20 miles of Roorkee, and had halted at about 5.30 A.M. for coffee and a biscuit, when word was received from the Officer in charge of the right flank guard that he was threatened by a large force of Sepoys. The men at once fell in in line facing the enemy, who was located in a field rather below them at a distance of about three-quarters of a mile. The rebel infantry was flanked on either side by a half battery of artillery, with his cavalry posted in rear. The morning was misty and the strength of the enemy was a matter of estimation. Two Rifle Companies were sent down to reinforce the flank guard, which was on the point of opening fire, when the sun rose, the mist disappeared, and the enemy vanished. The villages in the neighbourhood were searched but no trace could be found of the rebels. The Riflemen eventually resumed their march, after sending forward information to the General at Roorkee. That Officer sent out a column to obtain intelligence, and it was eventually ascertained that the rebel force was merely the reflection of a mirage, but that a column of the enemy corresponding in strength had been on the move that very hour at a place some 60 miles away!

4

The troops concentrated at Roorkee and designated the 'Roorkee Field Force' comprised in addition to our battalion the 1st Sikh Infantry, the 1st and 17th Punjaub Infantry, a Squadron of the Carabineers, the Multanee Horse—a fine Corps, finely commanded—a Field Battery, and two 18-pounders. It had been placed under Colonel John Jones, who received the appointment of Brigadier-General, the Infantry Brigade being commanded by Brigadier J. Coke, and the Rifles by Major Palmer. The Staff Officers of the Column were Major Muter, D.A.A.G., Captain Tedlie, D.A.Q.M.G., and Lieutenant Herbert Deedes, now A.D.C. to General Jones, all of our Regiment. The strength of the force was 670 Cavalry, 2,408 Infantry—the 60th, 568 rank and file—with 6 guns.

> 'Along the foot of the Himalayah Mountains runs a belt of forest land inundated in the rainy season, and always covered with a tropical vegetation: a region of fever and a den of wild beasts. In droves the towering elephant crushed down the underwood, the crouching tiger hides in the thickest lairs, and the screech of the hyæna and the howls of wolves and jackals are heard without cessation through the night.'

It was in this jungle that General Jones's column was about to operate.

On gaining possession of Lucknow the Commander-in-Chief had decided to clear the province of Rohilcund, and by means of converging columns to drive the enemy into the wilderness described above, generally known as the Terai, and to give him the option of death by disease or death by the sword.[1]

To this end three Columns were destined to co-operate. The first, at the outset under General Walpole but subsequently joined by the Commander-in-Chief in person, advanced into Rohilcund in a north-easterly direction from Lucknow; the second, under General Penny, entered it from the south-west; and the third, under John Jones, was, as we have seen, destined to operate from the northwest, the idea being that the three Columns should converge upon Bareilly, the capital of the province, which in a straight line was about 140 miles distant from Roorkee and Lucknow.[2]

The theatre of operations comprised the basins of the Jumna and the Ganges with their tributary rivers. Railways were non-existent; in fact the only line of importance in India at this date was that from Calcutta to Raneegunge, about 120 miles in length. But for part of his march at all events Walpole had the benefit of the Great Trunk Road connecting Peshawar with Calcutta. Excepting for the Terai the country was level, well cultivated, and studded with numerous towns and villages, in many of which the country people were well disposed to the British. The head of the insurrectionary movement in this district was the Moulvie of Fyzabad. The arrangements for the capture of Lucknow had unfortunately

---

[1] 'Our advance through the edge of the Terai,' writes Major W. F. Carleton, who was present, ' was a sight to remember. As our men skirmished through the trees and heavy jungle all sorts of game got up in front of them. Deer, pigs, pea-fowl, and later on rebels, who having been told that we were only native troops had the temerity to attack us. But having previously been at Delhi they quickly recognised us, and with loud cries of " The Rifle Regiment," " The Rifle Regiment " (in their own language, " Ruffel ka-Pultan "), took to their heels. But we got some, and the Cavalry cut up a lot of them.'

[2] Although by these combinations Sir Colin Campbell was treating the problem as a purely military one, it is only fair to say that he was at the same time urging upon the Governor-General the importance of an amnesty to the less guilty, and to avoid driving them to desperation.

occupied the whole winter, and it was evident that the present campaign would be conducted in heat which would shortly become intense.

On arrival at Roorkee on April 13 Jones immediately despatched to Kunkhul under Major Churchill of our Regiment a force consisting of a Squadron, 2 Companies of Riflemen, a wing of the 17th Punjaub N.I., and 2 guns for the protection of the bridge of boats which the Engineers were then throwing across the Ganges. On the 15th the main body of Jones's Column came up and encamped by the bridge of boats, the heavy guns and stores having already been sent to the ford opposite Nagul, where a Field Officer was directed to divert the enemy's attention by making a feint of crossing.

On the 17th Jones crossed the river, and moved into the Hurdwar jungle; his advance guard, commanded by Major Muter, being composed of a Company of the 60th in extended order, supported by another with two guns and a troop of cavalry. The main body comprised a troop of cavalry, a battery, the infantry brigade, and the Mooltanee regiment of horse. Flank guards were thrown out on either side. The column began its advance, and about 4 miles had been gained when the enemy was discovered in force, although the thick jungle made it difficult to locate his position and impossible to estimate his strength.

Major Muter cleverly occupied a piece of high ground, and having posted a company of Rifles thereon and brought up the cavalry and guns of the advance guard, opened fire. General Jones at once ordered up the Mooltanee horse and Austin's battery at a gallop; and having deployed the infantry into line with proper support and covered its flanks with his skirmishers, advanced upon the enemy, whose position was indicated by the fire of his artillery.

The plan of the mutineers had been to effect a surprise upon the party constructing the bridge; but finding themselves foiled in their object, and shaken by the destructive fire of our artillery and rifles, as well as by the charge of a troop of the cavalry on their left flank, they withdrew in great confusion, leaving behind them 4 guns. In this action, which was known as that of Bhaggawalla, Assistant Sergeant-Major James Roper of our Battalion —an excellent N.C.O.—was killed.

Speaking of this action in his subsequent despatch, Brigadier Coke writes in high terms of the way in which the Riflemen skirmished through miles of thick forest, and of the unwearied energy and resolution which enabled them to work for eight hours in such a country and under such a sun. General Jones praised the manner in which his troops manœuvred in difficult country. His loss was happily slight, being only 2 men killed and 16 wounded.

Next day the force, moving in the same order, reached and captured Nujeebabad; 8 guns were taken, and the town was destroyed by camp followers. Jones's immediate objective was now the town of Nugeena, some 11 miles distant. It was known that the enemy was concentrating his forces to offer battle. Wishing to strike at the rebels in a body, the General halted for 36 hours, partly to complete his concentration, partly to allow time for the arrival of 8 guns of position from Roorkee. The enemy's force was estimated at about 7,000 men.

At 12.30 A.M. on the 21st Jones put his column in motion. Progress was slow, and it was not until 8 A.M. that the advance guard under Major Muter reached a canal about a mile north of Nugeena and crossed it by a bridge. Then bearing to his right Muter followed the road which for a time runs parallel to the canal. The head of the main body had in the meanwhile halted on the bridge, where the men had been allowed to fall out and the horses taken to water. It is evident that there was some defect in the communications between the advance guard and the main body, for Muter was unaware of the halt. A Vedette reported to him that the enemy was posted parallel to the road on his left front, occupying more than a mile of ground, but concealed by groves of trees. The advance guard was clearly in some danger, but communication with the main body was speedily re-established; the 60th and the field artillery quickly came up, and formed line against the enemy. The 1st Sikh infantry prolonged the line of the Rifles to the left, and opened fire.

The rebels were in point of fact taken unawares; they had intended to dispute the passage of the canal, but miscalculated the hour of Jones's arrival. By this time their position was thoroughly located; their left rested on the canal while their line, which occupied between two and three miles, faced north-west. Spies gave their numbers at 2,000 cavalry and 10,000 infantry. The guns quickly opened fire; the 60th and the 1st Punjaub Infantry advanced to the attack with the 17th Punjaubees in support. The 1st Sikh Regiment swept the further bank of the canal, driving off a body of Sepoys which had crossed it and was threatening our right rear. The enemy was given no time to get our range. The Riflemen and Punjaubees charged and captured a battery of 5 guns. About the same time a squadron of Carabineers supporting the right of our line carried the guns on the enemy's left flank at a gallop. The rebels now attempted to retire into the city, but General Jones rapidly changed front to the right, threw his left forward at the double, forced them past the town and pursued them for nearly two miles with the artillery, the Rifles and the 1st

Punjaubees. By his manœuvre Jones undoubtedly saved his force from loss, for the city had been barricaded and prepared for defence. Bands of the enemy sought shelter in the large walled Serai, and were there cut to pieces. Nearly 200 were shot, and the 17th Punjaub Regiment, entering Nugeena, killed a great number.[1] The Mooltanee Horse galloping round the town headed the fugitives. Then, emerging from ambush in a grove of trees, they charged a body of cavalry and infantry, cut up the sowars, and captured some guns and 6 elephants. The rout of the enemy was complete. Jones's loss was astonishingly small, comprising only one killed and six wounded; of the latter, four were Riflemen. The enemy's loss was upwards of 1,000 men and 15 guns.

Moradabad, 70 miles distant, was reached on the 26th. It was in British occupation, but had for some days been infested by a strong band of rebels who, at the approach of the relieving column, fled in the direction of Bareilly.[2]

General Jones by this time had made such rapid progress that he was comparatively speaking far ahead of the Commander-in-Chief, and it consequently became necessary for him to halt for several days to allow the column of the latter to reach Bareilly simultaneously.

[1] 'The Serai,' writes Major Carleton, 'was a very difficult place to enter, and it was necessary to try and breach the high walls with the 9-pounders. The place was full of armed men. We got in at last and killed a lot of them. The rest were caught as they tried to escape at the rear of the enclosure, some 70 or 80 of them, who were afterwards shot by the Sikhs, as we never let our men turn executioners in cold blood.

'Inside the enclosure was a pitiable sight. A young girl—she could not have been more than 15, if as much—was lying dead, with a baby, also dead, in her arms. She had met her death from a shell, and a piece of her skull had killed the baby. It was quite pathetic to see what our men did in the midst of the hubbub. They pulled off the clothes from some of the dead bodies lying around and reverently covered up the poor little couple.'

[2] 'Our political officers found a number of Baboos, all rank rebels, quarrelling as to who should rule Moradabad, unaware of the fact that we were in the place. The episode is somewhat typical of the Oriental character. The dispute was settled by seven or eight being hanged next morning' (Carleton).

On the 14th it had met with a check at the Fort of Rooyah. In this action Brigadier Hope was killed. Adrian Hope was the youngest son of Lord Hopetoun, better known to the military world as Sir John Hope, one of the ablest men whom the war with France had produced. His son Adrian had been brought up in our Regiment; he had, as we have already seen, served with the 2nd Battalion in South Africa, and had been a Brigade Major in the Crimea. On promotion to Field rank he was posted to the 93rd, and it was in command of a Highland Brigade that Hope met his death. His military capacity was great, and his loss lamented by the Army at large.

On May 3 the Roorkee Field Force quitted Moradabad, and on the morning of the 5th approached the enemy's outposts at Meeragunge, some 18 miles north-west of Bareilly. General Jones at once made arrangements for the attack; the Rifles were deployed on the east side of the road, with the 1st Punjaub Rifles still further to the left. On the right were posted the 1st Sikhs flanked by 4 guns R.A., a squadron of Carabineers, and the Afghan Horse. The Mooltanee Cavalry and the remaining 2 guns R.A. were on the left. The rebels did not attempt to oppose our advance, but retired upon the Dojura River. Before they could reach the stream the cavalry on our right flank overtook them, charged, and captured their guns. The enemy then fled into Bareilly, while Jones crossed the river and encamped on the left bank. Early next morning the General struck his camp and advanced close to the north side of the town. He had no positive news of the Commander-in-Chief, but such information as he had led him to believe—correctly as it turned out—that Sir Colin Campbell was encamped in the Cantonment on the south side of the city.

On the north side Bareilly is covered by the Dhuranea

River, the bridge over which was commanded by some of the enemy's guns. Upon these our heavy guns, escorted by the Riflemen who were thrown into the gardens through which the road led, opened fire with great effect. The enemy's artillery being silenced, the Riflemen advanced.[1] Captain G. Bliss MacQueen, skirmishing on our left, took advantage of the river-bed, which protected him from the enemy's fire from the adjacent houses, and worked round until close to the guns, then opened fire upon them with such accuracy that the rebels could neither reload nor carry them off. MacQueen soon made a dash, and having captured the guns, entered the city upon the heels of the enemy, followed immediately by the rest of the Battalion and the 17th Punjaubees. In the street fighting which followed D Company under Lieutenant Cromer Ashburnham once more distinguished itself. A party posted on the roof of a house was warned of the approach of a body of Ghazis or desperadoes. The men dropped from the roof; Colour-Sergeant Henry Baily fell, covered with sword-cuts, and Lieutenant Ashburnham barely escaped the same fate. A stroke from a tulwar hardly missed his head, and his own sword was too blunt to cut. A point therewith, however, finished the career of his assailant. The rebels were soon put to flight: rapid progress was made with slight loss, and by 2 P.M. nearly half the city was in our hands.

During this day Captain MacQueen was witness of one of those tragedies inseparable from the capture of a city. Terrified at the approach of the British soldiers, and at the thought of what their countrymen had done at Cawnpore, some men of Bareilly had hurled into a well many feet below the level of the street a dozen or

---

[1] The Companies (Commanded by Ashburnham and MacQueen) were extended: two were in support, and two in reserve.

fifteen of their girl relatives. Some were seen to be lying with their heads just out of the water. With great gallantry one or more Riflemen descended into the well and brought up the girls. Five or six were still breathing. Beside the bodies of dead and living an old woman on her knees was pouring out her soul in grief, yet restrained herself on MacQueen's approach and bowed to the ground before him in gratitude and admiration.

At nightfall the Battalion received orders to feel its way up to the Katwallee or Court-house. Barricades were erected in the streets, and the ground occupied was made good.

Since its departure from Roorkee the Field Force had captured no less than 36 guns.

5

The Column under command at the outset of Brigadier General Walpole had quitted Lucknow on April 8. But despite a start of nine days its advance was much slower than that of John Jones. On the 27th it was joined at Inigree by the C.-in-C. in person, who took command and started next day for Bareilly via Shahjehanpore, which was occupied on May 1. Leaving there a garrison under Colonel Hale of the 82nd, Sir Colin next day resumed his march and was joined by the Meerut column, whose commander, General Penny, had just been killed in action. On the following day the combined column, about 8,000 strong with 19 field guns, reached a point a day's march south of Bareilly. On the 5th Sir Colin deployed and attacked the enemy, who had taken up a position five or six miles south of the city. A sharp fight ensued, so sharp indeed that the force opposed to Sir Colin was allowed to retire unmolested. On the 6th the Commander-in-Chief made a further advance, and next morning on entering Bareilly he found it had been captured by General John Jones the previous day.

Sir Colin became aware of Jones's success in a rather ludicrous manner. As he entered Bareilly with all due caution he came upon two Riflemen and loudly demanded to know who they were, and what they were doing. 'It's me and my rear-rank man,' was the naïve reply; 'we was ordered to scrimmage through the town.'[1]

The Commander-in-Chief and General Jones met at the Kutwallee.

That evening the former invited Captain MacQueen to dinner and spoke of the time which he had spent in our Regiment, particularly in the 5th Battalion at Gibraltar during 1817–18. He described it as the happiest of his life, and after inspecting the Riflemen on parade next morning repeated the statement to them.

By order of the Commander-in-Chief the Roorkee Field Force was now broken up. On leaving the Rifle Battalion Brigadier J. Coke wrote to Major Palmer so kind and appreciative a letter that it deserves to be recorded *in extenso*.

'I cannot,' he said, 'allow H.M.'s 60th Royal Rifles to leave the Brigade without endeavouring to express my opinion of the distinguished Regiment under your Command.

'I have before this, in 1849–50, when the 60th was commanded by that excellent Officer the late Colonel Bradshaw, seen the Corps on service in a very difficult country at Sugoo and Pallee in Euzofzye; and in the Kohat Pass the way in which your men worked in those hills excited my admiration. At Delhi I saw them

---

[1] It was rumoured that Sir Colin had intended to enter Bareilly in triumph at the head of his Highland Brigade, and that he was not best pleased at finding himself forestalled by General Jones!

when their discipline and gallantry under no ordinary trials showed them to be the *élite* of that army.[1]

'On the 17th April the attack on the enemy in the Hurdwar jungles and their subsequent skirmishing through many miles of heavy forest showed not only what perfect skirmishers they are, but their unwearied energy, which enabled them to work for 8 hours through such a country and under such a sun.

'On the 21st of April at Nuggeenah the advance of your line to the guns had all the steadiness and solidity of a corps trained alone in compact formation.

'On the 6th of May at Bareilly the rush of Captain MacQueen's Company on the guns and the advance up the street had a spirit and dash in it that was delightful. What has specially struck me was the advantage taken of the bank of the stream which protected the advance both from the fire from the guns and the houses. This is the perfection of training which in my opinion is seldom seen, when the lessons of the drill ground are made use of in the moment of difficulty.

'I am afraid lest these remarks on such a regiment as the 60th Royal Rifles may seem presumptuous. I trust that they may not be thought so, but be accepted as they are meant. I much regret our sudden separation. With best wishes for the welfare of yourself, Officers and men, I am, etc. etc.,

'JOHN COKE.

'To Major Palmer,
  'Commanding H.M. 60th Royal Rifles,
    'Shahjehanpore.'

Hardly was Sir Colin Campbell in possession of Bareilly when a note of alarm was received from the detachment of the 82nd Regiment left at Shahjehanpore to guard his communications. It had been forced to take refuge in the gaol, where it was besieged by a large force of insurgents, some 8,000 strong with 12 guns. Sir Colin at once despatched to its relief General John Jones, at the head of a column consisting of a squadron of Carabineers, the Mooltanee Horse, the 60th, 79th, a wing

---

[1] The discipline seems to have impressed others as well. General Sir Sidney Cotton, G.C.B., remarked to a Rifle Officer that 'It has always been a wonder to me how such perfect discipline exists in your battalion.' The reply was that it was due to Lord Melville, Colonel Bradshaw, and latterly to Kelly, the Adjutant.

of the 82nd, and the 22nd Punjaubees, with a field battery and some heavy guns. Quitting Bareilly on the 8th, Jones reached the outskirts of Shahjehanpore early on the morning of the 11th, and by daylight had reached the river, the passage of which was essential for the relief of the garrison. A ford proving impracticable for the guns of position, Jones withdrew that portion of his force which had crossed the river and advanced upon the bridge of boats. The enemy's force, consisting principally of cavalry led by the Moulvie of Fyzabad in person, was driven across the river; the town and fort were then shelled for two hours, and the latter set on fire in several places. Judging correctly that the place was abandoned, Jones advanced into the city, and opened communication with the beleaguered garrison. Continuing the advance our troops reached the open country beyond, where the enemy's cavalry was still massed. It was, however, soon dispersed by the fire of the skirmishers, and retired in the direction of Mohumdee. The actual loss was only two killed (both Riflemen) and two wounded, but the troops were under arms from 2 A.M. till 7 P.M. The day is described as being the hottest ever known even to people acclimatised, and several men were struck dead by the sun.

The overwhelming numbers of the enemy's cavalry made pursuit impossible. It was soon reinforced by fugitives from Bareilly, and the Moulvie prepared to make a counter-attack, which was not long deferred. Within a few days he made a vigorous assault upon our lines, which was, however, repulsed by General Jones with great slaughter. But even now the Moulvie was not quite done with, and a few days afterwards the Commander-in-Chief arrived at Shahjehanpore in person. Desultory fighting still continued, and Sir Colin, who was on his way to Futteghur, gave Jones orders to resume the offensive on the following day. In pursuance of this order, that officer, who had been reinforced by a brigade of Punjaub Infantry, crossed the river by the bridge of boats during the night of the 23rd, and formed in order of battle in front of the village of Loodipore. At daylight the force advanced and found the enemy in position at the Fort Bunnai. The heavy guns in the centre moved along the road, flanked on the right by the 1st Brigade, consisting of the 79th and 1st Sikhs supported by the 82nd, and on the left by the 2nd Brigade composed of the 60th and 1st Punjaub Rifles supported by the 64th Regiment. The right flank of the line was guarded by Carabineers, the Scinde Horse, and a battery; and the left by the 9th Lancers, the Mooltanee Horse, and Tombs' Battery H.A. Austin's Battery was held in reserve. The enemy gave way with little resistance; but the heat was appalling, and during this and the following day no less than 27 British soldiers died of sunstroke. On the 26th the fort of Mohumdee was taken and destroyed, and Jones, having completed his task, returned to Shahjehanpore.

One other small operation completed the share of our Regiment in the Rohilcund campaign. At 6 P.M. on the 31st a wing under command of Captain Maguire formed part of a column entrusted by General Jones to Lieut.-Colonel Taylor of the 79th. The force marched for Shahabad, which was on the following morning reached shortly after daybreak. At the edge of a grove of trees bordering the west side of the town a force of the enemy's cavalry with 2 guns opened fire. Three Companies of Riflemen and three of the 82nd pushed forward in extended order into the city, while the cavalry and H.A. trotted round to the further side. The city was found to be unoccupied and deserted; the only casualties were two men wounded, one of them being a Rifleman. Having accomplished his object Taylor returned to Shahjehanpore, which he reached on the morning of June 2.

Thus ended the campaign in Rohilcund, remarkable so far as General Jones was concerned for the rapidity of his movements, the unchequered brilliancy of his success, and the astonishingly slight losses sustained. Between April 17 and May 27 the force under his command had swept the whole province of Rohilcund from north to south, fought one battle, defeated the enemy in three actions, assaulted and captured a large city, the stronghold of the enemy, and relieved two others; had destroyed two forts, and taken 37 guns. If it be objected that Jones had nothing much to beat, the answer is that he had to deal with precisely the same men as those who had inflicted numerous checks upon our other British columns, and who at all events in fighting behind walls and entrenchments had shown high qualities of tactical skill and courage.

Jones received the K.C.B. and the appointment of Quartermaster-General in India. In the history of our Regiment nothing is more remarkable than the meteoric rise of this Officer to fame. He had no chance of showing whether he could command a large force; in the command of a small one he was unsurpassed, and the skill and generalship with which he executed his operations is evidenced by the surprisingly small number of his casualties and the decisive nature of his success. It was said of Jones that he never encountered an enemy whom he did not defeat, never attacked a town that he did not take, never had a gun pointed against him that he failed to capture.

6

During the hot weather Lord Clyde wished to give the troops rest, and the Battalion remained quietly at Shahjehanpore. On September 25 it was re-armed with the short Enfield Rifle.

Early in October the Begum of Oude began to create disturbance on the frontier of Rohilcund; and Sir Thomas Seaton, the Brigadier-General in command at Shahjehanpore, found it necessary to take action. On the 8th he moved out with a column, of which our Battalion under Captain Maguire formed part, attacked and defeated a large body of rebels at Bunk-a-gong. Two guns were taken, and the column returned the same evening to Shahjehanpore.

By this time the plans of Sir Colin Campbell—now raised to the peerage under the title of Lord Clyde—for the subjugation of Oude were nearly ready. The proposed advance was facilitated by the fact that Fyzabad, Sultanpore, Pertabghur, and Soraon were already occupied. It was intended that each Brigade should be complete in all arms, and thus able to act independently. The operations were to be simultaneously directed from two points, viz. from the frontier of Rohilcund with the object of drawing the rebels in a north-easterly direction towards the Gogra, and from the south-east against the district forming the watershed between the Ganges and the Goomtee.

Sir Thomas Seaton was directed to organise two columns: one at Shahjehanpore under Brigadier Colin Troup, the other at Futteghur under Colonel Hale. Various columns—the principal one being commanded by Sir Hope Grant—were also directed to advance from the south, the main object of all being to drive the enemy over the frontier into Nepaul.

The main roads were held in force; the theatre of operations was flat and open. Excepting the river there were few natural obstacles, but strongly built hill forts concealed by thick bamboo plantations formed the chief defence. The rebel force in Oude was probably over-estimated at 150,000 men—35,000 of whom were Sepoys.

It was expected that the numerous columns would afford mutual support, and that the mutineers escaping from one would fall into the hands of another.

On October 16 the Battalion, under command of Captain Conyngham Jones, joined the Column of Brigadier Troup destined to disperse the various bodies of rebels which had long been infesting the Rohilcund frontier under the leadership of Khan Ali Khan, Khan Bahadoor Khan, etc., and afterwards to reduce the country between Seetapore and the Gogra River.

In pursuance of his instructions, Troup starting on the 18th, attacked the enemy next day near Pusgaon, and captured three guns. A halt was made until the 25th, when the column advancing over the Deoha found the enemy strongly posted at Rissoolpore. Troup at once attacked, and drove Khan Ali Khan from his position with the loss of two guns. The rebels retreated over the Gogra River. On the 27th the column crossed a branch of the Goomtee, and reached Nurungabad, where it again halted. On November 3 Troup marched to Nikana. Resuming his advance on the 7th he approached the Fort of Mittowlie and reached it next day. The fort proved formidable. Just outside the walls it had been strengthened by a double line of 'live' bamboos, which almost concealed it and proved impervious even to our

18-pounders. When morning broke on the 9th it was found that the enemy had abandoned the fort, leaving behind him six guns as well as a large quantity of ammunition and stores. The fort was then demolished.

The Battalion was commanded for a few days by Captain MacQueen, who then handed it over to Captain C. P. Ellis; but Colonel Dennis now joined the column, which on the 17th advanced northwards to Aligunge, and at about sundown came up with the enemy, who hastily retreated. From Aligunge Troup marched southward, parallel to the Gogra, until December 1, when he discovered and routed the rebels at Biswar. Quitting Biswar on the 6th the column reached Baragaon on the 23rd. Here it was divided into two parts, of which one under Colonel Dennis, comprising the Rifles, a party of Irregular Horse, and 2 guns, marched northward the same day, crossed the Chouka, the upper stream of the Gogra, and drove the enemy through the Kyreeghur jungles. After clearing them the column returned to Baragaon on January 1, 1859. Its casualties during the Oude campaign had been 2 Riflemen killed, Captain Jones and 3 Riflemen wounded.

Thus ended the part taken by the 1st Battalion in the suppression of the Indian Mutiny.

Colonels (afterwards Sir Charles) Reid of the 2nd Goorkhas, who throughout the siege of Delhi had commanded the main Piquet and advanced posts by Hindoo Rao's House, observing that no notice had been taken of his almost daily ' chits '—hurriedly written in pencil—in which he had recorded the performance of Rifle Officers and men, took the strong step of writing a letter to the C.-in-C., in which he specially brought to his notice the conduct of Lieutenant R. W. Hinxman,[1] and also that of

[1] In later life Colonel Commandant of our Regiment.

Captain C. Jones, Lieutenants H. P. Eaton, J. D. Dundas, H. G. Deedes, J. Hare, C. Ashburnham,[1] and G. C. Kelly, the Adjutant.

The letter had no tangible result; the reply being that too long a time had elapsed for the consideration of further recommendations.

7

In the following Spring the Battalion went down country, and on April 6 met the 2nd Battalion at Benares for the first time since the regiment had been concentrated in the Ionian Islands.

Hardly had the Sepoy Mutiny been suppressed when trouble arose with the European troops in the pay of the East India Company who, *nolentes volentes*, were being transferred to the Queen's service. The men considered that they were unfairly treated in being thus transferred without their own consent. The concession of a trifling bounty would fully have satisfied them; but the Governor-General and the law advisers of the Crown, with the lamentable want of knowledge of human nature so often shown by legal luminaries, refused to make any concessions, and fanned discontent almost into mutiny.

With a view to overawing the malcontents, superior force was employed, and a wing of the 1st Battalion was despatched for this purpose to Allahabad.[2] Despite

---

[1] In later life a Colonel Commandant of our regiment.

[2] A curious incident occurred. The malcontents sent a deputation to our men in the hope of inducing them to refuse to fire should an outbreak take place. The Riflemen invited the deputation to discuss the matter in one of the 'godowns.' The 'Dumpies,' as they were nicknamed from their small stature, unsuspectingly agreed. But when they had entered the place the door was locked; the members of the deputation were laid face downwards on 'charpoys,' and with the Riflemen's belts received the punishment they deserved, after which they were turned out and told what to expect should they refuse to enter the train which had been prepared to take them away next morning.

When the time came the Battalion was marched down to the station and drawn up on the platform. The 'Dumpies' had, however, entrained like lambs, and as the train moved off they actually cheered 'The Rifles'!

COLONEL SIR JOHN JONES, K.C.B.

their previous immunity the men were now attacked by cholera, and 15 died.

In July Rifleman Valentine Bambrick was awarded the Victoria Cross for conspicuous bravery whilst engaged in the assault and capture of Bareilly in the previous year. He had had a hand-to-hand combat with two Ghazees by whom he was attacked, one of whom he despatched.

On September 6 the Battalion quitted Benares for Dum-Dum, whence, early in October it was transferred to Fort William, Calcutta, where a ball in honour of the officers was given by the European inhabitants. It had been intended to despatch the Battalion to China on active service, but the Duke of Cambridge, Commander-in-Chief at home, decided that its period of foreign service had already been unduly prolonged. The 2nd Battalion of our Regiment therefore went to China in its place, reinforced by a good many volunteers from the 1st Battalion.

Previous to its departure from India the Governor-General had issued the following farewell order which as a mark of appreciation was perhaps unprecedented.

'General Order by His Excellency the Governor-General of India.

'Camp, Deenanugger, March 17th, 1860.

'The 1st Battalion of H.M.'s 60th Royal Rifles is about to embark at the Presidency to return to England.

'His Excellency the Governor-General cannot allow this very distinguished Regiment to leave the country without publicly acknowledging its services in India.

'In October 1845 the 1st Battalion 60th Royal Rifles landed at Bombay from England.

'Towards the close of 1848 it formed part of the column of troops from the Presidency of Bombay which co-operated with the army of Bengal in the campaign of the Punjaub. The Battalion was engaged in the siege of Mooltan, and in the capture of that fortress in January, 1849; at the battle of Goojerat in February of the same year; and in the brilliant pursuit of the fugitive hosts of Sikhs and Afghans, which terminated in the establishment of the British power at Peshawar.

'While at Peshawar for a considerable period the Battalion distinguished itself in several operations against the border tribes.

'In 1857, soon after the breaking out of the late Mutiny, the Battalion was engaged in the important action on the Hindun; and having joined the army before Delhi, its services were pre-eminent in the memorable siege and capture of that stronghold of the rebel forces.

'The Battalion subsequently formed part of the retrieving column under Colonel Sir J. Jones, which, marking its progress by successive victories over the rebels and mutineers, proceeded into Rohilcund and assisted in taking the city of Bareilly.

'Subsequently the Battalion participated in the final operations in Oude, directed and carried out to a completely successful conclusion by the Right Honorable the Commander-in-Chief.

'But it is not more by the valour of its Officers and men, conspicuous as that has been on every occasion, than by the discipline and excellent conduct of all ranks during the whole of their service in India, that this Regiment has distinguished itself. The Governor-General tenders to the Battalion his warmest acknowledgments for the high example it has set in every respect to the troops with which it has been associated, in quarters as well as in the field; and he assures its Officers and men that the estimation in which their services are held by the Government of India confirms to the full the respect and admiration with which they are universally regarded.

'In bidding farewell to the Battalion, the Governor-General desires that it will accept his best wishes for the welfare of every Officer and man belonging to it.'

For their services in the Mutiny and more particularly at the Siege of Delhi the following honours were conferred upon officers of the Battalion :—

Lieut.-Colonel Jones, Brevet Colonelcy and K.C.B.
Lieut.-Colonel Palmer, C.B.

Captain D. G. D. Muter, brevet Majority and Brevet Lieutenant-Colonelcy.

Captains Sir E. Campbell, H. F. Williams, John Maguire, J. R. Wilton, W. Tedlie, Conyngham Jones, and H. G. Deedes, Brevet Majorities.[1]

On March 17, 1860, the Headquarters of the Battalion —by this time reduced to 12 Officers and 402 other ranks under command of Captain R. E. Robertson—embarked for England;[2] and on August 6, after a voyage of 140 days, via the Cape of Good Hope, disembarked at Gravesend en route for Dover. So bronzed by the Indian sun were the Riflemen that as they marched through the streets of Dover bystanders were heard to exclaim, ' Why, they are black men! We thought they were British soldiers! '

A party of Navvies shortly afterwards struck work and came to enlist. The Colonel said he was sorry to be obliged to decline such a fine body of men, but that his establishment was complete. He therefore advised them to enlist in the Guards. But the men all said ' No ; we want to enlist in the 1st Battalion of the 60th Rifles, but not in any other regiment.'

[1] Sir E. Campbell received also a brevet Lt.-Colonelcy in October, 1860.
[2] About 95 men went home in another ship. A large number had volunteered to remain in India ; some, in order to proceed to China with the 2nd Battalion on the 9th ; some to the Rifle Brigade.

CHAPTER XI

DESPITE the outbreak of the Indian Mutiny in 1857, that year passed away quietly for our 2nd Battalion in the Cape Colony. There is a story that the authorities in India applied in vain to those at the Cape for reinforcements sorely needed, but that whether rightly or wrongly the request was refused. Early in 1858 the Cape Colony authorities reconsidered their decision, and on March 26 Headquarters with four companies of the 2nd Battalion, viz. D, F, G, and H, under command of Major Webbe Butler, marched from King William's Town to East London, where on April 6 they embarked on the screw steamer *United Kingdom* for India, the remaining four service companies being left in Cape Colony under command of Captain T. B. Roe, Lieut.-Colonel Spence having gone home probably on account of ill-health, for he never rejoined the Battalion. On May 15 the half Battalion under Butler landed at Calcutta and was quartered in the Town Hall. Its officers in addition to the C.O. were Captains H. E. Warren and the Hon. Athol Liddell; Lieutenants Knox Gore, W. F. Carleton, G. K. Shaw, K. G. Henderson, J. S. H. Algar, and Lieutenant & Adjutant M. Tilford. The Paymaster was Francis Fitzpatrick, who occupied that position in the Battalion for upwards of 20 years; the Quartermaster, Luke Fitzgibbon. The half Battalion contained 23 Sergeants, 16 Buglers, and 316 of other ranks. A few days after landing it was reinforced by a draft from England consisting of 3 Subalterns and 64 O.R.

The change of climate proved detrimental; during the four weeks in which the Companies remained at Calcutta they lost, from cholera and heat apoplexy, no less than 25 officers and men. On June 22 the half Battalion went by river steamers to Dinapore, where it landed on July 10, and two days later marched to Arrah. Here it was attached to a force under command of Lieut.-Colonel Walter, 35th Regiment, which formed small Flying Columns, constantly engaged with bodies of the mutinous Sepoys and insurgent villagers of the Shahabad district. On September 9 a company was engaged with the mutineers at Raunpore Puranu, and on the 23rd an action took place at Kerlasab.

By this time Colonel Spence had resigned his command and was succeeded by Lieut.-Colonel F. R. Palmer, C.B., previously Senior Major of the 1st Battalion. He joined the 2nd on October 1. A few days later a detachment of 200 men, under Webbe Butler, by this time promoted to the rank of Lieut.-Colonel, formed a part of the Flying Column under Colonel Walter, which was engaged with the Sepoys at Nonada on the 20th, and in the Jugdespore Jungle on November 25. This detachment returned to Arrah before the end of the year, by which time Headquarters had been reinforced by drafts from England, to the number of 4 officers and 76 of other ranks.

Meanwhile Roe's detachment in Cape Colony, consisting of A, B, C, and E companies, embarked at East London on September 25 for Calcutta, where it arrived on November 14. Under Captain Roe the following officers accompanied this detachment: Captains J. Fraser and E. Robertson; Lieutenants L. E. Traherne, D. Watts Russell,

J. Morrah (Acting Adjutant), the Hon. R. Vereker, E. C. Allen, and F. S. Brereton. At Calcutta the detachment remained for a fortnight, and then went on by railway to Raneegunge, whence it proceeded in detachments by bullock train to Benares, where the last party arrived on December 7. Previous to quitting Calcutta this half Battalion was armed with short Enfield Rifles, but the Headquarter wing at Arrah was not re-armed until February, 1859.

In the month of July the practice of designating companies by letters was temporarily discontinued, numerals being substituted.

On March 8, 1859, Battalion H.Q. marched from Arrah to Benares, but the four companies, now known as 4, 6, 7 and 8, remained as a detachment at Arrah under Colonel Butler. Captain Roe's detachment had received its medals of the Kaffir War 1851–'53 while on the voyage to India, but those for Butler's half Battalion were not awarded until April 7, 1859.

By this time the Indian Mutiny to all intents and purposes had been suppressed, but here and there the embers of rebellion still flickered, and on April 5, 1859 a party of 3 officers and 196 of other ranks quitted Headquarters for service with the Flying Column, under Brigadier-General Turner, C.B., in pursuit of Sepoys near the Grand Trunk Road. The mutineers however eluded observation, and on the 18th the party returned from its fruitless errand. During the same month the 1st Battalion under Colonel Dennis arrived at Benares, and the two Battalions thus met one another for the first time since 1838, when quartered together in the Ionian Islands.

On November 18 Colonel Butler's half Battalion joined Headquarters from Arrah, on quitting which the C.O. received a complimentary letter from the Civil

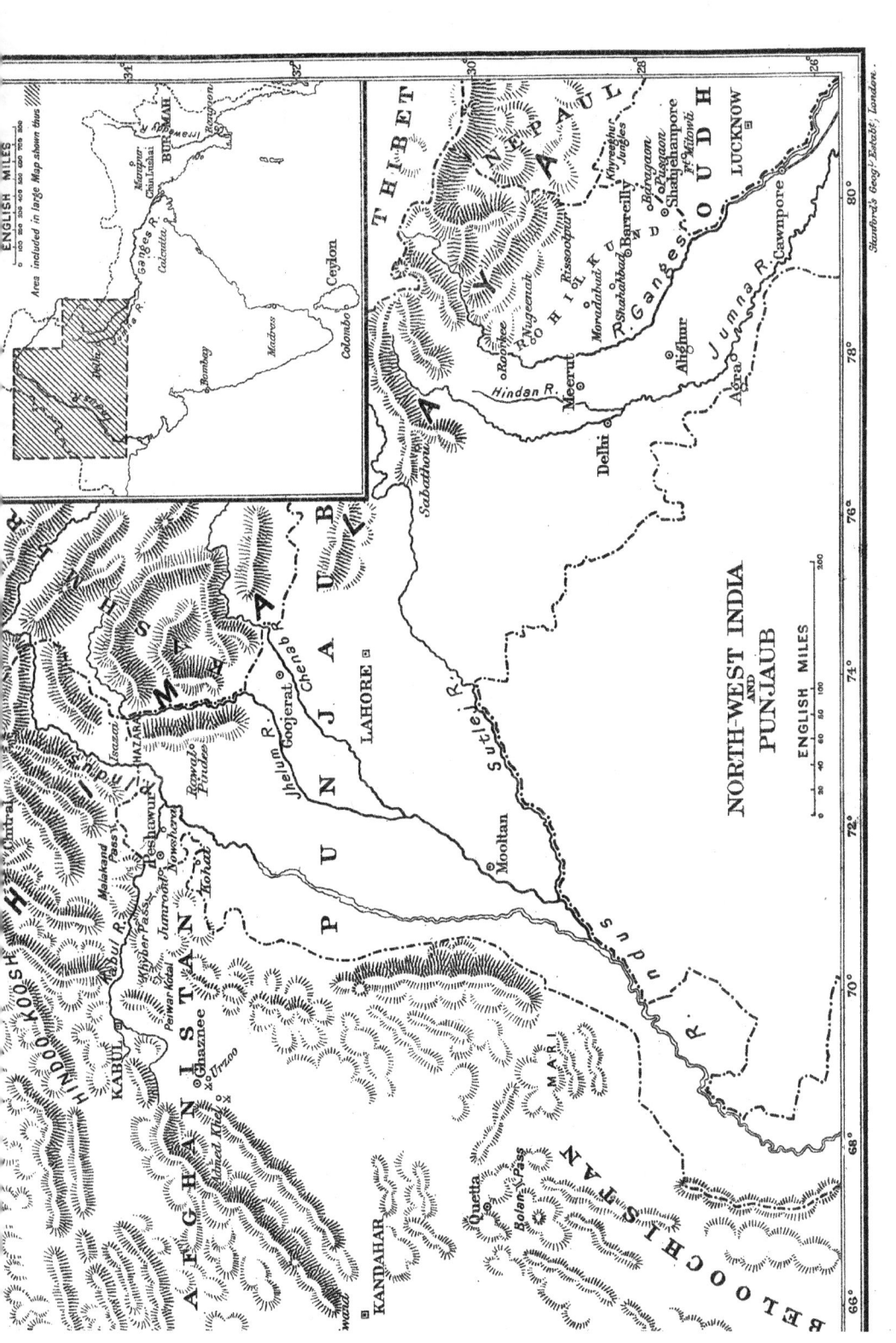

Magistrate, recording the good feeling which had existed between the Riflemen and the natives, and the absence of complaints made against any of our men. From this letter it may be inferred that the process of reconciliation after the horrors of the Mutiny was slow, and that the good example set by the Riflemen was greatly appreciated by the civil authorities.

2

On January 21, 1860, a new prospect of active service appeared, for the 2nd Battalion was ordered to form part of a force under Lieut.-General Sir Hope Grant, K.C.B., which was proceeding to China.

The Battalion accordingly marched down to Calcutta, where it was encamped in the glacis of Fort William, the 1st Battalion being quartered inside the fort preparatory to embarkation for England.

The difficulties between Great Britain and China were almost of a chronic nature. Although the conduct of the Chinese Government, which looked on us as barbarians and characterised us as 'foreign devils,' was extremely annoying and provocative, it may be doubted whether the English point of view was always the correct one, and whether it was entirely justified in its attempts to force our opium trade upon the Chinese, whose superior officials appeared to be anxious, and rightly so, to prevent its importation. In 1841 war had broken out between the two countries, and a force commanded by Sir Hugh Gough had occupied the country and captured Chin-Kiang. In this campaign two Riflemen took part, viz. Major-General Schoedde and Lieutenant Cunynghame.

The former will be remembered as an officer serving in our 5th Battalion throughout the whole of the Peninsular

War. In 1829 he had been promoted to the rank of unattached Lieut.-Colonel. In China he commanded the Left Column at the action of Chapoo, and in the following year, 1842, the 2nd Brigade at the storming of Chin-Kiang Foo. He received handsome mention in the C.-in-C.'s Despatches, and his name was subsequently included in a vote of thanks from both Houses of Parliament for the 'energy, ability, and gallantry' shown in the various services performed. For his share in these services Schoedde received the K.C.B., and was placed in command of the garrison at Chusan until relieved, in 1844, by his old brother officer Colin Campbell.

Lieutenant Arthur Cunynghame was A.D.C. to Major-General Lord Saltoun in the same campaign. He was present at the capture of Chin-Kiang Foo, and led the column of attack on the Makinihaow Heights. Thirty-five years later Cunynghame, by this time a General Officer and G.C.B., was appointed Colonel Commandant of our 2nd Battalion, and occupied the position until his death in 1883.

In 1857 the mercantile difficulties with China having once more led to a crisis, a force was sent thither for the purpose of insisting on our demands. The outbreak of the Indian Mutiny had, however, necessitated the diversion of this force to India, and the Chinese campaign was perforce postponed until the suppression of the rebellion. Despite our victorious campaign in 1841-42, the Chinamen still looked down upon us with contempt; and as all our bluff and threats were treated with scorn, it was evident that force of arms alone could ensure respect for past Treaties and enable us to gain our object.

For the present Expeditionary Force Lieut.-General Sir Hope Grant, K.C.B., had, as already mentioned, been selected. This officer had seen a great deal of active service, and although his selection for Staff employment in the last Chinese war had been due as much to his skill on the violincello as to military ability, Grant had done well and returned from the campaign with a considerable reputation; a reputation enhanced by his conduct in the Sikh War of 1845–1848, and still further in the Indian Mutiny, wherein, after commanding the Cavalry Brigade in the siege of Delhi, he had gained well-deserved renown in the independent command of a column. Sir Hope was in some respects a re-incarnation of a Cromwellian General. His strong sense of religion was entirely puritanical; and although cheerful and pleasant enough in society, he is said to have had a horror even of a theatre. Of him Lord Wolseley writes :—

'Sir Hope Grant's military instinct, mellowed by war's experience, invariably prompts him correctly; a soldier and leader of men, he possesses keen, bright views of war in its many phases. He is a man of strong opinions and plenty of ideas—and good ones, too—but either from faults of education, or want of practice in putting his views into words, he could not always clearly describe to others what it was he wanted done.'

Death had no horror for him. A few days before his end a young A.D.C., visiting him in his illness, burst into tears, but Sir Hope in his usual cheery way merely said, 'My dear boy, to die is nothing; it is only going from one room into another.' So it was to him then, and had always been in action, where no thought of personal danger ever seemed to pass through his mind.

Although the interests of France in China were not very large, the Emperor Napoleon III., at that time on the throne, expressed a wish to send a contingent and co-operate with the British force. He had been our ally during the recent war with Russia, and our Government seems to have felt that it would be impolitic to refuse him.

It was accordingly arranged that the force under Sir Hope Grant should not exceed 10,000 men, and that the French should provide 7,000, which were placed under command of General de Montauban; the two C.-in-C.'s being independent of each other. The British troops were, of course, drawn from our Army in India; but the French had the whole voyage from home.

The following was the British Order of Battle :—

Lieut.-General Sir James Hope Grant, K.C.B., C.-in-C.
Lieutenant Robert Biddulph, R.A., Military Secretary.
Colonel F. A. Stephenson, D.A.G.
Colonel Kenneth McKenzie, D.Q.M.G.

Cavalry Brigade.

Brigadier Pattle, C.B.

King's Dragoon Guards (2 Squadrons); 1st Sikh Cavalry; Probyn's Horse; Fane's Horse; Battery R.A.

1st Infantry Division.

Major-General Sir John Michel, K.C.B.

1st Brigade (Brigadier C. Staveley).

1st and 31st Regts.; Loodianah Regt.; 2 Batteries R.A.; 1 Coy. R.E.

2nd Brigade (Brigadier Sutton).

2nd (Queen's Regiment); 2nd Bn. 60th Rifles; 15th Punjaub Regt.

2nd Division.

Major-General Sir Robert Napier, K.C.B.
Brigadiers Jephson and Reeves.

3rd Brigade.

3rd, 44th Regt., and 8th Punjaub Infantry.

4th Brigade.

67th, 99th, and 19th Punjaub Infantry Regt.; Two Batteries R.A., a Company R.E.

A Battery of Mountain Guns and a Siege Train accompanied the force, which also included 250 Madras Sappers. The Field Artillery comprised two batteries of the newly constructed Armstrong breech-loading rifled guns, in addition to two of the old-fashioned 9-pounder brass muzzle-loaders. The Armstrongs proved a great success, but the R.A. experts disliked the breech-loading principle and after this campaign reverted for nearly half a century to the muzzle-loader. The Infantry was armed with the muzzle-loading Enfield Rifle. Breech-loading rifles were not adopted until seven years afterwards.

The effective strength of the force was about 14,000 men, for the Government in England had forgotten until too late to inform the Viceroy of India of the arrangement made with the French, under which it was limited to 10,000!

It is worthy of note that at least three members of the Staff of such a comparatively small force reached eventually the rank of Field-Marshal. These were the two Generals of Division, and Colonel G. J. Wolseley, D.A.Q.M.G.

3

While at Calcutta the 2nd Battalion received from England a draft of 2 officers and 248 other ranks, and was further augmented by 52 volunteers from the 1st Battalion and 17 from other regiments. Two new companies, numbered 9 and 10, were added to it previous to embarkation, which took place on February 28, 1860.

Colonel Palmer took Nos. 1, 2, 3, and 4 companies with him in the *Alfred*, while 5, 6, and 7, under Lieut.-Colonel Butler, sailed in the *Indomitable*, and 8, 9, and 10, under Major Rigaud, in the *Hougoumont*.

In addition to the 3 Field Officers, the following embarked with the Battalion, the strength of which was about 950 of all ranks : Captains H. E. Warren, R. W. Brooke, F. C. Fletcher, E. Bowles, F. D. Farquharson, and J. W. Medhurst ; Lieutenants The Hon. R. P. Vereker, G. K. Shaw, K. G. Henderson, M. Tilford, F. S. Brereton, A. S. Heathcote, V.C., K. A. Campbell, C. H. Cox, and H. T. Treeve ; Ensigns R. F. Barry, P. O'B. Butler, R. Meade, C. B. Prust, Arthur Morris, Redvers Buller, H. M. Pryor ; Lieutenant & Adjutant J. S. H. Algar ; Paymaster F. Fitzpatrick ; Surgeon-Major Schooles, M.D. ; Assistant-Surgeons G. Young, O'Hagan, and J. Doran.

The start was unpropitious, for 9 men died of cholera even before reaching the Sand Heads where the tugs quitted the convoy, and the three ships bumping against one another had to be fended off with spars. As far as Singapore a dead calm prevailed ; it was intensely hot, and the Bay of Bengal is described as being like a sea of molten silver. The *Alfred* made its own way ; but the *Indomitable* and *Hougoumont*, after drifting about for three weeks, were perforce taken in tow by a gunboat, which brought them to Singapore. Next day the voyage to Hong Kong was continued, and that destination reached by B.H.Q. on April 25. The weather was found pleasantly cool after India. The vessels were sent round to the further side of the island, and the troops disembarked at Stanley, where there was a small barrack. On May 18 Headquarters, with the Right Half Battalion, having re-embarked in the *Alfred* and the Left Half Battalion in the *Indomitable*, proceeded to the rendezvous of the British Force at Talien Wan Bay in the Gulf of Pechili.

The Fleet of transports encountered terrible weather, but the troops landed on and about June 29. Talien Wan Bay, on which Port Arthur is now built, could have contained the Fleets of the whole world. Owing to lack of any large water supply it was found necessary to separate the larger units. The 1st Division was encamped on the west side of Victoria Bay, the Cavalry Brigade and the 2nd Division on the east side. The Fleet, under Admiral Sir James Hope, comprised 100 transports and 70 ships of war in addition to gunboats. The French force was at Chefoo. The camp of the British 1st Division was on a fairly level plateau with some low but steep and barren hills in rear. Five bell tents per company were issued, which made rather a tight fit, as the strength of the companies exceeded 80 rank and file. The officers' mess-tent was merely a sail hung over a spar. The rations consisted of salt beef, pork and biscuit baked with rice flour in horrible condition, and so hard that it was uneatable without soaking. These rations were supplemented by a tot of rum, of which 60 went to the gallon.

In this encampment the Battalion—whose effective strength on July 11 was 30 officers and 794 O.R.: that of the whole army being just under 11,000 of all ranks—remained for some weeks waiting for the French, who during the whole campaign did little but hamper the movements of the British Army. 'They used our stores, got in our way at all points, and hampered our movements,' was the remark of Sir Harry Parkes.

On July 29 the Army re-embarked, the British transports being formed in two long lines, to which the French added a third, and anchored next day some 8 miles off the shore near Pehtang. On the 31st it blew hard, but on the day following the 2nd Brigade landed in the men-of-war's boats, being towed ashore by 2 gun-vessels, each boat carrying 50 men. The last mile was too shallow for the ships' boats, and the troops had to wade through a mile of mud flat. The Brigadier (whose command of the Queen's English was so great that he was popularly known as 'Blaspheming Billy') having discarded trousers, boots, and socks, jumped into the water and gallantly led the way. In appearance he was short, somewhat fierce-looking, and bandy-legged. Attired in a big white helmet and a dirty jacket of red serge, beneath which for a very few inches appeared the tail of a slate-coloured flannel shirt, the Brigadier presented a remarkable appearance as he trudged through the mud sometimes up to his knees, carrying his boots and trousers over his shoulder on the end of his scabbard. The host of onlookers was convulsed with laughter; but during the whole mile by unceasing cursing and swearing at the top of his voice, and a wealth of Billingsgate language which all might envy but few attain, he fully maintained his reputation!

The Brigade, which was supported by a 9-pounder and a rocket battery, bivouacked in line of Battalion columns on the Pehtang River, the Riflemen being furthest away from the evil-smelling little town of that name, which was about nine miles north of the Pei-Ho river, at the point near its mouth guarded by the Taku Forts. The night was cold and wet, and a few mounted Tartars rode up close to the line, whereupon the Brigade, whose nerves were perhaps a little unstrung, rose simultaneously with a wild yell and fired a volley into them. Next morning the town of Pehtang was occupied without opposition, for the British were received as friends by the inhabitants, who had suffered much from the Tartar patrols, their dislike of whom they expressed in a somewhat gauche manner, saying that 'they'—the Tartars—'stink even more than you English.' On August 3 a reconnaissance, in which 300 of the Rifles under Colonel Butler took part, was made by the Brigade, and a skirmish took place in which Rifleman John Wright of the 2nd Battalion was wounded in the left breast. The landing of the remainder of the allied forces and the stores occupied several days—our allies being terribly slow—but at length, on August 12, the Army gladly quitted the unpleasant spot.

The object of Sir Hope Grant's strategy being to take in rear the Taku Forts situated on the left or northern bank of the Pei-Ho, he decided to march south-west to Sin Ho, and thence in a south-easterly direction upon the Forts. The 1st Division went along the direct causeway constructed through the surrounding marshes. The 2nd Division took a line on the right which had been reconnoitred a few days previously by Lieut.-Colonel Wolseley, D.A.Q.M.G., and was attacked by a body of Tartar Cavalry about 3,000 strong, armed chiefly with bows and arrows. They were charged by the British Cavalry, which soon put them to flight; but although our horsemen followed in pursuit, their horses were in such bad condition after being cooped up on board ship that they were unable to catch the little Tartar ponies, and the enemy made good his retreat behind the Pei-Ho river. On the causeway the 1st Division had in the meanwhile come into action and opened fire upon the enemy's entrenchment with the new Armstrong guns at a range of about 1,000 yards. Later on in the day the little town of Sin-Ho was occupied by the Allies.

On the 13th the Battalion marched back to Pehtang for its packs, and on returning in the evening 500 Riflemen under Colonel Palmer formed a covering party for the works thrown up in front of the entrenchment at the Fort of Tang Ku, situated halfway between Sin-Ho and the Taku Forts. The Chinese threw a few fire-balls at the riflemen, who were otherwise undisturbed in digging a shelter trench. At daybreak on the 14th Nos. 3, 4, 5, and 6 companies, commanded respectively by Lieutenants Vereker, Shaw, Morrah, and Captain Warren—the whole under Major Rigaud—formed an escort to a couple of guns, detailed to silence the Chinese battery on the further bank of the river and some junks sailing thereon. This was soon effected ; and the four Coys. crossing in front of the Division occupied the trenches constructed during the previous night. 'Looking behind me,' says Colonel Arthur Morris of our regiment, who as a subaltern was present in the action, ' I saw 24 guns advancing at a gallop and behind them the 1st and 2nd Divisions in line of column. Their scarlet coats, fixed bayonets, flying colours, made a grand sight.' Of the guns two Batteries were the new rifled Armstrongs, while the other two were respectively made up of four brass 9-pounders and two 24-pound Howitzers. The guns opened fire and the Riflemen joined in. Sir John Michel, the Divisional Commander, was up in the front line of our Battalion, with which in the Kaffir War he had as a Field Officer been so often associated. His horse was shot. The enemy brought into action 14 guns which were quickly silenced. No. 4 Coy. of the Rifles, ' Gallantly led by Lieutenant Shaw,' says Lord Wolseley in his ' Memoirs,' contrived to effect an entrance into the fort at a point where the enemy's works touched the river. The other three Rifle Companies quickly followed, and the French with great gallantry effected a simultaneous entry at the main gate, which had been partly broken down by artillery fire. Further advance was stopped by heavy fire from the north Taku Forts, and the next few days were occupied in bringing up heavy guns, ammunition, and provisions from Pehtang.

The Taku Forts defended the mouth of the river, and in attacking them the previous year Admiral Sir James Hope had met with a severe repulse. Preparations were now being made for their capture. The weather was perfect, the days being cool and the nights warm. A bridge of boats was thrown across the Pei Ho near Tang Ku, but by a curious and extremely bad arrangement half was made by the British and half by the French. The fort was now closely reconnoitred by the French and British Commanders-in-Chief. Sir Hope Grant strongly urged the capture of the fort on the northern or left flank of the river, but General Montauban was strongly in favour of taking the fort on the other flank. To such a pitch was the disagreement carried that the French General wrote a strongly written protest; Sir Hope Grant, being a man of strong will, nevertheless insisted on having his own way, and it is unquestionable that his opinion was the right one. At 5 A.M. on August 21 fire was opened by eight of our heavy guns and three 8-inch mortars, supported by the two Armstrong 12-pounder batteries and the Rocket battery. The enemy replied with his available artillery, including two 32-pounders which had been taken from Admiral Hope the year before. A most graphic account of the capture of the fort is given by Lord Wolseley in his *Story of a Soldier's Life*, but as the 1st Division was not engaged, it will suffice here to remark that, despite the fact of two of their magazines being blown up, the Chinese made a gallant resistance, and it was only after a fierce struggle that the forts were taken. The British loss was 17 killed and 184 wounded. The Southern fort thereupon capitulated without firing a shot.

On the 30th Lieut.-Colonel Butler with Nos. 1, 2, 9, and 10 Coys., under respective command of Lieutenant Heathcote, Captain Fletcher, Lieutenant Tilford, and Captain Bowles, was left behind to guard the bridge of boats thrown across the Pei Ho. The remainder of the Battalion marched with the first Division to Tien Tsin, where it arrived on September 2, and was rejoined a week later by Butler's detachment, which had been delightfully encamped among the vines on the other side of the Pei Ho, where it got abundance of flowers and fruit.

On September 12 the Battalion marched for Hoo-Seo-Wu, which was reached on the 25th. It marched again and on the 27th joined General Headquarters encamped at Tung Chow, some ten or twelve miles from Peking. In the meanwhile much had happened. Envoys had been sent by the Chinese Government with a view to stopping the march of the Allies and arranging terms for a treaty of peace. Negotiations were conducted by Lord Elgin, the diplomatic officer attached to the Army, without consulting Sir Hope Grant, who had had too long an experience of the East to trust in the promises of Orientals. Lord Elgin ingenuously made up his mind that the overtures of the Chinamen were made in perfect good faith, and that to all intents and purposes hostilities were at an end. On September 16 Messrs. Parkes and Loch, British Consuls, who despite considerable experience of the country were apparently as much deceived as their chief, proceeded to Tung Chow, to prepare Lord Elgin's reception. With them went Colonel Beauchamp Walker, A.Q.M.G., and a small escort to arrange details as to camping ground and supplies. A further arrangement was made by Lord Elgin that the Allied Army should halt about two miles short of Chang Kia Wan, whence with an escort of 1,000 men he proposed to proceed to Tung Chow for the settlement of the terms of peace. The camp at Chang Kia Wan, some three or four miles short of Tung Chow on the road to Peking the capital, was reached on the 18th.

Meanwhile our envoys in Tung Chow had found out that treachery was intended. They were allowed to leave that place on the 18th, and hurried back to rejoin our Army. Chang Kia Wan was passed without molestation, but when between that town and the British camp the party was stopped by a troop of Tartar Horse; Parkes was pulled off his horse and taken before the Chinese Commander-in-Chief, Sang-Ko-Lin Sin (popularly known in the British Army as Sam Collinson!). Parkes was treated with the greatest contumely and his face rubbed in the dust.

On this day Sir Hope Grant with about 2,000 men of the 1st Division, followed by about the same number of French, had started at 5 A.M. for Chang Kia Wan; but only four or five miles had been made when a large body of the enemy, occupying a line of about five miles and supported by heavy batteries, were observed barring the road. The Chinese Infantry was drawn up behind a large watercourse to the right front of the British Army. The Cavalry was attempting to turn our flanks on both sides. The Chinese Army was probably some 20,000 strong. Just at this moment, while the allied forces were being deployed, up galloped Mr. Loch with a few Sowars. Loch brought a letter from Parkes to say that negotiations were making good progress; but his own experience contradicted this favourable news. He stated that with Parkes, Colonel Walker, and a few troopers and Sowars,[1] he had started from Tung Chow at 5 A.M. that morning, leaving there Lieutenant Anderson, 17 Sowars, and 2 English civilians. As the party came along, the concentration of large bodies of the enemy was observed on the very ground which had been suggested by the Chinese for our encampment, near Chang Kia Wan. Thereupon Mr. Parkes, with perhaps more gallantry than discretion, resolved to return to Tung Chow with a single trooper in order to ask the Chinese officials what it all meant. He then directed Loch to gallop on to the British Army, but asked Colonel Walker with the rest of the party to await his return. Mr. Loch, as we have seen, duly executed his mission and gallantly

[1] 'Sowars' are the troopers in Indian Cavalry regiments.

volunteered to return at once to Chang Kia Wan to bring in Walker's party. Sir Hope concurred, saying, 'I will send Wolseley with you,' but Captain Brabazon, R.A., told the Chief that Colonel Wolseley had not yet come up, and was given leave to go in his place. It was fortunate for the future Field-Marshal that he had been left behind to sketch the country, for Brabazon was captured and beheaded a few minutes afterwards. Between 10 and 11 A.M. Colonel Walker with his small party galloped in to the British lines, having cut his way through the enemy who had surrounded them.

By this time the Allied force was deployed, and our guns wrought havoc among the enemy's masses. Despite the disparity of numbers the Allied Generals did not hesitate in taking the offensive. On the right of the British, Montauban dealt with the left flank of the Chinese and enfiladed them with his guns. Then the French were charged and their guns were almost taken by the Tartar Cavalry, when a squadron of Fane's Horse, which had been lent to our allies, aided by a few French orderlies, charged in turn and put the enemy to flight. Meanwhile, on our left Sir John Michel, who had only a British Battalion, a 6-pounder battery, and some native cavalry, was attacked by such masses of the enemy that he had difficulty in holding his ground, till his front was cleared by Major Probyn, who charged with 100 of his men. After a time the whole Chinese Army retired. The French were too much fatigued to follow, but Sir Hope Grant, continuing his advance, captured the town of Chang Kia Wan and occupied the country two miles beyond. Eighty of the enemy's guns fell into our hands.

As a punishment for the Chinese treachery Chang Kia Wan was given over to plunder. The British did not halt until they were two miles beyond the town.

ADVANCE ON PEKING

Notwithstanding this success, the position of the Allies, in view of the large masses of enemy troops, gave cause for some anxiety, and all hope of immediate peace was, of course, at an end. Two days after the action the arrival of a French Brigade raised Montauban's force to 3,000, and Sir Hope Grant sent an order to Sir Robert Napier to march up with as little delay as possible from Ho-Si-Wu with two regiments, one of which was to be the 60th. Just at this time the commissariat stores arrived by river from Kian Sing.

On the 21st another action took place at the bridge of Pa-le-chaiao, which was captured by the French.

In pursuance of the C.-in-C.'s order the 60th joined G.H.Q. near Tung Chow on the 27th. A few days were occupied in bringing up stores, ammunition, and reinforcements. On October 5 the Allied forces marched upon Peking. Next morning the march was resumed. The Allies took it in turn to head the column; and on this day it was the turn of the English. The main body of the column marched along the road, which although now much out of repair had originally been constructed of enormous blocks of stone. The country on either side was enclosed, and Sir Hope, of course, moved with a strong advance guard and flanking parties. The Cavalry was ordered to take a wide detour on the right. The march was short but fatiguing, and a halt was eventually made in one of the suburbs at the north-eastern angle of the town. It had been arranged between the two commanders that the French should co-operate in this movement; but when Sir Hope went to confer with General Montauban, that officer and his army were nowhere to be found. It subsequently transpired that the French contingent, which should have been on the left of the British force, had halted until the whole of it had passed and then moved forward on our right, reached the famous Summer Palace, and lost no time in despoiling it. Our Cavalry on the right flank had also disappeared, but its disappearance was unintentional, and it returned to the main body in due course. At the Summer Palace Colonel Wolseley, D.A.Q.M.G., discovered our allies next morning; and on getting his report, Lord Elgin and Sir Hope rode over to see the French Commander.

'In the distance,' says Sir Hope in his 'Journal,' 'we at last perceived the Palace, beautifully situated amidst gardens and woods, and a range of large shrubs in the front. We passed the Park walls by a fine old stately gateway, and proceeding up an avenue came to a range of handsome dwellings roofed over with china tiles, turned up at the end in Chinese fashion. In different parts of the grounds were forty separate small palaces in beautiful situations. The park was carefully kept, the paths and roads were clean and in excellent order, and there were various pretty trees and ornaments. We found that the French had encamped near the entrance of the great Audience Hall, and it was pitiful to see the way in which everything was being robbed. . . . The principal palace was filled with beautiful jade stone of great value, and carved in a most elaborate manner, splendid old china, enamel, bronze and numerous clocks and watches, many of which were presents given by Lord Macartney (about 1793) and ambassadors from other countries. . . . General Montauban and I agreed that all that remained of the prize property should be divided among both armies; a quantity of articles was set aside for us, and I determined to sell them for the benefit of the officers and men. The French General told me he had found two staves of office, made of gold and green jade stone, one of which he would give as a present for Queen Victoria, the other he intended to give to the Emperor Napoleon. On returning to camp we found a letter from Prince Kung, the Governor of Peking, evidently written in great fear, saying that the prisoners would be sent to us to-morrow, and that the High Commissioner would meet any delegate he might choose to send at a house outside the gate of the city.'

Mr. Wade was appointed to meet the Chinese Commissioner, who promised to deliver up the British prisoners next day, and said that the Emperor had fled with the army.

On the following day a quantity of gold and silver and a room full of the richest silks and furs were found in a temple of the Summer Palace, and divided between the French and British. Supplies of food were plentiful; sheep and oxen were in abundance, and the fields were full of sweet potatoes and other vegetables.

At 3 P.M. on this day Messrs. Parkes, Loch, and five Frenchmen came into the camp, and narrated the events which had happened since their disappearance on September 18. It will be remembered that on that day Mr. Loch and Captain Brabazon had volunteered to ride into Tung Chow to find Mr. Parkes. It now transpired that they had fulfilled their mission and collected the whole of the party, consisting of Parkes, three officers or civilians, a trooper of the King's Dragoon Guards, and 19 sowars. They started on their return to the English lines, but having been fired at and intercepted, were brought before the Chinese C.-in-C., Sang-Co-Lin Sin.[1] He abused them and ordered them to be made prisoners, whereupon their hands were tied behind their backs with cords, over which water was poured to increase the tension. Their legs were tied and they were thrown into a cart and taken to the common prison in Peking and loaded with chains, one of which was round their neck and fastened them to the roof, so that at the outset they were unable even to lie down. In the prison they found a herd of criminals, who however treated them with the greatest kindness, and gave them part of their own scanty food. After a time the chain attaching them to the roof was removed and they were able to sit down. The prisoners were kept in chains for 9 days, and constantly threatened with death. After this their captors appeared to get nervous; Parkes and Loch were taken out of prison, given good quarters and

[1] Brabazon, as already mentioned, was beheaded.

the best of food. In the meanwhile, however, nearly all their fellow-prisoners had died of torture. On October 13 eight Sikh sowars, the sole survivors, were returned to the British Headquarters. The bodies of some of the dead prisoners were also returned and identified; on the 17th they were buried with military honours at a public funeral. The band of the 60th played the Dead March and the Battalion furnished the firing party.

Meanwhile the city of Peking had not been surrendered, the Mandarin in command attempting to make excuses and negotiate until informed that our siege guns would open fire if the gates of the city were not opened at noon on the 13th. Day dawned and the hour approached; but the Chinese made no sign. Then the guns of the siege battery, only 200 yards from the walls, were loaded, while Colonel Wolseley stood by, watch in hand. The Chinese delayed until the last minute; then they opened the gates. The troops marched in and occupied the ramparts, which were 50 feet high and broad enough on top to allow four carriages to be driven abreast.

As a punishment for the treachery of the Chinese, orders were given to burn the Summer Palace. The decree was carried out by the 2nd Brigade. Colonel Arthur Morris, of our regiment, describes the scene:

'The palace was surrounded by a garden wall five miles in circumference. In the centre was a large building called the Hall of Audience, which was full of furniture, porcelain, rolls of yellow silk, etc. Round the Palace and throughout the park were scattered the residences of the Court, and a perfect maze of trees, lakes, pagodas and buildings of every kind, round which a labyrinth of streams flowed crossed by quaint bridges. The Palace was filled with priceless treasures, silks and embroidered dresses and rooms of cloisonné enamel.'

Captain Fletcher and Lieutenant the Hon. R. P. Vereker

bought a very handsome set of enamels, which they gave to the officer's mess of the 2nd Battalion. On its return to England the enamels were valued at £1,000. They are still part of the mess property.

After carrying out its orders the Brigade returned to Headquarters, and on the 24th the Rifle Battalion found a guard of honour under Captain Warren to accompany Lord Elgin into Peking for the purpose of ratifying the treaty. So far as the British Army was concerned, its share of the spoil was sold by public auction. It realised £8,000 ; and specie amounting to £18,000 was handed over to the British Army by the French. Every private soldier of our Army received about £4 of prize money. The Chinese paid to the British £100,000, and to the French £67,000, for the benefit of the families of the murdered prisoners. An additional indemnity amounting to £2,700,000 was paid by the Chinese Government.

The treaty of peace was signed only just in time ; winter was fast approaching, by the end of October the nights were already cold. Our Riflemen were quartered at the An Ting gate of Peking. The Army was gradually withdrawn ; and on November 9 our Battalion, which was the last to leave the Imperial City, quitted Peking for Tien Tsin, where it arrived on the 19th, forming with Fane's Horse, 2 Batteries R.A., the 31st and 61st Regiments, the garrison under command of Brigadier Staveley, which it had been decided should be left there for the winter. Fur caps, long boots, and sheepskin coats were served out to the garrison. The Taku forts were also occupied by British troops.

Thus ended the campaign which Lord Wolseley describes as being most efficiently conducted.

The health of the Army had been good throughout, and although our Battalion, which was chiefly composed of young soldiers, had the highest proportion of men on the sick list, it never exceeded 5 per cent.

'The commercial advantages which we had obtained,' observed Lord Wolseley, ' were great, also we had carried on a most successful war at a distance of 17,000 miles from England. Fighting side by side with the most military nation of Europe, our organisation, staff, commissariat, etc., has at the very least proved equal to that of France . . . in the execution or results of the war there is nothing left to be desired.'

Lord Wolseley adds: 'I sincerely hope that every future war may be as ably planned and as well carried out as this was by Sir Hope Grant.' For Sir Hope Grant himself, the campaign may have been said to have been carried out too efficiently. Had there been any bungling, any mishap, any regretable incidents, the interest of the British Public would have been aroused, and Sir Hope would have received the reward that he so thoroughly deserved. But as everything went through without a hitch he was denied the Peerage which, without other exception, has been bestowed on the Commander of every successful military expedition of the same magnitude.

4

On November 23 Colonel Butler assumed command of the Battalion in place of Colonel Palmer, who had gone to England on leave. The winter was long and dull, and the cold intense; even the sea was frozen 100 miles from the mouth of the Pei Ho. For nearly four months all communication with the outer world was severed, but the houses happily were comfortable, and there was plenty of food; game was also abundant. Skating on the Pei Ho was the principal amusement. The gunboats on the river were all thatched over. On the further side was the

French contingent, but little or nothing was seen of them. The Riflemen rigged up a theatre and performed burlesques, written by an officer of the Commissariat, the scenery being painted by Captain Fane, who as an artist was no less brilliant than as a leader of cavalry.

Spring at length arrived, and on May 26, 1861, Lieut.-Colonel Butler, hitherto 2nd Lieut.-Colonel of the 2nd Battalion, having been promoted to the command of the 3rd Battalion, quitted Tien Tsin, handing over command of the 2nd to Colonel Rigaud.

In July a draft commanded by Lieut.-Colonel D. D. Muter, which had left England just twelve months previously, but having been unable owing to the ice to land at Ta Koo, had returned to Hong Kong, joined Headquarters at Tien Tsin. With Colonel Muter were Captains H. P. Montgomery, J. H. Archer, and A. W. Knox Gore; Lieutenants N. J. Pauli and C. Gosling; Ensign C. P. Cramer; one Sergeant, one Corporal, and 189 Riflemen. By this time the Battalion was suffering not from the cold but from excessive heat, the thermometer on July 21 standing at 108° in the shade. The health of the men suffered and the sick-list at this time rose to about 172. On quitting Tien Tsin at the end of September a monument was erected to the 94 Rifle N.C.Os. and men who had died in China.

On September 30 the Battalion went down in gunboats to Pei Ho and embarked on H.M.S. Troopship *Simoon*.

The strength of the Battalion was 27 officers, 874 O.R. On arrival at Hong Kong it was decided that for a long voyage the vessel was overcrowded. Captain Montgomery's Coy., D—for by this time letters had again been substituted for numerals—and all the sick men were left at Hong Kong for conveyance in a sailing transport. The numbers of the Battalion which proceeded in the *Simoon* were 22 officers and 700 men. Up to this point the Battalion had been commanded by Lieut.-Colonel Rigaud, but Lieut.-Colonel Muter being senior in brevet rank to Rigaud, although junior in the Regiment, took command of the troops in the *Simoon*. The other officers who proceeded home therein were Captains Farquharson, Laurence Archer, Knox Gore, and Black; Lieutenants the Hon. R. P. Vereker, Algar, Tilford, Brereton, Pauli, Campbell, Cox, Treeve, and Meade; Ensigns Redvers Buller and Cramer; Lieutenant & Adjutant Morrah; Paymaster Fitzpatrick; Quartermaster Storey, and Assistant-Surgeon G. Young.

While at Hong Kong seven men of the Battalion died, making a total of 101 deaths from disease since the Battalion had quitted India.

The *Simoon* eventually started from Hong Kong on November 2. Shortly afterwards the ship encountered a hurricane, and for a time looked like being lost. A passenger on board thus describes the situation: 'There was not a movement on deck, 1,100 men awaiting the result calmly and steadily, although they knew that every moment might be their last.' The storm was happily weathered. The Cape of Good Hope was reached on January 3, 1862, and Spithead in the evening of February 24.

Meanwhile Captain Montgomery, Lieutenants Gosling and Morris, and Assistant-Surgeon Doran, who together with 168 men had been left at Hong Kong, embarked on December 20 in a sailing ship, which, despite its name of the *Flying Cloud*, did not reach Portsmouth until April 19, 1862. The Battalion, whose strength had recently been reduced to 38 officers and 868 O.R., was quartered in the Cambridge Barracks at Southsea. The two depôt companies at Winchester had a strength of 6 officers and 144 O.R.

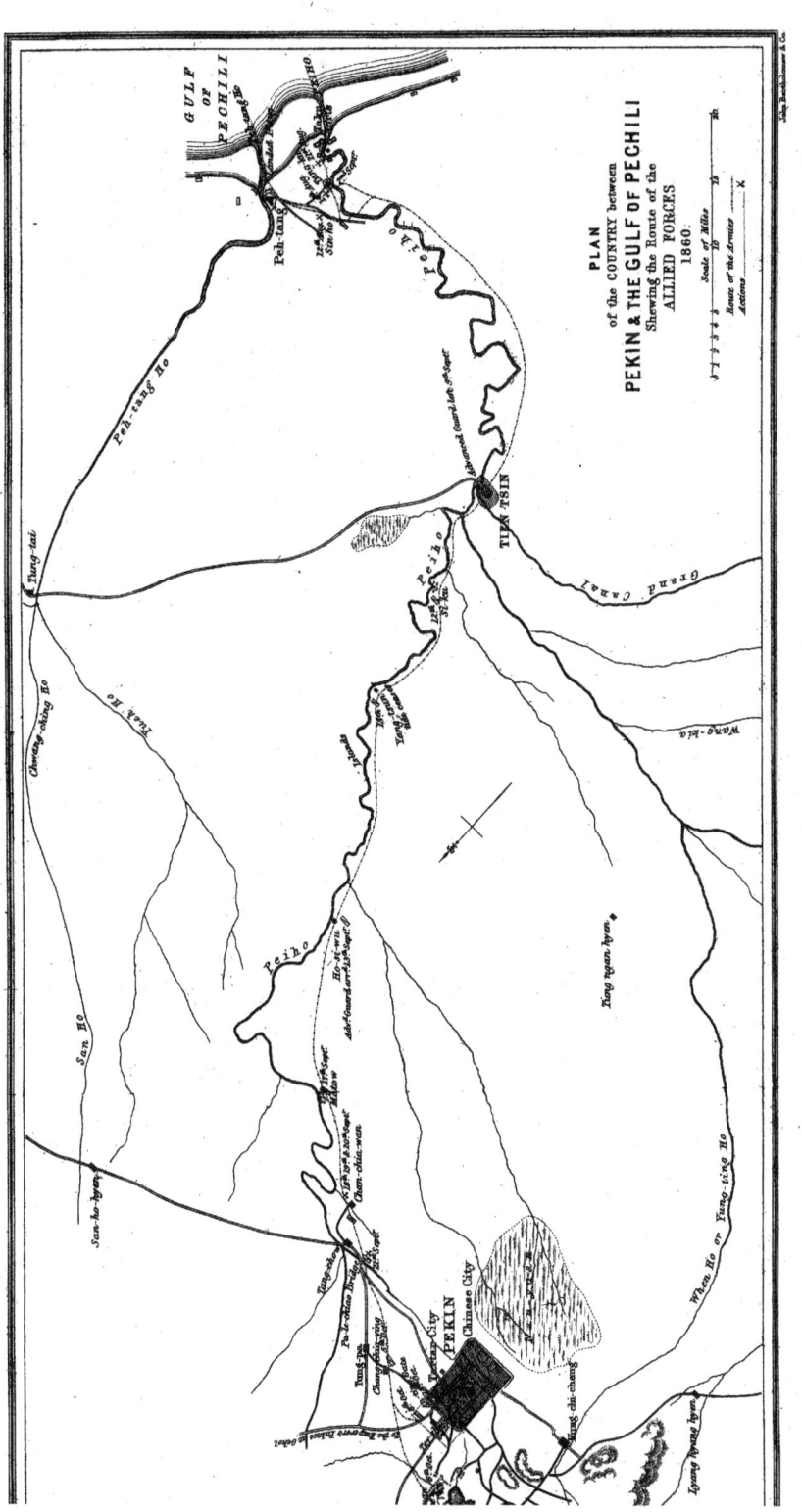

In June a further reduction was made : the establishment being 10 Service companies of 39 officers, 837 O.R., and 2 depôt companies 6 officers, 144 O.R.

In the month of March medals for service in India during the Mutiny were given to the officers and men of the Right Half Battalion, and in July the China War Medals with clasps for the Taku Forts and Peking were issued to the whole Battalion.

For their services in China Major Rigaud received the brevet of Lieut.-Colonel, and Captain R. W. Brooke that of Major.

CHAPTER XII

The Rifle depôt has been for so many years at Winchester that it is difficult to realise that it was ever stationed elsewhere. In point of fact, its locality has been constantly changed. At the time when the Regiment was originally raised the Depôt was at Albany in the State of New York. In 1763 it was apparently established at the Isle of Wight, where it remained until about 1824, in which year that of the 1st Battalion was changed to Chatham, in 1827 to Plymouth, and 1828 to Portsmouth. During the next four years that of the 2nd Battalion, which had hitherto remained in the Isle of Wight, was in Jersey. The Depôt of the 1st Battalion was in turn at Stockport, Newcastle, Sunderland, and Hull. From 1840 to 1844 inclusive the Depôt was at Dublin and other places in Ireland. From 1845 to 1857 the Depôt of the 1st Battalion was at Chatham, but that of the 2nd was constantly moving about in Ireland. In 1858 the Depôts of the 1st and 3rd Battalions were at Colchester, those of the 2nd and 4th at Winchester; since that year the Depôt of the whole Regiment has been stationed at Winchester.

Ensigns posted to battalions on foreign service joined at the Rifle Depôt for a few months prior to embarkation. Among others who thus arrived about this period were two destined to future distinction, viz. Redvers Buller and Francis Grenfell.

2

H.R.H. Adolphus, Duke of Cambridge, who had been appointed our Colonel-in-Chief in 1827, died in 1850 and was succeeded by H.R.H. Prince Albert, better known perhaps by his later designation of the Prince Consort. On the death of the Duke of Wellington in 1852 Prince Albert was transferred to the Rifle Brigade. General Lord Beresford, who had been Commander-in-Chief of the Portuguese Army during the Peninsular War, was made our Colonel-in-Chief, but held the position for a very short time, as he died in January, 1854.

In regard to the Colonels Commandant, on the reduction of the Regiment to two Battalions at the close of the war with France, Generals N. C. Burton and the Hon. E. Phipps, who had received the appointment in 1806 and 1807 respectively, continued to hold it until 1835, when Sir John Maclean, K.C.B., was appointed C.C. in place of Burton. In 1837 General the Hon. Patrick Stuart succeeded General Phipps. In 1842 General Sir William Davy, who as a Major had taken the 5th Battalion out to Portugal in 1808, succeeded Maclean, and held the appointment until his death in January, 1856.

In 1843 Sir William Eustace, who had fought in the Irish Rebellion of 1798, at Maida in 1806, and in the Peninsula from 1811 to 1813, succeeded General Stuart. On Eustace's death in 1855 General Thomas Bunbury, already mentioned in these pages as the well-known C.O. of the 1st Battalion, became Colonel Commandant. In 1856 Sir William Moore, K.C.B., nephew of the great Sir John Moore, succeeded Sir William Eustace. Moore had served with the 52nd in the Peninsula and at Bayonne as A.D.C. to Sir John Hope, with whom he was severely wounded and taken prisoner. In 1862 he was succeeded by General J. Paterson.

3

After the capture of Peking in 1860 it so happened that not a shot was fired by the Regiment on active service for over 18 years. The period was by no means wasted, and it will be shown in due course that during the interval the progress of the Regiment was great; but the piping times of peace, however profitably employed in the art of military training, and however desirable in other respects, do not lend themselves much to the pen of the historian.

The 1st Battalion, on returning from India, was, as already stated, quartered at Dover, where the Town Council paid it a compliment by erecting a monument in memory of the Riflemen who had fallen in India. The Battalion remained at Dover exactly a year, and during its stay received medals for the Indian Mutiny, which were presented on a Brigade Parade by Major-General Craufurd, G.O.C. at Dover.

On August 6, 1861, the Battalion, under command of Lieut.-Colonel C. N. North, moved to Aldershot, where it was quartered in the North Camp. In January, 1862, on the retirement of Sir John Jones, Colonel Henry Bingham from the 3rd Battalion assumed command.

On January 8, 1863, the Battalion left Aldershot for the Tower of London; three companies being detached at Woolwich. In March it took part in the reception of H.R.H. the Princess Alexandra, on the occasion of her arrival from Denmark for her marriage with the Prince of Wales, afterwards King Edward VII. The ceremony was thus described in a memorandum from the Horse Guards dated March 30 :

'Proceeding to London by the North Kent Rail Her Royal Highness was received, on reaching The Bricklayers Arms Station, by a guard of honour of the 3rd Battalion of the Grenadier Guards (3 officers, 5 Sergeants, and 100 rank and file, with colours and drums and fifes), the 1st Battalion 60th Royal Rifles from the Tower (having called in the detachment from Woolwich) being also present here; its band after "God Save the Queen" playing the Danish National Hymn, which all the military bands had been ordered to practise for the occasion.'

On the 10th, the day of the Royal Wedding, the Battalion marched to Hyde Park and fired a *feu de joie*.

In April Lieut.-General Paterson, Colonel Commandant, died and was succeeded by the distinguished Rifleman Lieut.-General Viscount Melville, K.C.B., who on appointment to the Colonelcy of the Battalion which he had commanded with so much *éclat* inspected it on June 10 at the Tower of London.

In September the battle honour 'Delhi' was granted to the Regiment.

The period of service at the Tower seems to have been thoroughly enjoyed. The officers were made honorary members of the Guards' Club, but of military achievement there is little to record, excepting perhaps the fact of a field day in Hyde Park, in which it was pitted against a regiment of Volunteers. At the conclusion of the field day the C.O. returned to the Volunteers, with his compliments, 66 ramrods, which in their enthusiasm they had fired into his Battalion.

On June 6 the Battalion embarked for Ireland, but before leaving the Tower a farewell Divisional Order was published by Major-General Lord F. Paulet, C.B., commanding the Brigade of Guards, who expressed himself in terms so kind and appreciative that the order deserves quotation in full.

'The Major-General commanding the Brigade of Guards cannot allow the 1st Battalion 60th King's Royal Rifles to leave London without expressing his satisfaction at their conduct during the time the Battalion has been quartered in the Tower, and his regret that they are no longer to be under his command.

'The smartness in appearance of the Battalion leaves nothing to be desired, and he especially congratulates them upon their behaviour under the peculiar circumstances of garrison life in the Metropolis, so trying to discipline.[1]

'Lord Frederick Paulet begs to return his best thanks to Colonel Bingham, the officers, and N.C.O.'s for the manner in which they have performed their several duties, and takes leave of the 1st Battalion 60th King's Royal Rifles with his hearty good wishes for their welfare and success in whatever service they may be engaged.'[2]

A day or two before quitting the Tower Whitworth Rifles of hexagonal bore were served out to the Battalion in place of the Naval Enfield.

The Battalion reached the Curragh camp on June 9 and there remained during the rest of the summer, but in the last days of September marched via Naas to Dublin, where its Headquarters was stationed in the Ship Street Barracks, while four Companies were detached at the Royal Barracks. In February, 1865, the Depôt Companies, consisting of 3 officers and 100 O.R., under Major Tedlie, joined the Battalion from Winchester.

Towards the end of May the Battalion returned to the Curragh. A month later five companies under command of Bt. Lieut.-Colonel H. F. Williams proceeded on detachment to Enniskillen. A few days later the seven remaining companies under Colonel Bingham went by train to Newry. On August 21 the Battalion was still further split up, for Captain Dundas was despatched with two companies to Londonderry. In November the remaining

---

[1] At this period the condition of the streets in the neighbourhood of the Tower was so bad that it was dangerous for men to walk out singly.

[2] The allusion is to the Fenian conspiracy then rife in Ireland.

five Headquarter companies were inspected at Newry by General Sir Hugh Rose, K.C.B., commanding the forces in Ireland. Sir Hugh was shortly afterwards raised to the peerage, under the title of Lord Strathnairn. He had done good service during the war with Russia and in Central India during the Mutiny, and was certainly one of the first soldiers of the day.

4

In November Colonel Bingham, who had served for 37 years in the regiment, retired and was succeeded by Randle Feilden, who purchased the Lieut.-Colonelcy over the heads of four brevet Lieut.-Colonels, viz. H. F. Kennedy, C. N. North, G. Rigaud, and Sir Edward Campbell. Feilden proved a good and very popular C.O.; but that an officer who had seen no active service should, owing to the fact of private wealth, have been able to purchase promotion over the heads of four officers of proved merit in the field, is a glaring example of the inherent vice of the 'Purchase System,' which was not finally abolished until 1871. On November 26 orders were received for the Battalion to proceed on foreign service to Halifax, Nova Scotia, but three weeks later the orders were cancelled; and on the last days of December the detachments were called in from Enniskillen and Londonderry, and the Battalion concentrated in Dublin; Headquarters with eight companies being quartered in the Richmond Barracks, and the remaining four in Linen Hall. The G.O.C. of the Dublin district was at this time Major-General Cunynghame, an old Rifleman, already mentioned as A.D.C. to Lord Saltoun during the Chinese War of 1841, who not unnaturally was pleased to have under his command the Battalion of the regiment in which he had long served.

In February, 1866, the Battalion was divided into 10 service and 2 Depôt Companies preparatory to foreign service. Two days previously our 2nd Battalion had arrived in Dublin, the Battalions thus meeting after an interval of 6 years; and rather curiously it happened that four companies of the 1st Battalion and five of the 2nd were quartered together in the Linen Hall Barracks.

On March 7 the 1st Battalion, whose officers had been recently entertained at a festive dinner by those of the 2nd, embarked under command of Brevet Lieut.-Colonel C. N. North in the *Simoom* for Malta, which was reached on the 16th. The embarkation state showed the following figures: 2 Majors, 8 Captains, 10 Lieutenants, 8 Ensigns, 5 Staff, 46 Sergeants, 38 Corporals, 18 Buglers, and 544 private Riflemen. The Battalion on landing was encamped outside Fort Manoel, but a few days later occupied the Floriana Barracks at Valetta.

In May Lieut.-Colonel North gave up the temporary command of the Battalion and went home on leave of absence pending retirement from the army. His services had been distinguished. With the 6th Regiment he took part in the defence of Aden against the Arabs in 1840–41. He joined the 60th in 1841, and served with the 1st Battalion in the Punjaub Campaign. During the Indian Mutiny he was separated from his Battalion and served with Havelock's Column in the first relief of Lucknow and in the subsequent defence of the residency until relieved by Lord Clyde. During the campaign he was wounded, and for his services was given the brevet of Lieut.-Colonel and a year's service for Lucknow.

On North's departure the command of the Battalion was assumed by Brevet Lieut.-Colonel H. F. Williams;

but on June 11 Lieut.-Colonel Feilden arrived and inaugurated his period of command by a happily worded Battalion Order, expressing his sense of the important and most honourable position in which he had been placed by getting command of the Battalion, 'which,' he added, 'bore a reputation second to that of no regiment in the Army.' He anticipated 'a continuance of the habitual, conscientious, and soldierly behaviour and attention to duty on the part of all ranks,' and expressed himself as being 'determined to do his utmost for the efficiency and if possible for the increased happiness of the Battalion.'

At this period General Sir Henry Storks was Governor of the Island, and among his A.D.C.'s was Captain Evelyn Baring, R.A., better known in after life as Lord Cromer, the great administrator of Egypt. The Island appears to have afforded no facilities for Light Infantry work, and parade movements were confined to Battalion Drill. The armament of the Infantry was still a muzzle-loading rifle. Short service had not yet been introduced. The atmosphere of the time was still that of the Crimea War, and indeed differed little from that of Wellington's days in Spain and Portugal.

The Navy was no better off, and the flagship of the Mediterranean Fleet was one of the old wooden three-deckers. In the case of both services the day of much needed reforms had not yet dawned, although it was now not far distant.

In regard to amusements, Cricket, Racquets, and Boating were the principal. There was no racecourse, but a meeting took place in which races were run on the highroad.

Polo was unknown, or had at all events not permeated beyond the bounds of India. As regards sport the shooting was pretty fair during the quail season.

A sort of tournament was arranged, under the conditions of which our Battalion matched itself in four events against the rest of the garrison combined. Of these we won the first three, consisting of cricket, racquets, and a mile race, our victorious champion in the last-named being Lieutenant N. W. Wallace. The fourth event was a swimming match, in which the regiment was to be represented by F. M. Lord Grenfell, our late Colonel Commandant, at that period a Subaltern. In the training for this event a horrible occurrence, very nearly ending in a fatal tragedy, took place, as may best be described in Lord Grenfell's own words.

'Two or three days before the match it was decided that I should swim a trial; and in order that my time should not be known, it was arranged that I should do it by night. A boat with a lantern was the winning post, and I jumped off a boat 500 yards from the goal. I had completed about half the distance, when I was seized by an enormous octopus, which clung round my arms and almost paralysed me. Overwhelmed by the weight of the creature and the horror of the situation I sank once or twice. Rising again I shouted for the boat, at the same time fighting the monster and tearing great bits off it. I was nearly beaten when the boat arrived, and was so exhausted that I was unable to get into it, and was therefore towed to the shore and landed. I was laid on the rocks and one of my brother officers ran for the Doctor. I felt very ill and was put to bed, the whole of my body being covered with large red spots, where the tentacles of the poisonous creature had clasped me. I had to remain in bed for a couple of days with a severe attack of fever. I never forgot, however, the horror of the encounter, and the feeling of being paralysed by the weight of the monstrous creature clinging to my body.'

The well-known Opera at Malta was of course an unfailing source of pleasure to all soldiers with an ear for music. During the hot summer evenings a great-coat over the mess-uniform was unbearable, and a light frogged jacket was invented for the occasion, and worn over the uniform by the officers. Among other occupations for the officers were frequent and interesting expeditions to Sicily and Italy. The other ranks of the Battalion had unfortunately fewer sources of amusement, but there was a body of Maltese police, conspicuous with tall hats and long whiskers. To knock off these hats and pull the whiskers was an irresistible temptation to which the soldiers of the garrison occasionally yielded; but the police, having little sense of humour, took the matter badly, with the result that a large number of private soldiers were summoned to the Court of Justice, or more accurately of Injustice; for, incredible as it may seem, the whole of the proceedings were conducted in Italian, and no translation was given to the prisoner until after pronouncement of the sentence by the Maltese Judge. Anything more abominable can hardly be imagined; and it was not until forty years later that, by the determined efforts of Lord Grenfell, at that time Governor of the Island, the system was abolished, and English soldiers were allowed to be tried before an English-speaking jury, while the proceedings of the Court were recorded in English as well as Italian.

Some of the older members of the Celer et Audax Club will remember a veteran officer with only one leg, a regular attendant at the Regimental Dinner, and an evident favourite among his contemporaries. This was Captain Streatfield, Paymaster to the 1st Battalion from 1858 to 1872. He had lost his other leg in the Indian Mutiny, and at Malta while coming home one evening to the Officers' Quarters had the misfortune to fall into a drain, whence he was pulled out by some Maltese, who, noticing his loss of limb, insisted on trying to carry him to the hospital, and were not unnaturally grieved when Streatfield, regaining his crutch, and mistaking their motive, not only thwarted their good intentions, but gave them a sound beating.

At the end of March 1867 the Battalion moved from Floriana barracks: Headquarters and six Companies to Pembroke Camp, while the other four were quartered at Fort Manoel.

On September 5 the Battalion, under command of Brevet Lieut.-Colonel B. E. Ward, embarked in H.M.S. *Himalaya* for Canada, and disembarked on October 1 at Grasse. A few days later four Companies were detached to Quebec, while Headquarters and the remaining six Companies went up the St. Lawrence on steamers to Montreal. After an interval of nearly half a century the Battalion was revisiting its old home.

In June 1868 the whole Battalion was concentrated at Point Levis, on the south bank of the St. Lawrence, opposite Quebec. Lieut.-Colonel H. F. Williams was in temporary command. Here the Battalion remained encamped until October 6, being employed in the erection of the Fort designed for the protection of the Citadel and town of Quebec. In the execution of this work the Riflemen received many compliments, including a somewhat exceptional one from the French Canadian inhabitants of Lauzan, Point Levis, who in an official letter signed by the Mayor expressed to Colonel Feilden their appreciation of the discipline and good conduct of all ranks in the Battalion.

5

The 2nd Battalion on its arrival from China was, as already mentioned, quartered in the Cambridge Barracks at Portsmouth.

On May 27, 1863, the Battalion proceeded to Aldershot and was quartered in the West Block, Permanent Barracks, one which since those days has often been occupied by a Rifle Battalion. On July 14 a grand divisional field day took place in honour of the Prince of Wales and his bride. Shortly afterwards the Aldershot rifle competitions were held, when Lieut. F. S. Brereton, Instructor of Musketry, won the Ladies' Purse and the Challenge Prize. In August the Battalion formed the advance guard of a flying column operating in Wolmer Forest, the force consisting of a regiment of cavalry, two batteries of artillery, and three battalions, reinforced later by a second cavalry regiment and another battery. Although the force engaged was insignificant, this was the nearest approach to army manœuvres as then known in England, and the Duke of Cambridge twice came down to see the operations, which lasted a fortnight. On returning to its quarters at Aldershot the Battalion maintained its reputation for rapidity of movement by marching the 15 miles in three and a half hours exclusive of halts.

The winter passed quietly away, and in May 1864 the Battalion was armed with the Whitworth rifle. At the subsequent Rifle Meeting Lieut. Brereton won the competition known as the Rifle Derby, for which Lieut. A. V. O'Brien, Assistant Instructor of Musketry, was second; the latter also won the Ladies' Purse.

On June 29 a Camp Industrial Exhibition was opened, in the absence of H.R.H. the Duke of Cambridge, by Lieut.-General S. J. Pennefather, commanding the Aldershot Division. To this Exhibition the Battalion made many contributions. The carving of Rifleman Farrell of C Company and the Lint-making Machine invented by Rifleman Southam of F Company were the theme of general remark, and the Lint-making Machine was purchased for the War Department by the Secretary of State.

In January 1865 the two Depôt companies from Winchester, strength 6 officers, 89 O.R., joined the

Battalion. On the arrival of this draft the 12 companies were equalised, each containing 57 private Riflemen, for the battalion had now lost a large number of men who had enlisted in 1854 under the Ten Years' Enlistment Act, and was far below its strength. On February 21 the Battalion, which had been for a year and nine months at Aldershot, proceeded to Dover, its effective strength being 44 officers, 806 O.R. Sir J. Pennefather thereupon wrote a private letter to the A.-G. at the Horse Guards, asking him to communicate to the H.R.H. the F.-M., Commanding-in-Chief, his high opinion of the Battalion, which 'he considered a pattern Light Infantry Corps.'

On October 3 the Duke of Cambridge came down to inspect the Dover garrison. The records of the 2nd Battalion describe the part taken by it therein in terms which after the lapse of 60 years appear almost amusing.

'The Rifles were worked by Colonel Palmer under H.R.H.'s direction: advanced in echelon of wings from the centre, 4 companies extended from the centre, 4 in support, 2 in reserve. The Battalion thus changed front in extended order on the 2 left wings, which was very smartly executed; 'Alarm' and 'Form squares'; closed up supports and so home, H.R.H. expressing his warm approval of what he had seen.'

Next day the Brigade Field Day took place, in which the work of the Riflemen won the compliments of H.R.H., and of which a newspaper reporter wrote, 'The admirable working of the 60th Rifles in light infantry order in which they manœuvred all day was especially admired. Other regiments would do well to copy the loose but perfect order in which the 60th work as light troops.'

By this time the Fenian movement in Ireland was coming to a head, and on January 24, 1866, the Battalion was directed to prepare for immediate service in that country. On the 31st it proceeded by rail to Liverpool, where it was met by Sir John Jones, late Colonel of the 1st Battalion, and at the present time Inspecting Field Officer. After various delays it reached Dublin, Headquarters, with D, E, F, H, I, K, and L Companies being quartered in Ship Street Barracks, and A, B, C, G, and M, under Major Brooke, at Linen Hall. The strength of the Battalion, temporarily commanded by Brevet Lieut.-Colonel Rigaud, was 22 officers, 822 O.R. On February 14 the Battalion marched to the Fifteen Acres, Phœnix Park, to be inspected by Sir Hugh Rose, K.C.B., Commander of the Forces, but on arrival at the ground the General, having in the meantime discovered that the day was Ash Wednesday, postponed the inspection until the following morning.

Conditions approaching those of active service prevailed. The Battalion was constantly under arms in Barracks, in expectation of a Fenian insurrection. Anticipating the suspension of the Habeas Corpus Act, the civil authorities arrested upwards of 100 suspicious characters connected with the Phœnix Park conspiracy. The Military powers, thinking this vigorous action might bring on a disturbance, gave orders for the piquets to be doubled and strong reserves to be kept ready. The sentries for the Magazine Fort in Phœnix Park were to be doubled, those posted at the angles of the Fort having their rifles loaded. Strong Cavalry piquets, their horses saddled and bridled, were prepared for instant action. For Kilmainham and Mountjoy Prisons strong infantry piquets were also furnished, for the warders were untrustworthy and aided the escape of a man named Stephens, known as a Head Centre of the Fenian movement.

In the following month, orders having been received for the reduction of the Battalion to 10 companies, L and M were broken up and absorbed among the remaining ten.

At the same time the strength was reduced to 750 N.C.Os. and men.

That the Battalion was in the habit of marching at a pace faster than that laid down by regulation was the subject of a remark by the General at an inspection held in May.

On July 3 the Battalion proceeded to the Curragh where it was concentrated, and towards the end of November went on to Cork. On December 29 the Battalion was armed, for the first time, with breech-loading rifles, the old muzzle-loading 5-grooved Enfield rifles having been converted into Snider breech-loaders.

The Fenian menace was still strong, and a general rising being anticipated in Killarney, A, B, and H Companies, consisting of 7 officers and 165 O.R., the whole under the command of Colonel Palmer, turned out at a short notice at 10 P.M. on February 13, 1867, and reached Killarney on the following morning about 3.30 A.M. This detachment remained for upwards of a month at Mallow in Killarney, and was employed in patrolling the country.

On March 12 a Flying Column, under Colonel Oakes, 12th Lancers, was formed and accompanied by D, E, and F Companies. The country being in a very disturbed state a great deal of hard work was needed in night patrolling, etc. At the end of May the open insurrection broke out, but concurrently therewith came a heavy storm of snow, and by the time the snow had melted the active revolt, which had necessitated the firing of only a few shots, was at an end.

The Battalion had not had a very long tour of home service, but during the summer orders were received to prepare for India, and on September 14 it embarked at Queenstown on board H.M.S. *Crocodile*. The list of officers is as follows: Colonel Palmer, C.B.; Lieut.-Colonel

Rigaud; Major Fitzgerald; Brevet-Major Brooke; Captains Bowles, Montgomery, Russell, Tilford, Byron, Moseley; Lieuts. Gosling, Morris, O'Brien, Farmer, Crofton, Chalmer, Gordon, Tilden, Parker, H. Ward, and Howard; Ensigns Forster, Michell Innes, Wood, Clarke, De Crespigny, Bagot; Lieutenant and Adjutant Cramer; Paymaster FitzPatrick; Quartermaster Holmes; Surgeon Cunningham; Assistant-Surgeon Kilroy; the Battalion contained 813 O.R. Captains Farquharson and Taylor with Lieuts. E. H. Ward and Cowan did not embark, but proceeded with the depôt companies to Winchester.

It will be remembered that at this period the Suez Canal did not exist, but the Battalion, by arrangement with the Khedive of Egypt, proceeded by what was termed the New Overland Route, being the first regiment to take advantage of it. Alexandria was reached on September 27; the troops disembarked and reached Suez by train, where they embarked on H.M.S. *Euphrates*, which sailed on October 4. The ship stopped at Aden and Trincomalee, and seems to have reached Fort William, Calcutta, on the 29th. G and F Companies were detached at Dumdum.

On February 10, 1868, the Battalion was inspected by Sir William Mansfield, K.C.S.I., Commander-in-Chief in India. In December, Headquarters with E, F, G, I, and K left Calcutta for Seetapore. Up to Cawnpore it went by train and the remainder of the way by march route through Lucknow, eventually reaching the destination on January 5, 1869. The remainder of the Battalion left Calcutta on the 16th of that month for Benares. In January 1870 its efficiency in musketry was the theme of a letter addressed to the C.O. by the Adjutant-General of Calcutta; Major H. P. Montgomery, who had taken temporary command at Benares, being singled out by name for special praise. The Battalion was reduced from ten to eight Companies, and about the same time the two Depôt Companies, which had hitherto formed part of what was known as the Depôt Battalion, was moved from Winchester, under command of Captain Arthur Morris, and attached to the 4th Battalion at Aldershot.

On November 16 Headquarters with D, E, F, and G Companies quitted Seetapore and marched to Peshawur, which was reached on January 3, 1871. At Peshawur it was joined by the half Battalion from Benares. In January 1872 the Battalion was concentrated at Nowshera. In April Colonel Palmer, C.B., retired from the command of the Battalion, which he had held since October 1858. He was succeeded by Colonel Rigaud, who went, however, to England at the end of the year and never rejoined his Battalion. In December the Battalion marched from Nowshera to a Camp of Exercise at Jullalia; its strength on January 1, 1873, being 17 officers, 657 O.R. During the month about 178 officers and men joined Headquarters from Fort Attock.

On the termination of the Camp of Exercise the Battalion marched to Rawal Pindi, where its parade state on February 24 showed a gross strength of 34 officers, 1,031 O.R.

CHAPTER XIII

THE 3RD BATTALION

THE fact of the re-raising of the 3rd and 4th Battalions, which had been disbanded at the end of the war with France, has already been noticed. Authority for raising the 3rd Battalion was received on March 31, 1855, and was carried into effect at Dublin, where the depôt for the 2nd Battalion was at that time stationed. Command of the Battalion was given to Colonel W. F. Bedford, and the list of the other officers appointed thereto was as follows :—

Majors.
The Hon. H. L. Powys and the Hon. Adrian Hope.

Captains.
C. N. North, W. P. Salmon, — Parker (Bt. L.-C.), A. J. Fitzgerald, F. A. St. John, F. Dawson, J. P. Battersby, I. L. E. Baynes, B. E. Ward (Bt. Major), R. Freer, F. C. Fletcher.

Lieutenants.
C. D. C. Ellis, W. A. D. Pitt, F. D. Farquharson, J. J. Phillips, A. Carlisle, J. Headley.

Ensigns.
F. V. Northey, W. F. Carleton, J. P. Shackle, R. M. Hazer, B. B. Forsyth, — Hogge, W. B. S. Conyers.

Adjutant.
J. Forbes.

Quartermaster.
H. Campbell.

Headquarters having been assembled at Ship Street Barracks, Dublin, 8 Sergeants and 530 Riflemen, transferred from the 2nd to the 3rd Battalion, joined Headquarters on April 15, and a few days later the new Battalion was further strengthened by the arrival of a Sergeant and 63 Riflemen, who had been transferred from the 1st Battalion. On July 10 it moved from Dublin to the Curragh, composed of 12 Companies, armed with the Long Enfield Rifle, and clothed in the double-breasted tunic which had just superseded the useless coatee.

Twelve months passed uneventfully. In the following year, 1856, peace was made with Russia, and in August the Battalion was broken up into 8 Service and 4 Depôt Companies preparatory to foreign service. The Service Companies—comprising 1 Lieut.-Colonel, 2 Majors, 8 Captains, 8 Lieutenants, 6 Ensigns, Adjutant, Quartermaster, Surgeon,[1] 2 Assistant-Surgeons, 7 Staff-Sergeants, 40 Sergeants, 40 Corporals, 1 Bugle-Major, 16 Buglers, and 760 Private Riflemen—were moved forthwith to Dublin and quartered in Richmond Barracks. It would appear that the Depôt Companies went in the first instance to Jersey, and thence to Chatham, where they joined those of the 1st Battalion. With them they proceeded in 1858 to Colchester, and finally to Winchester in 1859.

At Dublin the Service Companies remained through the winter; but on May 13, 1857, orders were received to prepare for embarkation, Madras being the destination. Three days previously the outbreak of the Indian Mutiny had taken place at Meerut in Bengal, but in the absence of telegraphic cables the news had not reached England, nor indeed was the fact known until some weeks later.

It was not until the first days of August that the

---

[1] At this time Surgeons were virtually officers of the Battalion and wore Rifle Uniform.

Battalion (which had in the meanwhile been re-inforced up to a strength of 39 Officers and 1,032 O.R.), having been distributed among five vessels, sailed for Calcutta, which was reached via the Cape of Good Hope towards the end of November. The Battalion was not employed in the field; but after a brief stay at Calcutta, was sent on to its original destination, the Province of Madras. The capital was reached on December 8, and Bangalore, its appointed station, on the 11th. Captain Ellis's Company was detached at Fort Bangalore, but the remainder of the Battalion was concentrated under Colonel Bedford.

Its average strength during 1858 was 1,057 of all ranks. The year was uneventful, the only incidents of note being the detachment of 3 Companies under Colonel Bingham, the officer second in comamnd, to Bellary in June, and the issue of Short Enfield Rifles in December. In February and March 1859 the Battalion moved to Jackatalla.[1]

It was enormously strong, its numbers averaging that year no less than 1,232. During 1860 they fell to 1,060. In that year Colonel Bedford resigned the command, and was succeeded by Colonel Henry Bingham; Major Roe, who purchased the step over the head of H. F. Kennedy, the senior Major, becoming Second Lieut.-Colonel.

Late in the year 1861 the Battalion quitted the Madra Presidency for Burmah. Colonel Roe was in command, for Bingham had been transferred to the 1st Battalion in England; and Webbe Butler, his successor, had not yet joined Roe, with the left half Battalion, comprising Nos. 3, 6, 7, 8, and 10 Companies, reached Thayet Myo early in 1862, while the remainder of the Battalion under

---

[1] Here, under the superintendence of Major Roe, theatricals among other amusements were successfully carried out.

Major Kennedy was stationed at Longhoo. Towards the end of 1863 the Battalion moved to Rangoon, which was reached by B.H.Q. and two Companies on November 27, the remainder arriving by successive driblets. By this time its strength had been much diminished, averaging for the current year only 722. In March 1864 the Battalion was inspected and well reported on for steadiness and good discipline. Its regimental institutions also received commendation. Colonel Butler now retired and was succeeded by Roe, whose place as Second Lieut.-Colonel was taken by Major Feilden from the 4th Battalion. At Rangoon in 1865 Captain the Hon. R. P. Vereker died. His company had recently rejoined Headquarters from detachment in the Andaman Islands. It was relieved by that of Captain Algar.

Late in the year came orders for a return to Madras, and, despite the protests of the local military authorities, who pointed out that the cyclones prevalent at this season risked the loss of the vessels and imperilled the lives of all on board, such trifling conditions had no effect upon the minds of the Indian Government, secure in the knowledge that none of its own members would share the dangers of the voyage. A word of caution or warning by military authorities is usually taken by civilian officials as a proof of 'timidity,' and it was customary to embark soldiers on any rotten old tub that offered itself.

The Battalion embarked at Rangoon in two sailing ships, viz. *The Star of India* and *Devonport*.[1] Headquarters and the Right Wing of the Battalion under Colonel Roe sailed in *The Star of India* on November 17 in fine weather, which continued until the 23rd. Early in the morning of that date a strong breeze set in from the N.N.E. with a heavy cross sea. The observation

[1] Some accounts give the name as '*Davenport*.'

at noon showed latitude 14° 16′ N., Longitude 84° 58′ E. At 4 P.M. some of the canvas was taken in; and as the heavy weather continued and increased sail was further shortened next day, and the course altered to N.W. During the evening the wind increased to a gale, still from N.N.E. At 6 P.M. it was estimated that the vessel was only 40 miles N.E. of Madras, but as the barometer was still falling and the sea rising Captain Holloway stood away from the land. In the early morning of the 25th there was every appearance of a cyclone coming from E.S.E. All ports were closed, and the ship, having altered her course to the south, ran 120 miles in the attempt to steer clear of the centre of the cyclone. At noon a sudden squall struck the ship; the remaining sails were furled and the ship ran before the wind under bare poles on the port tack. That evening the reading of the barometer was 29·40. On the 26th all soldiers were sent below, the watch placed in the cuddy, and the hatches battened down. At 6 A.M. it was blowing harder than ever, and the starboard gig was washed away from the davits. About 8 A.M. the ship was lying at a very dangerous angle, and by order of the Captain the topmasts and top-gallant masts were struck and lowered to the deck. The rolling of the vessel was then appreciably reduced.

But the worst was now over. At 9 A.M. the wind began to lull and the barometer to rise. So rapidly did the weather improve that in the evening it was found possible to set sail again and open the hatches. At noon on the 27th the weather was fine and the ship was found to be 113 miles from Madras. Light winds continued, and at 9 P.M. on the 29th the ship was able to anchor in the Roads. The seamanship and skill displayed by Captain Holloway were beyond all praise, in view of the kind of vessel he had to handle; but, despite the strain to which the ship was subjected from the severity of the storm, little water was found in the hold.

2

The S.S. *Devonport*, with the left half of the Battalion under Major Thomas Biggs, had meanwhile left Rangoon on November 11, 1865, in order to call for the Company of Captain Algar, which had been on detachment in the Andaman Islands. Port Blair was reached on the 17th; and the Rifle Company having embarked, the passengers on board comprised 1 Major, 1 Captain, 3 Lieutenants, 2 Ensigns, 1 Assistant-Surgeon, 1 Apothecary, 350 of other ranks, 24 Women, 45 children, and 49 natives.

At 5 P.M. on the 20th the *Devonport* sailed out of Port Blair harbour, and helped by a strong fair wind anchored about 11 A.M. on the 24th in the Madras Roads. But the danger flag was seen to be flying at the Master Attendant's Office, and heavy surf prevented the landing of the troops. During the night the ship rolled heavily, and at 8 A.M. on the 25th Captain Lodwick the Commander, in response to a signal from the Master Attendant, slipped his anchor and stood out to sea; the barometer was falling and the weather threatening. About 5.30 P.M. most of the sails were furled. The wind and sea rose, and at 8 P.M. a gun got loose, badly injuring a sailor and a native. The gale continued to increase, and at 10 P.M. sail was reduced to close-reefed topsails.

At midnight the main topsail was blown away, followed immediately by the mizen and foretopsail. By this time the gale had become a hurricane, and one of the boats was broken to pieces by a huge wave and washed away from the davits. At 2 A.M. on the 26th Captain Lodwick felt it necessary to tell Major Biggs that the situation was one of imminent danger, for the vessel lay between a cyclone and a lee shore. It was obvious that the centre of the cyclone must pass very near, and if the ship were caught thereby the peril would be extreme. At 6.30 A.M. the Captain reported that the centre of the cyclone must be close at hand. About 8 A.M. the wind abated and it was hoped that the worst was over. The troops were quickly undeceived, for in a few minutes a terrific squall struck the vessel: the foremast was blown away by the deck; the main and mizen masts were immediately afterwards broken off 10 or 12 feet above it. Yards and spars, which fell in all directions, destroyed three more of the boats. The main and the cross-jack yards struck the poop-deck and tore it up on the starboard side, carrying away compass, skylight, and barometer. The ship then became unmanageable, and for several hours the sea broke over her, flooding the poop-cabins and cuddy, and carrying away all movables. The vessel was in imminent danger of having a hole knocked in her timbers, for some of the yards which formed part of the wreckage were hanging over the side, and at every roll of the vessel acted as a battering ram. The crew being called upon by the Captain to cut away the wreckage, refused to go on deck, saying that it was all over and useless to attempt such dangerous work! In view of this refusal the fate of the ship appeared to be sealed, when Ensign Henry Lindesay, an officer of little more than two years' service, went up to the Captain and volunteered for the service. The Captain refused, saying that the Ensign would not know how to set about the task; but Lindesay insisted. The Captain at length consented, and gave him as well as he could the necessary instructions. Henry Lindesay then called upon a few Riflemen to accompany him. With them and a single sailor he got up on the poop; and at imminent risk of their lives this gallant band after a hard struggle succeeded in clearing away the wreckage. By their efforts the lives of 500 people on board were undoubtedly saved.

During this time one of the ship's officers openly stated that the vessel was sinking and nothing could save her; but a ray of hope was shed when the Captain coming up from below said that the ship was making no water, although in the troop deck there were about three feet which had been taken in by shipping seas. The saloon was also under water, and furniture, baggage, etc., were floating about in it. Major Biggs placed gangs of men at the pumps; but owing to the extreme violence of the gale and the fact that the seas were constantly sweeping over the deck, raking it fore and aft, little progress could be made, and for a moment the Riflemen were disheartened, when the 3rd Mate declared that there were 7 feet of water in the hold and that the ship was foundering. The men at the pumps ceased working, but when called upon by Lieut. Barry, the acting Adjutant, at once resumed their task, and the pumps were kept going during the whole day.

About 11 A.M. the storm began to lull; but the peril was even now not over, for at 6 o'clock in the evening a large ship appeared to windward, utterly helpless and drifting towards the *Devonport*. A collision seemed imminent, and in the opinion of Captain Lodwick would have been fatal to both vessels. By the mercy of Providence they cleared each other but by a few yards only.

Next day, the 27th, the Captain was anxious to rig up jurymasts, and Major Biggs directed all Riflemen who were carpenters, smiths, etc., to lend a hand in the work, which was at once begun.

But now another danger arose. The Captain reported

that some bags of biscuits, soldiers' hammocks, bedding, etc., had became heated in the hold, and could remain there only at the risk of setting the ship on fire. The Major in consequence ordered a party of his men to bring the articles up out of the hold and throw them overboard.

From the 28th to the 30th the *Devonport* drifted so far south that the Captain feared it would be necessary to put into Trincomalee in Ceylon. But during all this time the Riflemen were at work at the jurymasts and other jobs, such as caulking the decks, etc., etc. On December 1 some of the jurymasts were put up, and the ship could be steered on her proper course. By running out into the centre of the Bay she escaped the current, and eventually anchored at 2 A.M. on December 8 in the Madras Roads, when the Commander was able to report all well on board, including even an infant born at the height of the storm!

During the gale four unhappy native followers had been washed overboard, and so intense was the cold that four others died from its effects. Among the troops—a term which no doubt included the wives and children—many were bruised and cut, but no lives were lost. In his official report Major Biggs states: 'On the day of the storm the whole work for the safety of the ship apparently devolved on Captain Lodwick the Commander, the 2nd Mate, two or three sailors, and the soldiers. The other ship's officers were drunk. Notwithstanding this the Captain met the difficulty of our position most nobly. He has taken occasion to speak to me in high terms of the assistance rendered him by Lieut. R. C. Robinson and Ensign H. P. R. Lindesay of the Wing under my command.'

'In closing this narrative I deem it my duty to bring to notice the admirable conduct of all ranks. Their ready obedience, their willingness to do any work that was required of them, and their cool and soldier-like conduct under most trying circumstances, were in my opinion, as well as in that of the Commander of the ship, the means of saving the vessel. I would particularly mention the assistance received from Lieutenant Barry the acting Adjutant, who by his presence and example encouraged and gave confidence to the men.'

By the skill of the Captain and the conduct and discipline of the troops thus ended happily an episode which for many hours appeared certain to terminate in the loss of the vessel and the lives of all on board.

It may be asked, what reward did Ensign Lindesay receive for his splendid gallantry ? The reply is, that as to a reward, substantial or honorary, there was none. Even in his own regiment the recollection of his bravery, like that of hundreds, nay thousands, of his brother Riflemen, has faded away. No report in detail was ever made of his conduct. Had it not been for the care of a single brother officer present in the ship the very story would have been forgotten. But Lindesay's reward lay in the consciousness of work nobly performed and crowned with success; work which—combined with the skill of Captain Lodwick—saved the lives of 500 men and women, magnificently maintained the traditions of the 60th Rifles and added a page to their records of discipline and heroism.

The Battalion remained concentrated at Madras for two years; but on December 30, 1867, a half battalion, consisting of C, D, E, F, and K Companies, under command of Major M. F. Battersby, was detached to Bellary, where it arrived on January 9, 1868. On June 30 of that year Headquarters and the remaining half battalion, under Brevet Lieut.-Colonel H. F. Kennedy, proceeded to Bangalore, which was reached on the day following. On November 24 it joined Battersby's detachment at Bellary.

On the retirement of Colonel Roe in 1869 he was succeeded by Colonel Kennedy, a veteran of the Punjaub campaign. Kennedy was no doubt a well-meaning man, and it is stated that he strongly protested against the order which in 1857 had consigned the Battalion to Madras in the place of being employed in the field, but—partly perhaps on this account—he quarrelled with the then C.O., and this quarrel had a detrimental effect on the Battalion. He was probably also a disappointed man, for, through the agency of the 'purchase' system, he had been passed over by a junior officer. Kennedy is described by one who served under him as a charming companion in plain clothes but an impossible person in uniform. He became anyhow very unpopular, and his words and acts were at times hardly consonant with the spirit of army regulations. On one occasion, noticing a man yawn on parade, he sent him to bed and kept him there for a fortnight, until the General, getting an inkling of the affair, made a sudden inspection of the barrack rooms and released the man.

But it was his manner and behaviour to the officers which chiefly showed his unfitness for command. Nagging and bullying were incessant on his part, and at length one day on parade the storm burst. A young Ensign, goaded to desperation, threw down his sword. This act of insubordination could not but cost the lad his commission; but at his trial by G.C.M. much sympathy was shown him by the witnesses, and the impossible nature of his C.O. was clearly brought out. H.R.H. the Duke of Cambridge, C.-in-C. at the Horse Guards, had no difficulty in realising the facts of the case. Kennedy in consequence retired on full pay, and Colonel Roe was for the second time given command of the Battalion.

By this time its period of foreign service was drawing to a close. On November 20, 1871, the Battalion, under command of Major H. P. Montgomery—an officer loved by all, and one whose charm of manner, combined with professional efficiency, went far no doubt to heal old sores—quitted Bellary, embarked for Aden, and on December 7 reached its destination. Headquarters with four Companies went into camp: two Companies to Steamer Point, and the remaining two—for during the previous year the strength of the Battalion had been reduced from 10 to 8 Service Companies—to Isthmus Position.[1] The Disembarkation State showed 21 Officers and 569 O.R.

On November 29, 1872, the Battalion, still commanded by Major Montgomery, embarked for England, landed on December 24, and was stationed at Shorncliffe. Its strength was 22 Officers, 540 O.R. The Depôt Companies, comprising 7 Officers and 146 O.R., left Winchester and joined B.H.Q. on the same date.

More than fifteen years had elapsed since the 3rd Battalion quitted England, and of the 1,032 men who had gone out in 1857 only 72 served in it for the whole period and returned therewith. The old soldiers had forgotten that fatigue duties performed in India by natives had to be done in England by themselves, and bitter were their complaints of being treated like 'b—— Coolies!'

The establishment of the Battalion was now fixed at 27 Officers and 578 O.R.

---

[1] The Depôt Companies were at the same time reduced from 4 to 2.

CHAPTER XIV

THE 4TH BATTALION

JULY 27, 1857, is the day on which authority was given for the formation of the 4th Battalion, although the commission of its first Lieut.-Colonel, E. J. Vesey Brown, did not bear date until September 4. Colonel Brown had begun his service in the 60th, quitted it, and came back thereto from the 88th regiment. The two Majors were Brevet Lieut.-Colonel Pretyman from the 33rd, and Major Robert Beaufoy Hawley from the 89th. All three field officers had seen service in the Crimea War, and Hawley came of a military stock, his father having served in the Peninsula under Wellington, while one of his ancestors was the General Hawley, second in command to the Duke of Cumberland.[1]

The officers of the new Battalion were almost without exception appointed from other regiments in which, on the reduction of the army in 1856 at the end of the war with Russia, they had been borne as supernumeraries.

Our regiment had no reason to complain of such arrangements, for the officers had been given all the promotion consequent on the raising of the 3rd Battalion in 1855, and any deviation from the spirit and traditions of the regiment which might have been expected from the

---

[1] The story that General Hawley was responsible for the cruelties enacted after Colloden was stoutly denied by his descendant, who averred that they were the work of the Duke himself.

introduction of all these strangers was obviated by the fact that within the next few months so many officers, whether by exchange or promotion, joined the 4th from the older Battalions that the new one, both in spirit and administration, quickly became amalgamated with the remainder of the regiment.

The remaining officers were as follows :—

Captains.	Lieutenants.
E. H. Stewart.	H. Brackenbury.
E. A. Stotherd.	W. N. Manners.
W. J. Holes.	T. H. A. Hamilton.
W. Paterson.	W. M. M. Fortescue.
R. Crowe.	E. W. Denne.
W. S. Cookworthy.	A. T. Ewens.
T. Aldridge.	G. Hatchell.
C. Williamson.	J. N. Sewell.

Ensigns.
J. H. Cowan.
J. D. Bitham.
L. C. Brownrigg.
I. Lovell.
W. T. Sainsbury.

The Adjutant was A. T. Ewens, the Quartermaster T. Walker.

Of these, Captains Stotherd, Crowe, and Cookworthy had served in the Crimea, and Paterson in the Burmese War, Lieut. Brackenbury had fought at Gujerat, and Dr. Lewis against the Boers at Boomplatz.

The men of the Battalion were principally volunteers from the Militia, of which many regiments were at this time embodied for service. The Battalion was also recruited from London, the south of England generally, and from Lincolnshire. Its first estalishment was 8 companies, comprising 1 Lieut.-Colonel, 2 Majors, 8 Captains, 10 Lieutenants, 6 Ensigns, 42 Sergeants, 16

Buglers, 32 Corporals, 608 private riflemen; but on January 13, 1858, the establishment was augmented to 12 Companies, and the Battalion comprised 1 Lieut.-Colonel, 2 Majors, 12 Captains, 14 Lieutenants, 10 Ensigns, 58 Sergeants, 24 Buglers, 50 Corporals, 950 private riflemen.

The Battalion was raised and quartered at Winchester; it was armed with Short Enfield Rifle and sword, and equipped with black waist and pouch belt, with ball-bag and cap-pocket. The ball-bag carried 50 and the cap-pocket 10 rounds of ammunition.

At Winchester the Battalion remained until May 8, 1858, when it went to Aldershot, and thence on August 19 to Dover, where Colonel Brown quitted the service and was succeeded by Colonel Pretyman, an officer of ability, who laid the foundation of the admirable system subsequently developed by his successor. Pretyman had the opportunity of showing his Battalion to H.R.H. the Duke of Cambridge, the General Commanding-in-Chief, who during a march past shouted out to the C.O., 'Well done, Pretyman, you have got a splendid Battalion.' But in May 1860 Colonel Pretyman, retiring from the service, handed over his Battalion to Robert Hawley, 'Clarum et venerabile nomen' among Riflemen. Hawley thus entered upon a period of command destined to last for almost 13 years. In September the Battalion moved to Ireland, being in the first instance quartered at Waterford with detachments at Kilkenny, etc., and a few months later in Dublin.

2

Meanwhile on the other side of the Atlantic matters in the United States were rapidly coming to a crisis. On the last day of December 1860 a large number of the

Southern States seceded from the Union, as the result of divergent interests, among which the retention or suppression of the slave trade in the South was among the most prominent. Civil War between the Northern or 'Federal States' and the Southern, termed the 'Confederate,' quickly broke out.

In every contest on a large scale the rights of neutrals are apt to be a bone of contention, and differences of opinion soon showed themselves between Great Britain and the Federal States. There was at this time only one regular Battalion of the British army in Canada, and the fact that the actual frontier line was in several places indefinitely marked added to the danger of hostile action. Under these circumstances it was determined to reinforce the regular garrison of Canada; and on June 25, 1861, the 4th Battalion embarked at Liverpool upon the S.S. *Great Eastern*, at that time by far the largest vessel in the British service. It also conveyed another Battalion and a Battery R.A., and reached Quebec on July 4, after the most rapid voyage hitherto accomplished.

The disembarkation State showed 1 Lieut.-Colonel, 2 Majors, 10 Captains, 20 Subalterns, 5 Staff, 47 Sergeants, 21 Buglers, 40 Corporals, 760 private riflemen.

The Battalion was quartered in the Citadel. Shortly after its arrival occurred an incident which threatened an immediate outbreak of war between Great Britain and the Federal States. Two gentlemen named Slidell and Mason had embarked on the British S.S. *Trent*, and were proceeding to England as envoys to the British Government from the Southern or Confederate States, when the *Trent* was stopped by a Federal Man-of-War, commanded by Captain Wilkes of the U.S.A. navy, who boarded the British vessel, and despite the protests of its commander, seized and carried off Messrs. Slidell and Mason. Great and not unreasonable was the wrath in England when this episode became known, and demands were at once made for the release of the Confederate envoys, and an apology for the insult to the British flag. It happened also that great interest was at this time taken in the fortunes of the Confederate States by the people of England; for the suppression of the slave trade in the South was not believed to be the real cause of the Civil War. To a large proportion of English men the attempt of the Federals to conquer the Southern States by force of arms was looked on as a pretext for tyranny; and the gallant resistance made by the Confederates, despite their numerical inferiority, evoked strong sympathy with their cause. Politicians of the Liberal Party in prominent positions were most unguarded in expressing their sympathies with the South, and the news of the capture of the Confederate envoys raised to boiling point the feelings of hostility towards the Northern States. A dispatch of undiplomatic violence was drafted by the British Cabinet in remonstrance; but, largely at the instance of H.R.H. the Prince Consort, wiser councils prevailed, and when forwarded to Washington the wording of the dispatch had been greatly toned down.

On the other side of the Atlantic President Lincoln and his Cabinet kept their heads under circumstances of no small difficulty. They were perfectly aware of the fact that the action of Captain Wilkes was indefensible. But, on the other hand, public opinion was bitterly disappointed that Great Britain, the first country in the world to abolish slave trade, should now be in sympathy with the slave-owning States; and consciousness of the fact that in the seizure of the Confederate envoys they were in the wrong made the Federals doubly sore at the violence of hostile feeling which it had evoked in England.

But although he could not have failed to share in the disappointment and annoyance of his countrymen, President Lincoln combined wisdom with patriotism, and insisted on the consideration of the main point only, viz. whether the U.S.A., which were fully occupied with the struggle in the Southern States, could afford to start war with England in addition. To this question he replied in an unhesitating negative.

Meanwhile the British Government—a Liberal one—was making active preparations for war, and despatched to Canada at a moment's notice a body of Staff officers belonging to the Q.M.G. Department. It was pointed out that the vessel on which they were embarking was extremely slow, and their arrival in Canada would be actually accelerated by the delay of a day or two waiting for faster conveyance. From the point of view of the Secretary of State for War the practical considerations were all much less important than the fact of throwing dust in the eyes of Members of Parliament, by an appearance, however unreal, of activity and instantaneous action.

The ship in which the Staff had embarked was not only slow, but unseaworthy, and known to be so. Meeting tempestuous weather in the Atlantic, its engines broke down and it nearly went to pieces. By the skill of a British R.E. officer the engines were however patched up, and the crazy old tub, unable to make Halifax, came perforce to anchor at New York. The Staff officers would have had no alternative but to surrender as prisoners-of-war, when to the pleasure and surprise of all concerned it was found that the crisis, so acute when they quitted England, was at an end. And now came a comic element in the episode, for by the permission of the U.S. Government, against which they had come to fight, they were allowed to proceed through American territory to their destination in Canada! Thus happily ended, amid jeers and laughter, an incident which might have had most dire consequences. It may be mentioned *en passant* that the regiment from England, for the preparation of whose arrival in Canada the Staff officers were thus fatuously hurried out, had landed in Canada some days previously!

The momentous dispatch from the British Foreign Office had long ago reached Washington. So critical was the moment, and so intent on peace was the American Government, that Mr. Seward, its Secretary of State, entreated the British Ambassador to allow him a private view of its contents before the document was officially presented, the reason of this request being the feeling that such a private perusal would admit of the alteration of any untoward phrase, which otherwise might set the American people on fire, and render war inevitable.

The request was complied with; the danger of war happily passed away, but a strong feeling was engendered at Washington that the British Cabinet had failed to appreciate the difficulties of the situation in which the U.S. Government had been placed, and that common courtesy was lacking in the attitude assumed. The soreness remained in the U.S.A. long after the episode had been forgotten in England.

This digression will at all events show that the 4th Battalion, and the other slender military forces in Canada during 1861, were in a somewhat critical position. The danger of war had disappeared, but so far as the British troops were concerned other difficulties arose. The forces of the United States were at first little more than a conglomeration of raw and untrained recruits; regular troops were badly wanted, and every artifice was employed by American agents to entice British soldiers to desert and enlist in their armies. These efforts were not entirely unsuccessful, but as regards the Riflemen, it is satisfactory to be able to record the fact that notwithstanding all the inducements held out to them during a most critical period, up to 1863 nine only deserted. Of these, several distinguished themselves in the American Army.

The 4th Battalion remained at Quebec nearly two years, but in 1863 went on to Montreal, where it remained until November 1865. From Montreal it proceeded to London, Ontario.

3

In the spring of 1865 the Civil War ended in the complete victory of the Northern States, and one of the results of the peace was the disbandment and discharge of a large number of men of Irish origin, who had fought during the war and now found themselves without occupation. In Ireland, as we have already seen, what was known as the Fenian movement was in full swing, and in America the Fenians were recruited by a large number of the above-named Irish soldiers, who, apart from politics and political views, appeared more partial to Guerilla raids and irregular warfare than to settling down to any form of hard and continuous employment in civil life. The danger of attack from some of these brigand bands was now evident to the Canadian Government, which realised at the same time how open and unprotected was the long and straggling frontier which divided Canada from the United States.

These Fenian bands established Clubs in the cities of the United States bordering Canada, and considerable numbers were—at all events on paper—organised in military units. Added to this was the fact that the United States Government, mindful of the very recent British sympathy with its enemies in the Southern States, was not sorry to have an opportunity of revenge, and used it by quiet countenance of the Fenians. The encouragement received from these high quarters was openly declared by the Irish leaders; and whatever the exaggeration of their statement, it had the effect of securing for them large subscriptions in America in aid of their project for invading British territory.

Our Intelligence Department was in the meanwhile quietly and unostentatiously gaining information. Reports were received that an attack on the Canadian frontier would be made in the summer of 1866, and that the basis of operations would be the cities of Buffalo and Ogdensburg in the State of New York, the former at the head of the Niagara river, and the latter 60 miles lower down, at the point where the St. Lawrence river emerges from the lake Ontario.

In view of the extent of ground to be defended, all that could be done was to form a kind of outpost line by small parties of selected soldiers under command of an N.C.O., who were posted partly to give notice of hostile movement, partly to prevent deserters crossing into the United States. Of this work our 4th Battalion took its share. In March 1866 the Canadian Government felt it necessary to call out 10,000 of the Militia; but it was found that the regiments had no equipment enabling them to take the field; and if time had been an object, the deficiency might have lead to disastrous results. Months however passed, but on June 1 came the alarming news that during the preceding night 15,000 Fenians had crossed the Niagara river at Buffalo and landed in Canada at the old ruined fort known as Erie. One or two trifling skirmishes took place. Two Companies of our 4th Battalion arrived under command of Captain Travers, the other officers being Lieuts. J. G. and J. D. T. Crosbie and H. D. Browne, and the rest of the Battalion was ordered up from London, Ontario; but by the time it reached the scene of action the Brigands, whose numbers had been greatly exaggerated, had already decamped, and thus ended the fiasco of Fenian invasion.

In May 1868 the Battalion was moved from London, Ontario, to St. John's, New Brunswick.

4

During all this time Colonel Hawley was training his Battalion and bringing it to the highest state of efficiency. In earlier life he had married but lost his wife shortly afterwards. It is evident from the letters written by him in the Crimea (to his father) that he had always been a keen student of his profession, endowed with all the ability needed for success therein; and in the desolation of his grief, a grief from which he perhaps never fully recovered, it was to his profession alone that he looked for some mental relief. To that extent it may be said, that however terrible to himself, the death of his wife led to the advantage of his regiment, and indeed of a circle far beyond it.

Hawley modelled his system upon what remained known of that of our 5th Battalion, which had earned so great a reputation under Wellington in Spain and Portugal; and it may easily be that, from personal intercourse with officers who had served therein, he gained a comparatively intimate knowledge of the history and doings of that Battalion. It was said of Sir John Moore, and it might equally have been said of Colonel Hawley, that his officers were trained for command, and his soldiers acquired such discipline as to become an example to the army, and proud of their profession. Although drill, field manœuvre, and rifle practice formed an important part of the instruction, it was not by such means only that the character of his men was developed. Every single item connected with the food, comfort, and training, moral or physical, of a Battalion was thought out by Hawley and gradually perfected. His system, also like that of Sir John Moore, was based on the cultivation of morale and of self-reliance on the part of the individual officer or man. Among those who largely owed to their commanding officer the distinction which they subsequently gained may be mentioned Field-Marshal Lord Grenfell, General Sir Redvers Buller, Lieut.-General Sir Edward Hutton, Colonel Donald Browne, and many of equal or lesser degree. Colonel Hawley was *facile princeps* in the Regimental branch of the army just as was Lord Wolseley on that of the Staff. He was a master of his art, and his influence extended far beyond the limits of his own Battalion. Lord Wolseley, at that time a Colonel, was stationed in Canada as Deputy Quartermaster-General; it was unfortunate that the two men failed to appreciate one another. Hawley's promotion had been quicker than that of the average officer, but the rapidity of that of Wolseley, who was twelve years junior in age, had been positively phenomenal, and his opportunities of distinction on active service had been far greater. Hawley perhaps regarded Wolseley as something of an upstart and ill-acquainted with the regimental side of his profession. In this feeling there was some foundation, for Wolseley, who joined the army in 1852, never did a day's regimental duty after 1858, and even during the interval was for the most part employed on the Staff. It was therefore perhaps not unnatural that in view of the good fortune which had deservedly attended his own career, Wolseley failed to appreciate the value of Hawley's 'spade work,' or to realise how much his own subsequent success was due thereto.

The conduct and the discipline of our 1st Battalion at Delhi, and of the 2nd Battalion in South Africa and China, gave evidence of regimental efficiency, and it is known that a happy feeling always prevailed between the officers and men. The regiment had had its share of good commanding officers, notably Colonel Molyneux, Lord Melville, and Colonel Bradshaw in the 1st Battalion, Colonels Nesbitt and Webbe Butler in the 2nd, but there are few Corps which are not the better for having from time to time the infusion of a little new blood. Hawley, as already stated, came to us from the 89th Regiment; yet, as remarked by Sir Redvers Buller at a regimental dinner long afterwards, 'Colonel Hawley had hardly been in command of the 4th Battalion two years before we thought him the finest Rifleman in the service.'

Hawley was once asked to what he attributed his successful régime, and his reply was, 'By feeding the men well, and giving the officers plenty of leave.' He had a natural capacity for business; he took great pains to ensure that his Battalion was supplied with the best bread and meat, and their issue was by no means a matter of form between the Quartermaster-Sergeant and the men. On the contrary, the orderly men from each company on being assembled at the ration stand were given every opportunity of inspecting the food; and any portion fairly criticised was rejected. In regard to the Canteen, the supplies were purchased wholesale from the markets direct, and the men in consequence obtained what they needed in the best possible condition and at the lowest possible prices, immune from any toll on account of the middleman's commission.

In regard to the Company officers, the Colonel took care that they performed their duty to the best of their ability. He expected unremitting attention to the individual instruction and development of their men, and on this basis discipline was perfected. There was no domineering, still less bullying; nor was Colonel Hawley ever heard to swear. But the officers were never denied leave; they were encouraged in all manly pursuits, and particularly in the cultivation of what may be termed the Hunter's instinct. Had the Battalion been in England this education would have been very hard to acquire; but in Canada there was ample scope for it, and officers in parties of two and three, accompanied by an Indian or two, would explore the prairie and the forest for big game, such as bear, elk, and caribou. In the pursuit of such game, which largely took place in the winter, the hunting parties were obliged to carry on their back such baggage and provisions as were essential. From such life privations were of course inseparable, and a man's very life depended on his own skill. Clad in furs from head to foot, equipped with snow-shoes, parties penetrated far and wide. In birch-bark canoes they ascended or descended rivers, sometimes half frozen, sometimes flowing in torrents, and crowded with trunks of pinewood. They skimmed dangerous rapids, where the life of the boat's crew depended upon the amazing skill of the helmsman with his paddle, and where the shifting even of a load of baggage might overturn the canoe and doom the whole of its occupants to certain death.

At the end of the day's toil it would be necessary to erect some sort of shelter—of snow if it were winter, of sail or tent in summer—while others of the party were scouring the rivers for salmon to provide an evening meal. In hot weather the difficulties of transport were no less, and experience of mosquitoes gained at painful cost. Flies in fact of all description made life as near as possible unbearable.

But when the little party of officers returned to their regiment they had received an education infinitely more practical than that of a University, for they had learnt to rely on their own resources. They could kill and cook their own food, they had acquired skill in all branches of the Hunter's craft. They knew where to look for their quarry; they readily recognised its tracks, and were able to follow them up until the culminating point, when success or failure terminated their efforts. They had learned a thousand little arts—tricks or dodges, if you like—from the Indians or half-breeds who had accompanied them; they had been able to gauge the mentality of such companions, and every moment of the expedition had been spent in acquiring an experience than which nothing could be finer for the student of the military profession, and which Oxford or Cambridge could never have given them.

Colonel Hawley set his officers a personal example in this education, and was an expert in the art of handling a canoe. Among his subalterns was Redvers Buller; and despite nearly twenty years' difference in age they were close associates. One day while together in a canoe the Colonel saw rapids ahead and prepared to disembark, but Buller refused to admit the danger and insisted in remaining on the river. The force of the current increased, and the peril very shortly became undeniable. Buller in his turn now proposed to turn to the shore, but this time it was Colonel Hawley who refused, 'No,' said he, 'I have come to this point for your pleasure and you must now go on for mine.' Buller was forced to obey, for a quarrel in the canoe would have meant instant death. Then Hawley, no less conspicuous for skill than for prudence, shot the rapid successfully and passed into calm water.

Among the regimental institutions of that period was

a pack of hounds, which were hunted by Lieutenant Donald Browne. Redvers Buller, who was one of the 'Whips,' was a man of enormous muscular strength, and under trees where the crust of snow 20 feet deep was so soft that the pack of fox-hounds sank up to their middle and could not flounder along, Buller would take a hound under each arm and soon snowshoe to a harder surface.

In regard to the actual training of his Battalion on parade, Hawley very rightly insisted on the utmost steadiness when it was a matter of barrack-square drill. At the same time he never kept a man standing at attention for a moment longer than absolutely necessary. At the conclusion of any movement the word 'stand easy' was at once given, either by the Colonel himself or individually by the officers in command of Companies. Hawley abolished superfluous words of command. At the word 'Steady' men standing easy stood properly at ease, and on the word 'Rifles' sprang to attention. Among other reforms in drill he introduced the word 'Change ranks' in order to supersede the cumbrous and lengthy movements hitherto necessary to effect a change of front. No one understood better than Colonel Hawley the fact that steadiness under arms is an essential preliminary to rapidity of movement: and rapidity was acquired not by use of the Double, but by training men to move on his word of command instantaneously, and not after an interval of one or two seconds, as usually happens under less experienced commanders.

Sir Edward Hutton, at this period a subaltern in the 4th Battalion, writes :—

'Hawley's battalion excelled in the highest degree. Quick and rapid movement, changes of front were made by signals or by whistle without notice or word of command. The system at present in vogue was commonly practised by Hawley and the 4th

Battalion sixty years ago, and at a time when the noise and consequent confusion caused by a very babel of words of command was a universal system.[1]

Every encouragement was given to skill in rifle shooting. A Rifle Club was formed, and in 1865 the 4th was the best shooting battalion in the army. At places affording no ground for manœuvres instruction in light infantry movements was given by Company Officers in the Barrack room, and illustrated by small blocks of wood, somewhat in the style of the modern War Game.

It may be mentioned incidentally, it was customary in the Battalion not to shave the lower lip, but to cultivate the adornment known as an 'Imperial.' This custom lingered on indeed long after the battalion had returned to England.

Years passed quickly amid the many delights of Canada, and the time came for returning to England. On June 27, 1869, the Battalion embarked in H.M.S. *Crocodile*. On July 5 it landed at Portsmouth. During the voyage the *Crocodile* had the experience not unusual off the Canadian shore of four days' dense fog, but otherwise the weather was fine. On landing at Portsmouth the Battalion went by special train to Farnborough *en route* to Aldershot. The officers were :—

Colonel R. B. Hawley.
Bt. Lt.-Colonel C. A. B. Gordon.

Captains.
J. J. Collins, K. G. Henderson, F. H. A. Hamilton, H. R. Milligan, R. F. Barry, R. H. Beadon, A. Tufnell.

Lieutenants.
R. H. Buller, W. Warren, P. J. H. Barne, R. C. Robinson, H. D. Browne, J. J. Wynne Finch.

[1] For further details readers are referred to Sir E. Hutton's 'Memoir of Colonel Hawley,' printed in the *K.R.R.C. Chronicle* for 1909.

Ensigns.

J. A. Williams, A. R. Liddiard, H. P. Barrard, E. T. H. Hutton, E. R. Wingfield.

Paymaster.

Captain E. C. Grant.

Quartermaster.

Lt. T. Jarvis.

Assistant Surgeon.

W. M. Harman, M.B.

The other ranks comprised 688 N.C.Os. and Men, together with 66 Women and 105 Children.

CHAPTER XV

On March 3, 1869, Field-Marshal H.R.H. George, Duke of Cambridge, was appointed to the Colonelcy-in-Chief of the Regiment. It will be remembered that his father had occupied the same position from 1827 to 1850.

2

In September 1868 the 1st Battalion, which had returned to Montreal at the conclusion of its work at Point Levis, went by boat to Ottawa, whence three Companies, under Brevet Lieut.-Colonel H. F. Williams, were sent on detachment to Toronto.

In June 1869 four Companies returned to Montreal and were quartered at St. Helen's Isle under canvas until September.

In April the establishment of the Battalion was reduced to 8 Service and 2 Depôt Companies.

In March 1870, on the abolition of the 7th (Rifle) Depôt Battalion, the depôt of the 1st Battalion left Winchester under command of Lieut.-Colonel Tedlie, to be attached to the 4th Battalion at Aldershot.

3

At the period of which we are speaking, despite the fact that our remaining Colonies on the Continent of North

America had been amalgamated for the purpose of forming the present Dominion of Canada, the bond linking them together was very loose, and enormous tracts of country which now contain important cities were at that time not traversed by railways, but were sparsely occupied by white men, and for practical purposes unexplored.

Now it happened that the Hudson Bay Company claimed exclusive right to govern all the British territory whose waters drained into that Bay. Its boundaries were ill-defined; the desire on the part of its officials to maintain exclusive rights of trading with all the Indians who inhabited that region discouraged not only immigration but even the visits of travellers or explorers. The object of such policy was, of course, to prevent the ultimate extinction of fur-bearing animals, which supplied the source of their principal trade with the natives.

It being impossible to admit such an *imperium in imperio*, the Dominion Government purchased all the territorial rights of the Hudson Bay Company for the sum of £300,000. But notwithstanding this settlement discontent prevailed. It will be remembered that when in 1763 Canada, which had been conquered by force of arms, was ceded by treaty to Great Britain the white population was exclusively French; and although French religion, law, and custom had been preserved, there was as time went on a certain bitterness of feeling in the fact that the country was gradually becoming less French and more English: it was therefore hoped that the territory of the Hudson Bay Company might be administered for the exclusive advantage of its ancient inhabitants, and might ultimately become a counterpoise to the British power further east. The Church of Rome, which appealed much more strongly to the imagination of the Red Indians than did the Churches of England or Scotland, was also an active factor in this problem, and did its best to give a religious aspect to the dispute between the English and the French inhabitants of what is now known as the province of Ontario. To make a long story short, in 1870 a French Canadian named Louis Riel raised the flag of rebellion in what was known as the Red River Settlement. He gathered a party of idle fellows, who took possession of Fort Garry—the site of the present city of Winnipeg—with the stores of the Hudson Bay Company contained therein. It unfortunately happened that Sir John Macdonald the Prime Minister of the Canadian Cabinet was ill, and in his absence his colleagues mismanaged the matter. Riel seized an Englishman who was acknowledged as an official surveyor, and brought him before an irregular court martial. The proceedings were carried out in French, a language not understood by the prisoner, who by sentence of the Court was immediately shot.

The British outcry on the perpetration of this murder was naturally loud; and after a very ineffectual attempt of pacification, the Government of Ottawa decided to despatch a military force to suppress the rebellion in the Red River Settlement. The Expedition consisted of a British Battalion with some detachments R.A. and R.E., together with two Battalions of the Canadian militia.

Command of the force was given to Colonel Garnet Wolseley, whom we have already met in the Indian Mutiny and Chinese War. He was now Deputy Q.M.G. in Canada; and having been stationed in that country for nine years had acquired a thorough knowledge of every detail connected therewith, whether political, military, or geographical. For his Staff and Special Service Officers Wolseley had collected men of ability, the best known of whom was a Subaltern who in later life became General Sir William Butler. Lieut.-General the Hon. James

Lindsay, G.O.C. of the troops in Canada, did all in his power to assist Colonel Wolseley, not only in matters relating to military equipment, but also in smoothing the way with the Canadian political authorities.

The task about to be undertaken, involving as it did a route of 1,200 miles, was no light one. The first stage of 94 miles was overland from Toronto to Collingwood on the eastern shore of Nottawasaga Bay. The distance from Collingwood across Lake Huron to Port Arthur, Thunder Bay, on the North-west coast of Lake Superior, was 534 miles. Port Arthur was the point of concentration, and the distance thence to Fort Garry was 612 miles, making for the entire journey a total of 1,240. The range of hills which formed the watershed between Hudson Bay and Lake Superior had to be crossed at a pass about 800 feet in height. On reaching the waters on the further side the troops were to be embarked in boats, for roads were practically non-existent. During the subsequent long voyage no supplies of any kind could be expected from the outer world; the consequence being that the whole of the stores, arms, and provisions had to be carried in the boats. The construction of these boats was extremely difficult; for while on the one hand they could not fail to be subjected to rough usage, it was on the other necessary to build them of light wood, since they would have to be dragged not only over numerous *portages*, but also over the steep and rugged heights between Lakes Superior and Winnipeg.

If the Expedition were to be successful there was no time to lose, for it was essential that the regular troops should be brought back to their barracks before the end of the autumn and the setting in of the hard frosts, to say nothing of the fact that even a quarter of an inch of ice on the water would have cut through the thin wood of the boats.

Canadian experts loudly phophesied failure and even the possible loss of the troops; but Colonel Wolseley made his own calculations and refused to listen to such forebodings. He reckoned that after embarking in the boats the voyage would occupy about 40 days, and that, although lightened of the bulk of the stores, the return journey might take as long. It was therefore necessary to pack into the boats provisions for three months.

4

The force selected for this expedition comprised the 1st Battalion of the 60th under Colonel Feilden with 23 officers and 350 other ranks; small parties R.A. and R.E. each 20 strong with a proportion of the Army Service Corps and Hospital Corps. There were in addition two Battalions of Canadian Militia, each of about 400 men, viz. the 1st (Ontario) Rifles, and the 2nd (Quebec) Rifles, both of which had been organised by Colonel Feilden. The whole combatant force was therefore about 1,200 strong, all the men having been selected after careful medical examination. Four 7-pounder guns accompanied the R.A.

In addition to the two Field Officers, Colonel Feilden and Major Robertson, the Battalion consisted of seven Companies as follows:—

A Company, Captain J. D. Dundas, Lieuts. D. Bingham and the Hon. Keith Turnour.
B ,, Captain N. W. Wallace, Lieut. R. C. Robinson, Ensign F. M. Ward.
C ,, Captain Redvers H. Buller,[1] J. H. Burstall.
D ,, ,, F. V. Northey, Ensign F. W. Archer.
F ,, ,, J. O. Young, Lieuts. E. L. Fraser and R. C. Davies.

[1] Buller, but recently promoted to the rank of Captain, was in England when the expedition started.

G Company, Captain E. H. Ward, Lieut. F. J. A. Wood, and Ensign A. St. Maur.
H   ,,   Captain C. M. Calderon, Lieuts. F. C. Coulson and A. F. Mitchell-Innes, Ensign W. H. Holbech.
The Adjutant was Lieut. H. S. Marsham, and the Quartermaster John Toole.

5

On May 14, the earliest date on which the ice on Lake Superior had sufficiently melted to permit of navigation, the first two Companies started from Toronto and went by train to Collingwood on the southern corner of Georgian Bay, the waters of which connect with those of Lake Superior.

From Collingwood steamers ran through Lake Superior, but only by the Ste. Marie River, which throughout its whole length of 50 miles forms the boundary between Canada and the United States. It contains the unnavigable rapid known as the Sault Sainte Marie, to avoid which the Americans on their side of the river had constructed a canal three miles long. To that extent our steamers would be obliged to pass through United States territory; but during the Civil War in America, 1861-1865, Canadian authorities had allowed a United States gunboat to pass through our canals on the St. Lawrence River, and it was in consequence hoped that on the present occasion a similar courtesy would be extended to ourselves, particularly as we had arranged to transmit stores only through the canal but to land our troops below the Sault on the British side of the river at the further end of the canal.

On the appearance of the British steamer at the lower end of the canal the United States officials, having received no orders to the contrary, allowed her to pass; and once through the canal the vessel was again in British waters. But the next steamer, although containing no war material, was stopped at the entrance to the canal; for the American Government, afraid of losing the Irish vote, yielded to the dictation of the Fenian organisation, which as usual spared no pains to thwart the projects of the British Government.

Although this prohibition caused a delay in the conveyance of stores, and it was absolutely essential that we should have the use of two steamers on Lake Superior, by a piece of good fortune it did not prove fatal, for at the critical moment an American Captain not only let his steamer to us on hire for work on Lake Superior but, entirely of his own accord, made an affiadvit to the United States authorities that he had not been hired by the British Government and had nothing whatever to do with the Red River expedition! It is perhaps only fair to add that in replying to the formal protest by the Governor-General of Canada the United States Government eventually threw open the canal to all our vessels which were not carrying actual munitions of war.

6.

Owing, however, to the delay it was not until June 21 that the whole of our Battalion was concentrated at Thunder Bay on the western shore of Lake Superior. The landing-place, which was named by Wolseley Port Arthur, proved to be a dreary waste and contained only a few shanties. Its vegetation had been recently destroyed by a fierce fire.

Another vexatious delay now took place. The Canadian Government had promised that a road for transport of stores and boats over the 48 miles separating Port Arthur from Lake Shebandowan should by this time be completed. It was found to be only half finished and in fact one section had not even been begun. Thus it happened that nearly a month was spent by the Riflemen in hard work upon this road, the difficulties being increased by continuous and heavy rains.

The two regiments of Canadian Militia had not yet come up, and it was found necessary to employ part of them in protecting the line of communication from the raids of Fenians in the United States.

7

The problem of completing the road and of carrying over it 150 boats during the current summer appeared almost insoluble. In order to relieve the pressure Colonel Wolseley, at the instance of Mr. McIntyre, the Hudson Bay official at Fort William, decided to send a Rifle Company up the Kaministiguia River, although every one but Mr. McIntyre declared the river to be absolutely unnavigable in consequence of its falls and rapids.

The officer selected for this purpose was Captain John Owen Young, whom Wolseley describes as one of the hardiest campaigners he had ever met. Young certainly was a remarkable character. He had joined the Battalion a year or two before the outbreak of the Indian Mutiny, during the early stages of which he belonged to the half Battalion which was left at Meerut for the purpose of keeping the surrounding country under control; but he joined the Headquarters of the Battalion at Delhi a few days before the assault of the city and took part in the subsequent operations.

Captain Huyshe, Wolseley's Staff Officer, describes Captain Young as he appeared early in July on the occasion of a visit of General Lindsay. 'Young's attire consisted of a red woollen nightcap, flannel shirt, sleeves rolled up, duck trousers up to his knees; no shoes, but a pipe unceasingly in his mouth, which he condescended to take out only when he shook hands with the General.'

Jack Young, as he was always called, was ever the first man to jump out of his boat in a rapid, regardless of the depth of the water. He was habitually wet through to the waist, yet never failed to keep his pipe and matches dry. One day when up to his chin in water a man of his Company, hoping to take him at a disadvantage, asked for a light, whereupon Jack Young produced a box of dry matches out of the loose end of his nightcap!

His Company was 'F.' He always called it 'the Ara(r)bians,' on the ground that the latter were 'a fierce and warlike nation.' Its critics declared, however—in mere jealousy—that the real reason was that it kept no sort of order on the march. Certain it is that Young had only two words of command. When it was time to advance he said, 'Time to get along, boys,' when he halted, 'Time to have a drink, boys.' His senior Subaltern, 'Friday' Fraser, also deserves a word of notice. Almost as contradictory as Redvers Buller, he was yet the most lovable character imaginable. It will be realised that during this expedition very little was seen of regulation uniform. The officers wore moccasins, which they dried at every opportunity, but 'Friday' Fraser always kept his in water all night, and when asked the reason by Colonel Wolseley said it was that he found them more easy to put on in the morning!

8

Young and his Company started on June 4, and were met by Colonel Wolseley in person, along the romantically beautiful country of Hiawatha. After ten days of terrific work (aggravated by the fact that in one night the river rose 6 feet), during which officers and men were half devoured by flies in the day and wet to the skin at night, Young forced his way through 50 miles of forest and rapids to a level of 800 feet over falls, one of which was known to be upwards of 120 feet in height, and up inclines of 45 degrees. Having crossed seven portages and laid trunks of trees as rollers over all, he at length reached Matawan Bridge, beyond which no boat could be taken. It was then decided to send the remainder of the boats, partly by road, partly by water, to the Oskondagee Creek, the furthest practicable point, whence they were transported on carts to the shore of Shebandowan Lake. Here they were once more floated, and by the middle of July the Battalion, with the other units belonging to the Regular Army, was concentrated at its eastern entrance.

9

The force now assembled consisted of 45 officers and 543 O.R. There were in addition 136 Canadian or Indian *Voyageurs*, men skilled in boat craft and in navigation of rivers. There were also 7 men hired as guides, who might have been useful but for the fact that they were ignorant of the route!

The flotilla was divided into 12 Brigades as follows :—

Letter.	No. of Boats.	Name of Commander.
A	6	Captain Young, 60th.
B	6	,, Ward ,,
C	5	,, Alleyne, R.A.
D	7	,, Dundas, 60th
E	6	,, Buller ,,
F	6	,, Northey ,,
G	7	,, Wallace ,,
H	6	,, Calderon ,,
I	6	,, Scott (Ontario Rifles)
J	1	,, Huyshe (H.Q. Staff)
K	6	,, McDonald (O. Rifles)
L	6	,, Henderson (O. Rifles)

[1] Captain Redvers Buller, having come out from England post-haste, had joined the Battalion on June 10th at Thunder Bay. Having spent many years

The boats were each about 30 feet long and 6 or 7 feet broad—some carvel, others clinker-built. Each weighed, when empty, about 7 cwt. ; when loaded, from 3 to 4 tons : they were pulled by six oars, and contained 11 or 12 men and 2 or 3 *Voyageurs*. The flotilla under Captain Wallace, which may be taken as a general example of the whole, consisted of 7 boats containing 5 officers, 58 men, and 14 Indian or Canadian *Voyageurs*, 77 in all. The cargo on board these seven boats comprised 40 barrels of biscuit (each weighing 100 lbs.), 42 barrels of flour (each 120 lbs.), 50 barrels of pork (each 200 lbs.), 7 barrels of sugar (each 150 lbs.), 7 cases of tea, 13 sacks of beans, 8 boxes of preserved potatoes, 9 tins of pepper, 19 axes, 11 picks, 22 hatchets, 13 kettles, 1 oven, 18 frying-pans, 13 shovels, 13 spades, 11 tents, 7 tins of mosquito oil, 13 boxes of medical comforts, boxes containing rifles and 6,000 rounds of ammunition, some boat-builder's tools, tin plates and plenty of white lead for patching up holes or other injuries incurred by the boats, together with blankets and water-proof sheets. The provisions were calculated to last for 60 days ; all wine and spirits were strictly prohibited.

The country about to be passed through was unknown except to the employés of the Hudson Bay Company, whose chief posts *en route* were at Fort William, where the Kaministiguia River falls into Thunder Bay ; at Fort Francis, about halfway to Fort Garry ; and at Rat Portage, where the Winnipeg River leaves the North end of the Lake of the Woods. The distance to Fort Garry from Shebandowan Lake was 612 miles. This lake, described as a beautiful sheet of water, comparatively narrow but

in Canada with the 4th Battalion, he had a greater knowledge of the country, lakes, and rivers than the officers of the comparatively newly arrived 1st Battalion. His Company C was the first to follow F up the Kaministiguia River, and his wider experience enabled him to catch up Capt. Young.

about 20 miles in length, is more than 800 feet above the level of Lake Superior.

'It was wonderful,' says Lord Wolseley in his 'Story of a Soldier's Life,' 'how quickly the little Londoners of the Rifles became good men in the boats and over the Portages. By the time they had made the trip to Fort Garry and back, both Officers and men had become good, many of them expert, axemen, and all more or less skilled in the craft of the voyageur.

'. . . The mosquitoes, sand-flies, and black-flies drew blood freely and rendered sleep difficult. I had provided each man with a veil, but after a little while it was difficult to make them use either the veil or the mosquito oil.'

Both appliances came in handy although in a way other than that intended. The veil was useful for straining the lake water, which was densely loaded with vegetable matter, and the oil to light their lamps.

A halt of a few weeks was necessarily made on the banks of the Shebandowan, for the boats had been injured in the rapids and on the sharp rocks of the Kaministiguia River. All the boats were overhauled, mended and fitted with oars, mast and sails. It was also essential to re-cooper the barrels of pork and refill them with brine.

All was at length ready, and the start fixed for July 16 ; but during the previous night a thunderstorm, unparalleled in the experience of all present, broke.

'While it lasted,' says Lord Wolseley, 'the heavens seemed at times to open and let fall great crushing weights of explosives upon the earth beneath, which apparently trembled at the shock. Then followed a rain the like of which I have never seen even in the Tropics. It fell upon us not in drops but literally as sheets of water in rapid succession.'

The storm ended as suddenly as it had begun, and the following day broke with a bright sun which soon dried the soaking clothes. It unfortunately happened, however, that a strong westerly wind raised a big sea, and not until nearly sunset did the wind begin to fall. At length about 8.30 P.M. the order was given to embark the first detachment, which comprised the Companies of Young and Ward—the latter, Colonel Wolseley's escort—small parties of the R.A. and R.E. with two 7-pounder guns, the whole under the command of Colonel Feilden.

'I fully understood,' says Lord Wolseley, 'the great natural difficulties they would meet with and would have to overcome. But I was equally certain that if determined courage, strengthened by the best and highest military discipline, could possibly overcome all such obstacles, Colonel Feilden and his men would do it.'

Lord Wolseley's confidence was justified. Be it remembered that the battalion contained a large proportion of the men who had fought at Delhi, although of the Officers Dundas, Young, and Toole only had taken part in that siege. Redvers Buller, recently promoted into the battalion from the 4th, considered the latter under Hawley's regime as perhaps rather the handier of the two, but spoke of the immense value in the great tradition of the 1st Battalion. Anyhow Riflemen had no dread of the difficulties ahead, and merely laughed at the imaginary terrors portrayed by French-speaking politicians in regard to the half-breed enemy who, they said, would certainly lure the British force to its destruction.

Once embarked in the boats the toil was by no means slackened. The weather at the outset consisted of little more than a succession of thunderstorms. It was difficult to find the correct passage through the numerous islands of the lakes, and hours of labour often ended in a *cul de sac* which necessitated retirement and the search for a new means of exit. Then occurred frequently the hard work at the *portage*, a term used either for the shortest road from one lake to another, or for a path along the river bank constructed to circumvent a rapid when the river is impassable for boats. Colonel Wallace gives a graphic description of the toil at these *portages* :—

'On arrival men at once are sent to fell trees along the path selected, which ought to be from 8 to 12 feet wide. These trees are then used as rollers for the boats to be dragged over; and while some men are path-making, others are unloading boats. The heavy weights are carried with a portage strap—a long thong of leather, or more generally untanned hide, about 14 to 16 feet long, 5 or 6 inches wide in the centre, and tapering off to a point; the rope-like ends are fastened round the barrel or box to be carried, leaving a small loop for the head to pass through. The broad part is placed on the forehead, and the hands are clasped over the back of the head, which is bent slightly forward; the barrel thus rests on the back, and the strain is on the vertebræ of the neck. In this way a man can carry from 200 to 300 lbs. An Indian can carry from 300 to 400 lbs.; and this, remember, not only on a level, or merely for a yard or two, but over rocky, hilly, and slippery ground, and for a distance up to 2,000 yards, each man having to make from four to five journeys over every portage, and sometimes encountering six or seven portages a day. When all stores are carried over, the boats, under charge of an officer, follow. About thirteen men can generally portage a boat, unless the incline be very steep. A rope is rove through the bottom of the stem post of the boat, carried over the bow and fastened round the two forward seats, by which means leverage is gained to lift the bow. Two men are stationed as bowmen, one on either side to lift the bow over rough ground and roots of tees; this work is the most arduous of all. Two men amidships keep the boat on an even keel. The remainder harness themselves with portage straps to the rope. At a given signal from the officer, who also takes his share of the work, a start is made and the boat walked along at a steady pace, the bowmen guiding. Should any hitch occur the pulling ceases till the bow is raised, and then the well-known shout of 'Together, heave! stick to her, boys!' sets her going again. In this way, extra hands being added, woods of any denseness, roads of any roughness, and hills of any steepness can be traversed. In going downhill a drag rope is run out over the stern, and three or four men are told off to it, to prevent her taking a shoot downwards. When all boats are safely over, launched, and loaded, a fresh start is made. Should any have been damaged or strained in transport, the mischief is soon repaired with oakum, tin, and white lead. So much for portage and the work.'

Wallace goes on to describe a day's doings on the road up :—

'Camp was roused by the sentry on duty between four and five A.M., fire lighted and tea warmed while we dressed, which consisted of getting out of a blanket and buffalo robe, occasionally, but not always, washing, and getting into a coat and red nightcap. For the dress of Officers and men was simple in the extreme : flannel shirts of every hue, caps of all descriptions, and trousers, which before long resembled Joseph's coat of many colours, kept up by a broad strap from which dangled a sheath knife and tin cup. One Officer invariably kept his boots and leather moccasins soaking in water all night that they might be comfortable : at least that was the reason he assigned to Colonel Wolseley, who inquired what the boots were doing in a bucket of water outside the tent.

'By this time our tents were down, and everything stowed in the boats, half an hour from the first call being allowed for all. The tea itself was capital, but a layer of grease always floated on it, owing to the usual secretion of pork fat from the kettle, which was the jack-of-all-trades : add a little sugar and I may safely say that the most skilful physician would be at a loss to prescribe a more nauseous draught. With it was served up a dry biscuit or piece of choke-dog—a pancake made of flour and water fried in pork fat (but not bad, I can assure you) ; and last, though not least, the only delicacy allowed us in the shape of meat, a piece of salt pork about half an inch thick, requiring a microscope to find out the proportion of lean to fat. And yet we eagerly devoured this our early repast, and were ready to jump into our boats, pull over a lake or shoot a rapid, until such time as the pangs of hunger assured us that eight o'clock breakfast hour had arrived.

'On landing, the usual question was put to our servants, "What have you got for breakfast?" "Nice cold pork, Sir, tea and biscuits; or if you prefer it, Sir, fried pork." Ravenous after our morning's work and our bath we fall to, and soon are ready for another start. The usual doubts about the weather, whether the wind is fair, the current strong against us, or a long day before us, pass away the few moments allowed for a smoke, while camp kettles are being packed up. The shout of "All aboard" from the Captain is heard, answered by the well-known "Aye aye, sir," and off we go. In about half an hour we arrive perhaps at a shallow channel, the first boat runs aground, and all the endeavours of her crew fail to move her. "Lift her, boys," cries the officer in charge, and over he jumps into the water, followed by his crew, and in less time than it takes to tell it, she answers to the shout of "Walk her along, boys," and is once more in deep water. The other boats follow in like manner. Another fair start; soon a rapid is seen ahead, consequently the shore is hugged until we assure ourselves whether it can be shot or not. The Indians jump ashore and inspect the seething mass of water, and return determined to run it. The best men take the oars. The Captain's boat, which carries the guide, leads; the others follow at an interval of 50 yards, and out into the current we pull. The Indian in the boat with his broad paddle guides it into the main channel, the helmsman with an oar astern keeps her from being swung round by the stream, the picked crew give way, and our boat, impelled at the rate of some 10 to 15 miles an hour, rushes downward into the smooth water at the bottom, where we lie on our oars and watch the fate of the remainder of our fleet as they shoot safely over. But not always *safely*. Once I saw the signal made from one of my boats, "I'm on a rock sinking and must throw my cargo overboard." Immediately my own boat was manned with Indians, and with great difficulty the sinking craft was reached, cargo picked up, and damage repaired.

'And now away we go again, singing and recounting dangers past, till the roar of a distant waterfall tells us that a portage is before us. Should noon be near, the order is given to get dinner ready while we portage. As each boat touches land one man springs out to secure a good place for unloading, while another rushes over the portage to select a convenient spot for re-loading. Officers and men vie in carrying the heaviest weights; the smell of the frying pork stimulates all hands, and the portage for the moment resembles an ants' nest, with its busy proprietors bustling to and fro. The baggage over, dinner is soon ready. Oh! what a sumptuous repast. "What have you got for dinner?" we enquire of our servants. "Nice hot boiled pork, beans, tea, and biscuits, Sir." What a delicious change! hot boiled pork instead of cold boiled pork! One short hour and to work again. Over the boats go, and a start is made for our camping ground, which we arrive at, if all goes well, about six or seven o'clock. But perhaps it is surrounded by sandbanks on which we all stick fast, working away in the dark for nearly two hours before we reach the camp fires, which we see brightly burning on the shore, kindled by the cooks sent through the water. In one instance I remember officers and men were from nine o'clock in the morning till eight o'clock at night in the water, poling and hauling and pulling at the boats, besides which we had to go over one of the most severe portages on the whole march : in fact after days like this, so weary often were we, that without supper and without pitching our tents we threw ourselves down in our wet clothes, and were soon oblivious of hunger and fatigue.

'But let us suppose ourselves arrived at our camping ground. As we sit over the fire and dry our clothes, or huddle up in our tent, while the heavy rain pours down, talking over our prospects, and trusting that we may, when we get to our journey's end, burn a little powder to repay us for our hardships, the meal of the day is preparing. "Well, Perks, what for supper ?" "Just making some pancake, Sir," and here it comes ; and not even the most fastidious can complain as regards quality, quantity, or variety. Boiled pork, hot and cold—fried pork, hot and cold, rare luxuries ! dry biscuits, "choke-dog," biscuits fried in pork fat, tea, and—can my eyes deceive me ?—fried potatoes procured from some mission garden in exchange for pork. Right good justice do we do Perks' cuisine, unless indeed he has made his bread with some of Riel's *starch* instead of baking-powder, as happened once, and then not even *our* digestions could tackle it, when he handed it to us in the morning, informing us that he had "sat up all night watching for it to rise, but it wouldn't." After supper we smoke our pipes, conscious of having done our duty to our stomachs and our Queen ; and sweeter never was sleep than ours, when tucked up in our "flea bags,"—as we called our beds—under a buffalo robe in our little tents, with perhaps a box or a stone for a pillow. Such was each day's routine, varied only occasionally by the catching of a few fish—I shot a sturgeon weighing 20 lbs.—the shooting of a few partridges, or the meeting with a few more than usually wild-looking Indians, and in this way working Sundays as well as weekdays, we reached on August 8 Fort Francis, our halfway house.'

Fort Francis, a post of the Hudson Bay Company, consisted of a palisade surrounding two or three wooden houses. Here Colonel Wolseley received a report from Lieut. (afterwards General Sir William) Butler, who had been sent through the United States to acquire intelligence, and had actually succeeded in reaching Fort Garry and having an interview with Riel. Butler's report was to the effect that the whole settlement was in a ferment and a general outbreak of the Indians imminent. Here also was received the disappointing news that the roads from the N.W. angle of the Lake of the Woods, which would have saved 150 miles, was impracticable for troops. The only possible course was therefore to continue the advance by boat, even though it involved the risk of the terrible rapids on the Winnipeg.

The information gained at Fort Francis induced Wolseley to push on at once; and within an hour or two of arrival the boats' crews re-embarked on the Rainy River below the neighbouring falls. During the brief interval the Colonel had had a visit from 'Crooked Neck,' a Chippewa Indian, whose tailor's bill could hardly have been a long one, for his apparel consisted of a body cloth only, while a coat of yellow paint and a nose ring completed his outward adornment. On receipt of a present of salt pork and flour the Chief granted to the force the right of passage through his territory.

The waters of the river were turbid and difficult. Seventy miles further on brought the boats to the Lake of the Woods, crowded with islands or with what appeared to be islands, but whose inlets in reality often ended in a *cul de sac*, leaving the disappointed boatmen no alternative but a return to the point of ingress and new attempts in other channels. The banks being covered with trees and rocks, and bordered by yellow sands, the scenery was delightful and romantic. Stormy weather was encountered on the third day, but on August 11 Rat Portage, another Hudson Bay station at the further end of the Lake, was safely reached. A halt of an hour or so was permitted, and the voyage then recommenced on the terrible Winnipeg River—the most dangerous section of the route.

The river is enclosed within precipitous cliffs, and in a course of 160 miles descends 350 feet by a succession of falls and rapids, of which there are no less than 27.

'No one,' observes Lord Wolseley in his 'Story of a Soldier's Life,' 'who has ever descended the Winnipeg River in boat or canoe is ever likely to forget that experience. The falls, the rapids, the whirlpools, the great rushing angry waters, and the many hair-breadth escapes are indelibly stamped on my memory. We had one or two boats wrecked, but no lives were lost. . . . The enthralling delight of feeling your frail canoe or boat bound under you, as it were, down a steep incline of wildly rushing water into what looks like a boiling, steaming caldron, exceeds most of the other maddening delights that a man can dream of. . . . No word can describe the rapid changes of sensation when the boat jumps through the last passage between rocks into an eddy of the slack water below.'

At Fort Alexander on Lake Winnipeg at the mouth of the river in comparative civilisation the force of regular troops was concentrated on August 20. Next day, Sunday, after Divine Service, Colonel Wolseley, although informed that armed resistance was probable, decided not to wait for the Canadian Militia, but to push on at once across the Lake to the mouth of the Red River now close at hand. A useful addition to the party was found in the person of the Governor of the Hudson Bay Company, Mr. Donald Smith, better known half a century later as Lord Strathcona. Appreciation of the approach of British troops was shown by loud cheering from the people on the river-banks. At 2 P.M. on the 22nd the leading boats, having crossed Lake Winnipeg, entered the Red River. The pace became slow, for they were now going up-stream, and the boats were ordered to keep in line by Brigades, led by that of Colonel Wolseley and Colonel Feilden.

The night, like most of its predecessors, proved wet. Soon after 4 A.M. next morning a start was made, and at 8 o'clock Stone Fort, some 10 miles below Fort Garry, was reached and utilised as a warehouse for surplus stores. The rifles were unpacked and distributed among Officers as well as men. Colonel Wolseley seized all the carts and ponies available and mounted Captain Wallace's Company (B) thereon. This was the first instance—at all events since the American War of Independence—of Riflemen being utilised as Mounted Infantry. Many who took long to mount their steeds found involuntary dismounting easy. Some thought it necessary to use the butt end of their rifles as a cutting whip before their mount could be induced to start. Wallace's orders were to act as a flank guard on the left bank of the river, moving about a quarter of a mile in advance of the boats.

It was hoped that Fort Garry would be reached the same day, but head winds prevailed and a bivouac was formed 6 miles short of the destination. A rumour said that Riel, with his rabble consisting of approximately 200 half-breeds and idle adventurers, meant to fight, and despite torrents of rain all were in great spirits. When day broke (August 24) the roadless country had been turned into a quagmire, and the idea of marching on foot was abandoned. The boats therefore started at 6 A.M., but a disembarkation was effected two miles short of Fort Garry, and as the Union Jack could be seen flying from the steeple of the Winnipeg Cathedral it was pretty evident that rebel rule was fast disappearing.

Fort Garry stood on the left bank of the Red River within the angle of confluence with the Assiniboine. It was about 100 yards in length and 85 in breadth, with a stone wall on three sides and a wooden palisade on the fourth. Each corner was flanked by a stone tower.

Colonel Wolseley's tactics were to encircle the fort from the west and by so doing to capture a bridge 200 yards distant over the Assiniboine and pin Riel and his men down within the angle of the two rivers. It would appear that Captain Calderon's Company, 'H,' led the advance. On approaching the fort the muzzle of a gun over the gateway looked threatening; but the next moment it was discovered that the walls were not manned, and the Riflemen to their disappointment entered Fort Garry without firing a shot. All the difficulties, hardships, and dangers of the advance from Thunder Bay had been borne not only with fortitude but positive joy at the idea of a fight at the end of it; and now, having reached the goal, it was found that Riel and his bandits had sneaked off across the river just before the bridge was taken. On the further bank were descried two men watching the occupation of the Fort. It was asserted—in joke more probably than in earnest—that they were the arch rebel and O'Donaghue, his secretary.

It was evidently at the last moment only that their nerve had failed them. Hot dishes and tea for their breakfast were found in the dining-room, and together with a half-packed portmanteau proved that the troops had arrived with surprising rapidity. Loaded rifles occupied every corner, and the guns of the Fort were also loaded. The only living creature was a black bear not fifteen months old, which was appropriated by Captain Wallace, and quickly becoming a regimental pet marched for some years at the head of the battalion with much dignity.

The delight of the loyal settlers at our arrival and the discomfiture of the rebels is indescribable. Had any of the latter been captured they would have been lynched, for Colonel Wolseley had been given no civil power, and was unable to stop the wild drunken rioting with which Indians, half-breeds and Voyageurs celebrated the restoration of law and order!

Riel escaped into United States territory. Not many years afterwards he once more raised the flag of rebellion; but being happily captured received the reward of his exploits by being hanged.

The stay at Fort Garry was short. On the 28th it was given up to the advance guard of the Canadian Militia battalions just arrived, and next day the Riflemen started on their return journey. Redvers Buller had always declared that the road between the Lake of the Woods and Fort Garry *was* practicable, and ought to have been the line of advance. He was given the chance of making good his words, and he succeeded, for he and his Company (C) performed the feat, although with great difficulty; and it would have been impossible for the whole expeditionary forces.

The remaining Companies re-embarked in their boats. This time the voyage, after passing Fort Alexander, was up-stream, and the ascent up the Winnipeg proved even more difficult than the descent had done. It was accomplished to some extent by what in Canada was termed 'poling,' 'Anglicé,' 'punting'; but for the most part the rapids were traversed by towing. A number of soi-disant 'voyageurs' had been engaged as experts; but many had in reality never handled an oar in their lives. Some of the Indians however did really good work. At the 'Seven Portages' were as many successive waterfalls.

'About halfway up,' said Captain N. W. Wallace, in a subsequent lecture, ' we had to cross the main stream of the river between two of them. Allowance had to be made for the currents, so we first pulled through the backwater as close as possible under the falls above us, then dashed out into mid-stream, the Indians in the bow straining every nerve to keep the boat from swinging broadside to the stream. The men pulled for dear life. We crossed safely, but by the time we were close to the other side we had been swept down nearly to the brink of the falls below. Drops of perspiration fell from the men as they rested on their oars, and we looked at each other, thanking God it was over.'

The perils of the passage were extreme. It is hardly too much to say that every man carried his life in his hands. There were many wonderful escapes from drowning, one of which may be taken as an example. At the Silver Falls above the Winnipeg the portage is only about twenty yards from the head of the cataract. Almost all of the Company's boats had safely negotiated the passage. Into the last but one an officer jumped, and having been assured that all was ready ordered the men in the bow to push off. The men obeyed the order with so much zeal that the boat shot out too far, and before the oars could catch the water the current swept her broadside on towards the Falls. To stem the torrent of water by means of the oars was impossible. The crew were stared in the face by death; but just as for a last resource the men were about to jump overboard an Indian belonging to the last boat appeared. Grasping the situation in an instant he shouted to the crew to throw out a rope. Dashing into the water he was just able to grasp the end. The sudden jerk checked the bow for an instant, and the stern, although by this time within a few yards of the brink, swung round. With the energy of despair the men seized their last chance and pulled with the oars in superhuman might. Not a single life was lost. All regained the bank in safety. The courage and composure of a single savage was an instrument of Providential protection.

Once over the Seven Portages the back of the homeward voyage was broken. On September 23 the first of the boat flotilla reached Shebandowan. This place, now known as McNeil's Bay, was reached at 10 P.M., and 48 hours later the advance guard marched into Thunder Bay.

Thus in brilliant success ended this military-naval

expedition. Bearing in mind the perils on the water, the difficulties of communication between the units of the force scattered over a distance of 150 miles, the danger of losing boats and stores and of the crews being left without food or transport in a country destitute of resources, the loudly expressed forebodings of the prophets before starting could certainly not be considered devoid of foundation. The impossibility of conveying either sick or wounded imposed another terrible risk on the Commander, for it would have been necessary to leave them on the shore exposed to the mercies or otherwise of Indian tribes.

It must also be realised that every single article of arms, equipment, or baggage had to be carried on the back of the Officers and men, or dragged by their main force. No fewer than 47 portages had been negotiated. Visualising all these difficulties, the risk arising from the fact that the arms were packed in chests and not immediately available in case of surprise or attack was, one may say, a comparatively minor affair.

The success of the Red River expedition was due in the first place to the extraordinary care and forethought exercised by General the Hon. James Lindesay, G.O.C. in Canada, and still more to Colonel Wolseley himself, by whom every single detail had been worked out in advance. It was due in the second place to the fact that from start to finish there was not a man sick. It really seemed that a sense of peril, the intensely hard work, and the rains, incessant for hours and days together, combined to produce this happy result! It should be added that with the exception of a very small modicum of brandy conveyed as a medical comfort not one teaspoonful of spirits was carried or tasted from beginning to end. Tea was the sole beverage. Despite all dampers, for the men were almost incessantly wet to the skin, the cheeriness of the expeditionary force was the theme of general comment. The only shade of disappointment lay in the fact that the rebels bolted without firing a shot.

The importance of the success gained was thoroughly realised throughout the Dominion of Canada. In England it attracted but little attention. This was partly due to the fact that men's minds were naturally enough absorbed by the struggle between France and Germany. The astonishing incidents of that war, the downfall of the Emperor of the French, and the victory of Germany left little time for the consideration of what was passing in one of our Colonies 5,000 miles away.

Fort Garry is no more. The little settlement of wooden huts has long ago grown into a great city, Winnipeg. Civilisation has altered the whole face of the country and covered it with a network of railways and other means of communication. In a few years' time it will be as difficult to appreciate the difficulties of approach to Fort Garry as at the present time it is difficult to appreciate that of the march in 1758 to Fort Duquesne, mentioned in the first volume of these Annals.

10

The Commander of the Red River expedition received the K.C.M.G., which he so well deserved. He also earned (what he probably appreciated more than the decoration) the entire confidence of the Officers and men comprising the force. Wolseley on his part reciprocated the confidence; and when three years later he had been selected as Commander of a force, destined to operate on active service in Ashanti, he asked, although as it happened in vain, for a Battalion of the 60th to form one of its units.

Colonel Feilden received the C.M.G., and two brevet majorities were awarded. All the Officers had done well; but at this distance of time it is perhaps not invidious to say that the names of Captains John Owen Young and Redvers Buller were those most frequently on the lips of their brother riflemen. In view of the fact that no fighting had taken place, it was, however, decided by the military authorities at home that the two brevet majorities should be awarded to the senior Captains, James Durham Dundas and Francis Vernon Northey.

Colonel Wolseley lost no time in expressing his acknowledgment to the troops under his command.

'Fort Garry, August 28, 1870.

' The following address from the officer commanding the Red River Expeditionary Force to the regular troops is published for general information.

'To the Regular Troops of the Red River Expeditionary Force

' I cannot permit Colonel Feilden and you to start upon your return journey to Canada without thanking you for having enabled me to carry out the Lieutenant-General's orders so successfully.

' You have endured excessive fatigue in the performance of a service that for its arduous nature will bear comparison with any previous Military Expedition. In coming here from Prince Arthur's landing you have traversed a distance of upwards of 600 miles; your labours began with those common at the outset of all campaigns, viz. road making and the construction of defensive works; then followed the arduous duty of taking the boats up a height of 800 feet, along 50 miles of river, full of rapids and numerous portages. From the time you left Shebandowan Lake until Fort Garry was reached your labour at the oar has been incessant from daybreak to dark every day; 47 portages were got over, entailing the unparalleled exertion of carrying the boats, guns, ammunition, stores, and provisions over a total distance of 15,000 yards; it may be said that the whole journey had been made through a wilderness, where, as no supplies of any sort were to be had, everything had to be taken with you in the boats.

'I have throughout viewed with pleasure the manner in which the officers have vied with their men in carrying heavy loads. I feel proud of being in command of officers who so well know how to set a good example, and of men who evince such eagerness in following it.

'Rain has fallen upon 45 days out of the 94 that have passed by since we landed at Thunder Bay, and upon many occasions officers and men have been wet for days together. There has not been one slightest murmur of discontent heard from any one. It may be confidently asserted that no force has ever had to endure more continuous labour, and it may be as truthfully said that no men on service have ever been better behaved or more cheerful under trials arising from exposure to inclement weather, excessive fatigue, and the annoyance caused by flies.

'There has been a total absence of crime amongst you during your advance to Fort Garry, and I feel confident that your conduct during the return journey will be as creditable to you in every respect.

'The leaders of the Banditti, who recently opposed Her Majesty's loyal subjects in the Red River settlement, having fled as you advanced upon the Fort, leaving their guns and a large quantity of arms and ammunition behind them, the primary object of the expedition has been peaceably accomplished. Although you have not therefore had an opportunity of gaining glory, you can carry back with you into the daily routine of garrison life the conviction that you have done good service to the State, and have proved that no extent of intervening wilderness, no matter how great may be its difficulties, whether by land or water, can enable men to commit murder or rebel against Her Majesty's authority with impunity.

'(Signed) G. J. WOLSELEY,
'Colonel Commanding Red River Expeditionary Force.'

Colonel Feilden and his men reached Toronto about the middle of October. A complimentary general order on the recent expedition was issued by H.R.H. the Duke of Cambridge, C.-in-C. of the British Army.

11

In November the Battalion moved from Montreal to Quebec, where the cold was intense. During the period

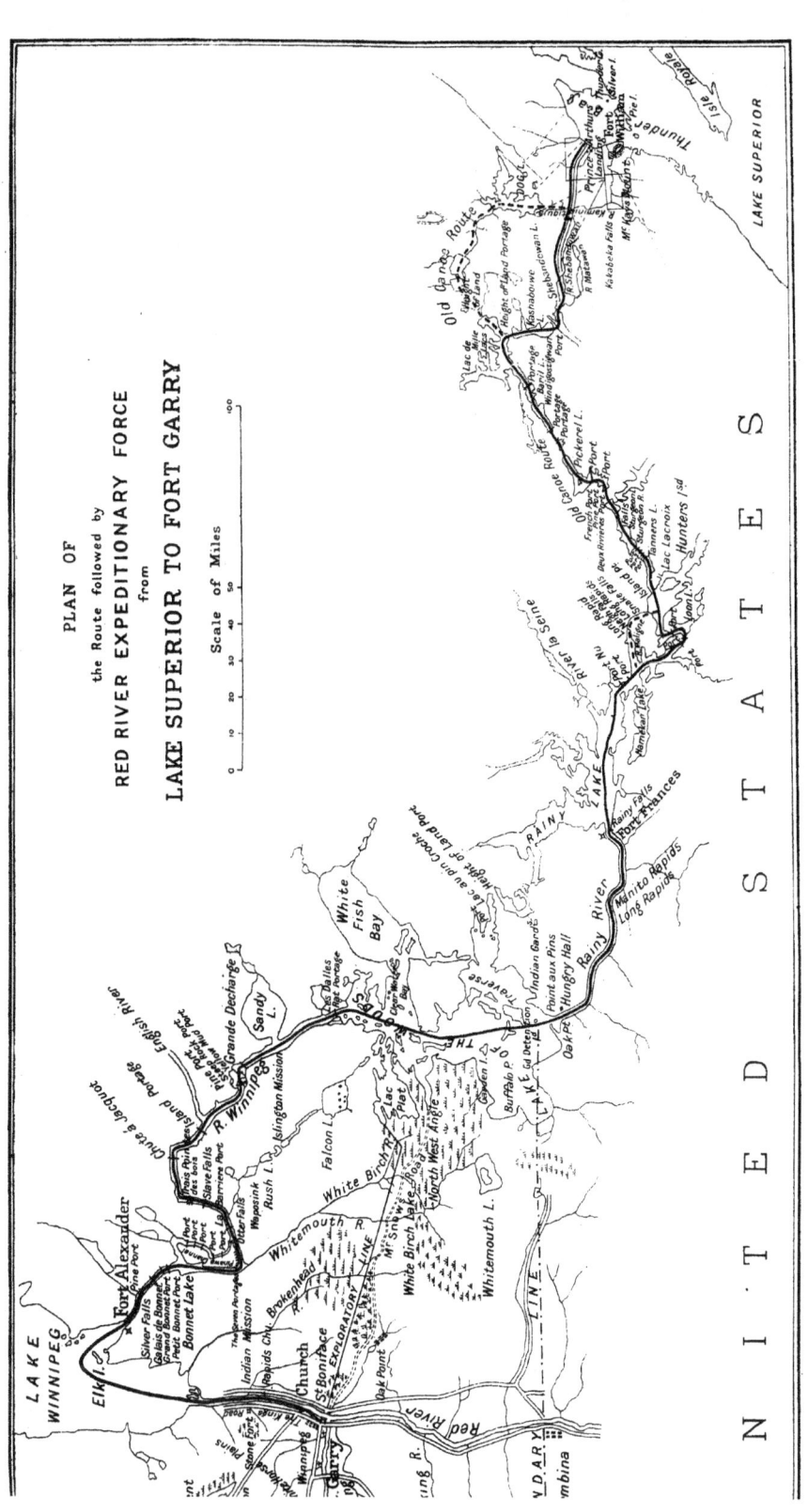

between June and November 1871 detachments of the Battalion were employed in the erection of forts Nos. 1 and 2 at Point Levis on the right bank of the St. Lawrence.

It had now been decided by the British Government to withdraw, so far as possible, all regiments from the Colonies, leaving the latter to make their own arrangements for home defence. In accordance with this decision all British regiments were withdrawn from Canada proper, and our Battalion was in consequence ordered to evacuate Quebec and to proceed to Halifax, Nova Scotia.

This Battalion had in September 1759 been present at the surrender of Quebec by the French and had seen the British Ensign hoisted on the Citadel by an officer of the Royal Artillery. After the interval of one hundred and twelve years it became the duty of the Battalion, as the last unit of the British Regular Army at Quebec, to consign the Imperial Flag to the keeping of another officer R.A., the flag of the Dominion of Canada being hoisted in its place.

The long association of The King's Royal Rifle Corps with the Dominion of Canada is graven on the memory of the regiment and, it is hoped and believed, equally cherished by the people of Canada.

On November 11 the Battalion embarked on H.M.S. *Orontes*, and on the 17th landed at Halifax, Nova Scotia. To the deep regret of all, Colonel Feilden, C.M.G., had recently retired on half-pay, and on arrival at Halifax the Battalion was met by its new commanding officer, Lieut.-Colonel Charles A. B. Gordon.

The happy days of Colonel Feilden's command were often subsequently recalled. He took no further part in military life, but a few years later became Member of Parliament for a division of Lancashire. Although without any claim to especial brilliancy, Colonel Feilden was a good soldier and the model of an English gentleman.

At Halifax the new Valise Equipment was issued to the Battalion in place of the time-honoured but anachronistic knapsack.

The establishment of the Battalion was now fixed at 30 Officers, 708 O.R. for the service companies; and 4 Officers and 108 O.R. for those at the depôt.

At Halifax also the Snider Rifle was returned into store and superseded by the Martini Henry. Here the 1st Battalion was united with the 3rd, and the 2nd with the 4th, the idea being that one out of each pair should be at home and furnish drafts for its fellow abroad. A year or two afterwards the 1st and 4th were united together, and the 2nd with the 3rd; but the system broke down, for the number of Infantry Battalions abroad was invariably greater than the number at home, and not long afterwards it happened that for several years the 1st Battalion was obliged to supply drafts to each of the other three.

Time passed uneventfully at Halifax. It was a most popular station and excellent for the training of officers and men in the ' hunter's art.'

Towards the end of 1875 Lieut. H. S. Marsham resigned the Adjutancy, which he had held for six years, and was succeeded by Lieut. Mordaunt Boyle. During the winter 1875–6 the Battalion sustained a great loss by the death of the Quartermaster, John Toole. At this time and for some years afterwards there were two names constantly on the lips of the officers of the Battalion. One was that of Captain John Owen Young, whose performance in the Red River has already been described. He was well-known as an excellent soldier and most amusing companion. The other name was that of John Toole, a man intensely loved and intensely respected by all. Of his origin little is known, but he was well brought up and educated by his parents and appears never to have lost an opportunity of adding to that education. He served with the Battalion at the Siege of Delhi, and happened to be Sergeant of the Guard on the day on which the bodies of the native princes executed personally by Major Hodson were brought in. As a Quartermaster, to the office of which he was appointed in 1866, he was second to none of the many talented Quartermasters whose names are household words in the Regiment. Almost his last words to his friend, Captain John Crosbie, as he lay dying were, 'It is not death we fear. It is the parting from our friends.'

In December 1876 the Battalion embarked for England in the H.M.S. *Tamar*. The cold was intense, the masts and spars covered with icicles, and for some days the Captain steered a due southerly course in order to reach a less inclement latitude. The stormy weather which so often pursued this Battalion at sea was not wanting. The gales were terrific, but for a Government transport the *Tamar* was perhaps exceptionally seaworthy, and on January 1, 1877, anchor was safely cast at Spithead.

CHAPTER XVI

On arrival at Aldershot in 1869 the 4th Battalion was quartered in the Permanent Barracks and attached to the Brigade of Major-General J. G. Carey, C.B., who inspected it on arrival and expressed satisfaction at its appearance. Here it remained until September 1870, when B.H.Q. proceeded to Colchester, and provided a detachment of 280 R. and F. for Landguard Fort.

On January 1, 1871, the strength of the Battalion and of the depôts of the three other battalions attached to it was as follows:

	Sergeants.	Buglers.	Riflemen.
4th Battalion	45	21	809
Depôt of the 1st Battalion	6	4	62
2nd Battalion	9	3	41
3rd Battalion	9	5	96
Total	69	33	1,008

The system of attaching to the Battalion at home the depôts of those on foreign service did not last long; but in the present instance, at all events, it had the advantage of enabling officers of other Battalions to realise Colonel Hawley's system and his standard of efficiency for Riflemen.

In May 1871 the Adjutant, Latham Brownrigg, who had held his office for upwards of 12 years, was promoted to the rank of Captain, and the adjutancy given to Lieut.

Henry Donald Browne, who proved himself one of the finest soldiers we have ever had in the 60th.

On September 2 (1871) the Battalion left Colchester—which it was destined to see no more until the lapse of nearly 38 years—*en route* for Aldershot, where it took part in the Autumn Manœuvres. In these Manœuvres Hawley's Riflemen (as they were commonly called) played a prominent part. To such an extent had military training in the army as a whole been neglected that the Riflemen were considered to be somewhat exceptional in having been taught such elementary arts as that of pitching tents and constructing Field Kitchens. In the field their alertness, rapidity of extension and manœuvring were the theme of frequent remark;[1] but in parades in close order the rapidity, as already remarked, was due not to running about but to the instantaneous execution of Colonel Hawley's word of command. An incidental result of this acquirement was that at Brigade Parades on the order being given to the line or line of columns to advance the Riflemen were a yard or two ahead before the other battalions had begun to move.

Another feature was the way in which the Colonel saved his men unnecessary fatigue. So nicely calculated were the time and distance of the march to the Brigade parade that the Battalion invariably arrived at the nick of time, instead of appearing a quarter or perhaps half an hour too soon, as was often the case with other units.

At these Manœuvres the Battalion was attached to the 1st Brigade of the 3rd Division, the Brigade and Divisional Commanders being respectively Major-Generals Brownrigg, C.B., and Sir Charles Staveley, K.C.B. The whole Army Corps numbered about 30,000 men. Personal

---

[1] The rate of marching was 120 paces to the minute. The rate of other regiments was 116.

command was taken by H.R.H. The Duke of Cambridge.

The manœuvres began on September 8, and at their conclusion on the 21st the Battalion quitted Aldershot for Winchester, where it arrived on the 28th. B Company, under Captain H. R. Milligan, was sent on detachment to the powder magazine at Marchwood on the west shore of Southampton Water.

On August 12, 1872, the Battalion, accompanied by one company made up of the attached depôts, marched to Blandford for the purpose of once more taking part in the Autumn Manœuvres. It encamped *en route* on Southampton Common, Lyndhurst Racecourse, and Woolbridge Common. On arrival at Blandford it formed part of the 2nd Brigade (Major-General F. P. Harding, C.B.) 2nd Division (Major-General S. Brownrigg) of the 1st Army Corps, under Lieut.-General Sir John Michel, who commanded the southern force operating against the 2nd or northern Army Corps. It will be remembered that in the China War of 1860 Sir John Michel commanded a division of which the 2nd Battalion of our Regiment formed a unit. He was a man of military talent and great independence of character.

The manœuvres took place on Salisbury Plain, and were marked by an incident which at the time was the subject of considerable comment. By common agreement the Infantry contained no smarter or more efficient battalion than Hawley's Riflemen. In the Cavalry the 10th Hussars, under the well-known Colonel Valentine Baker, were unsurpassed; and between these two corps existed a certain healthy emulation. One day the Battalion while lying down in line by the side of a narrow ridge was charged on the right flank and rear by the 10th, who had concentrated unseen on the further side of the ridge. Colonel

Hawley was not for an instant taken about by this unexpected charge. At his word of command the riflemen turned about and changed ranks—the supernumeraries lying down under the swords of the new front rank—and met the Cavalry with the full volume of its fire. But by this time the 10th were pulling up at the prescribed distance and the firing accordingly ceased. Had the cartridges contained bullets the charge must have failed; but Colonel Sir Garnet Wolseley, Chief Umpire, coming up at the moment placed the Battalion out of action, on the ground that—as claimed by the 10th—it had 'been taken in rear.' Hawley refused to admit the justice of the decision. 'Understand, Sir,' cried he in a voice of thunder to Wolseley and Baker, 'that the Rifles have no rear.' Wolseley adhered, however, to his decision, on the ground that although the Colonel's action would have repulsed the charge, the command 'Change Ranks' was not to be found in the Field Exercises of that day. By the rules for Manœuvres at that time in force the decision was justified; but it was quite contrary to the spirit of Wolseley's own ideas and instruction; and even his *fidus Achates*, the late General Sir Frederick Maurice (Senior), in one of his writings quotes the incident as an instance of inconsistency on the part of his hero.' Sir Garnet's experience of regimental duty was very slight, and it was believed by some that he was actuated by a certain jealousy of Colonel Hawley's pre-eminence as a battalion commander; but it is just possible that he wished

---

[1] Colonel Hawley distinctly told the writer that his neglect to post a sentry on the ridge behind which the 10th concentrated was due to the fact that the 'Cease Fire had sounded.' But this statement, made more than 20 years after the incident, is not confirmed by any other Rifleman who have related it. General Astley Terry, present as a Captain, saw Valentine Baker go up to Wolseley—evidently to point out his intention. Terry reported the fact to Major Carleton, and the latter to Hawley, but by that time the charge was in full swing. Both General Terry and Colonel Donald Browne, at that time Adjutant, considered that Hawley—for a wonder—had been caught napping.

to show that the Field Exercises were out-of-date. Strict adherence to the rules laid down therein to achieve the equivalent of 'Change Ranks' would have needed ten minutes, for the manœuvre of 'Counter Marching' was singularly cumbrous.

Although from a modern point of view the Manœuvres of that period were of a somewhat primitive nature, the troops were undoubtedly the better for them. But in consequence of the opinion that more 'spade work' was needed before the Army should be ready for combined operations on a large scale, Manœuvres were abandoned for nearly a quarter of a century. As regards those of 1872, Colonel Donald Browne in a MS. memoir of the 4th Battalion writes :

'It is probable that no Regiment in the two opposing forces was better known either to the soldiers or the the public than the 4th Battalion, which was constantly being quoted as a model of smartness in camp and quickness of movement in the field.'

These comments are valuable, for Colonel Browne was not in the habit of giving or appreciating indiscriminate praise.

In March 1873 Colonel Hawley was appointed to the post of Assistant-Military Secretary to the Commander-in-Chief. His long period of command thus terminated.

On the evening preceding his departure Colonel Hawley, in accordance with regimental custom, dined at the Mess on the invitation of his brother officers, and his health was drunk with every token of respectful affection. Hawley had set his face against speechifying at Mess, and in returning thanks apologised for breaking his own rules. 'But,' he added, 'there are occasions when an exception must be made,' and in a few touching and impressive words expressed his deep regret that a period of command which had been to him one of unqualified pleasure, had at last come to an end.

It is not too much to say that every officer of the battalion felt that he was losing one who had been almost a father to him. Never was a man more loved and honoured by every one under his command.

Colonel Browne, at that time Hawley's Adjutant, writes :—

'It has probably been given to few Commanding Officers in time of peace to obtain a greater hold of those who served under him than he gained and maintained during the 13 years of his command, and his name is still fresh in the Battalion though few remain who served in it with him.

'His farewell remarks published in Battalion Orders bear a lasting testimony to the esteem in which he held all those who had been associated with him in his duties.

'Battalion Orders, March 28, 1873.

'The Field-Marshal Commanding-in-Chief having been pleased to select the Colonel commanding for the appointment of Assistant Military Secretary at Head Quarters from the 1st April,

'Colonel Hawley this day relinquishes his trust as Lieut.-Colonel of the 4th Battalion with a feeling of deep obligation to those who have assisted him to carry on the duties of the Battalion to the satisfaction of his superiors. The generous aid he has received from the Field Officers, the never flagging interest which the Company Officers have taken in the welfare and rights of their men, the intimate knowledge which the Staff Officers have shown of their constant duties, the excellent bearing and good judgment displayed by the Staff and Company Non-commissioned Officers, the sobriety, intelligence and activity of the Riflemen have caused the Battalion to be known far and wide as an efficient and model force.

'That God's blessing may be with one and all who have so faithfully associated with him during his command is the prayer of their friend, who now bids them " Adieu." '

When appearing on parade for the last time as Commanding Officer of the 4th Battalion he made an attempt to say a word of farewell ; but the effort was too much for him, and after a pause painful to his hearers he could only mutter the word 'Dismiss!' He took pains to keep to himself the moment of departure, but it nevertheless leaked out, and the whole Battalion turned out in the Barrack Square as a last token of love and respect.

Hawley's period of command was long looked upon as the 'Golden Age' of the Battalion; but his influence extended far beyond the limits not only of the Battalion but even of the regiment; and gradually, although no doubt unconsciously, permeated the atmosphere of the whole Army. It is wonderful even now (1924) to hear the opinions of Colonel Hawley expressed by officers of other regiments who had come into contact with him. No branch of regimental life escaped his notice. His institutions were good and efficient. The regimental workshops were exceptional. His capacity for business, aided, no doubt, by good and loyal Quartermasters, enabled him to purchase for the canteen, etc., in the open market articles of the best quality and at the cheapest rate. The food and messing of the whole regiment was his particular care.

Colonel Hawley was a deeply religious man, from whom bad language or violence of censure was unknown. In regard to non-commissioned and other ranks his was a great educative force. He was intimately acquainted with the characters of his men. He was frequently called upon to furnish drafts to other battalions, and it was noticeable that in their new battalion 4th Battalion men were selected for special employment. Punishment was resorted to only when unavoidable, and it was known throughout the Battalion that it was not on punishment but on regimental esprit de corps that he relied. On one occasion a man was brought before him for an offence calculated to entail an entry in the Regimental Defaulters'

Book. Although Hawley knew the man's character, he referred as a matter of form to the Captain of the Company. 'Bad, sir,' was the reply; 'but I have reason to believe that if given a chance he will do better.' The Colonel looked for a moment at the Officer, then turning to the prisoner said in his deep voice, 'You hear what your Captain says! Admonished!' The result thoroughly justified his leniency.

The next year the Commander-in-Chief in his notes on the inspection made particular remark on the absence of crime in the Battalion, which he attributed to Colonel Hawley, 'its excellent late Commanding Officer.'

At the period of which we have been speaking Company training in the present sense of the term was unknown, but it was Hawley's practice from time to time to strike a Company off duty in order to enable it to be drilled and manœuvred at its full strength by the Company Officers. He was also a great believer in oral instruction as supplementary to that on the field; and—particularly in places devoid of manœuvre ground—lectures illustrated by small blocks of wood were habitually given by Company Officers in the Barrack Room.

The manner in which under his auspices Battalion drill was simplified and unnecessary words of command eliminated has already been touched upon. At a regimental dinner many years afterwards, Sir Redvers Buller, in proposing the health of General Hawley, observed that the manœuvres introduced into the Field Exercises for the first time in 1896 had been habitually performed by Hawley and the 4th Battalion in 1862. A person who is 34 years in advance of his age is certainly a great man.

As Assistant Military Secretary and later on as Deputy Adjutant-General Hawley did good work, but it was not the work that fitted in best with his own genius, which shone brightest in the personal command of men. He should undoubtedly have been given command of a Brigade at Aldershot or of larger bodies of men at summer drills. Had this been done his influence would have extended still further and more quickly to the advantage of the Army in general.

In 1877 he was promoted to the rank of Major-General, and six years later, when Deputy Adjutant-General, was retired at the age of sixty-two.[1] In 1890 he became a Colonel Commandant of the Regiment and spent his last years at Cirencester, where in 1898 he passed away.

Upon August 9 he was borne to his rest by a privileged few of his old comrades. By those Riflemen who followed him to the grave it was felt that there had no doubt been other men as great—nay, greater as the world reckons greatness—but that there were few who have left stronger or more lasting impress upon their contemporaries than did General Hawley. Memory recalled to them the fact that it was largely due to Hawley and to Hawley's teaching that in the last fifty years The King's Royal Rifle Corps has attained and maintained its high standard of efficiency and of military renown, and that it was also largely due to their great Colonel that so numerous a band of Riflemen, acquiring through him—directly or indirectly—their inspiration, have done great and lasting service for the Regiment, for the British Army, and for the Empire. The name which The K.R.R.C. holds to-day is his lasting monument and the reputation of its sons his best epitaph.

Among General Hawley's pupils who have now passed away were four outstanding figures, the characteristics of whom deserve to be rescued from oblivion.

1. REDVERS HENRY BULLER was a remarkable per-

---

[1] At the time when Hawley was D.A.G. Lord Wolseley was Adjutant-General. There is no doubt that the two men failed to understand each other.

sonality, of independent opinion and habit of thought. Endued with unusual physical strength and clever with his hands, he had in a high degree three qualities—an astonishing capacity for work, whether of mind or body; great love of argument; and a personal magnetism which gained for him the love, confidence, and devotion of every N.C.O. and private soldier with whom he came in contact. Buller was the last man to curry favour with them; but that an electric current of sympathy flowed incessantly between him and them is undeniable. Such a power is given to few English soldiers. Marlborough may perhaps be the only exception. With officers Redvers Buller was not always tactful; but those who knew him well realised the fact that a manner at times brusque concealed a most kindly and sympathetic heart.

Although again and again distinguished for courage, resource, and coolness in the field—he earned the Victoria Cross three times on the same day—his greatest work was undoubtedly executed as Quartermaster-General and Adjutant-General at the War Office; and his re-organization of the Army Service Corps was a masterpiece, the value of which was abundantly shown during the war with Germany.

The Duke of Cambridge, the C.-in-C. under whom Buller served, had the highest opinion of him, and an affectionate regard enhanced by appreciation of his loyalty and counsel. Sir Redvers, had he wished it, could have succeeded the Duke as Commander-in-Chief, but stood aside in favour of Lord Wolseley.

Hard work at the War Office told on Buller, and he began to age comparatively early in life. Although his administrative powers shone brightly during his command in South Africa, he had—at the age of sixty—passed the culminating point of his intellectual vigour in the field. Sir Redvers' abilities were of a very high order, and included great moral courage, a quality as rare as it is unappreciated by politicians.

2. FRANCIS WALLACE GRENFELL was a man of very different characteristics. Intensely popular with his brother officers and essentially a *bon camarade*, he made no attempt in his earlier days to study his profession. But Grenfell found himself the object of Fortune's embraces which he had never solicited. His career was marred by no reverse. Success followed upon success; but although exploited by his own natural abilities and by the willing service of his subordinates, he could never quite make up for the idleness of his first fourteen years in the service. For ten subsequent years, while in the prime of life, he was, however, almost incessantly engaged in warfare, and on several occasions sucessfully commanded a force in action. But it was comparatively late in life and in a civil capacity that Grenfell did his best work. Shortly before the close of the last century he was appointed Governor and Commander-in-Chief at Malta. Internal difficulties and keen political feelings among the population demanded tact combined with firmness, and the success with which he managed a difficult situation amply justified the peerage conferred on him.

With increasing years Lord Grenfell appeared to gain rather than lose intellectual power and activity; and a great debt of gratitude is due from us to his memory for his administration of our regimental affairs while occupying the position of senior Colonel Commandant.

3. EDWARD HUTTON was a man of lovable and most generous nature. His energy and enthusiasm were unbounded. His life was spent in the determination to develop his abilities and broaden the range of his knowledge by careful and unceasing study. His opinion on general

subjects was marked by a depth and breadth of view at times quite remarkable.¹ The fruits of his studies and reflection were given to his profession. No one could have done more than he did to encourage his brother officers in professional zeal and study. His influence in this respect extended far beyond the circle of his own regiment. Hutton took a leading part in the Mounted Infantry movement, which, although now defunct, produced some of the best soldiers in the Army. It was stated on good authority that the Division entrusted to him at the beginning of the Great War was the best trained of all the new Divisions. But his greatest and most *impériale* achievement lay in the successful organisation and training of Colonial forces in Canada and Australia. The results of this work were amply shown by the War, and can hardly be overestimated.

To Sir Edward Hutton must be given the chief credit for the re-organisation and expansion of the Celer et Audax Club, begun in 1908. At the outset his ideas met with opposition but are now firmly established.

4. HENRY DONALD BROWNE differed from the trio mentioned in the fact that—to use a phrase common on the Turf—his form was never exposed. This was due to lack of opportunity alone. His abilities were second to none, but whereas fortune, as already noted, exhausted her favours upon Lord Grenfell, to Colonel Browne she denied them entirely. The latter combined handsome features with great charm of manners. It may be said with confidence that none of the other three could have

---

[1] A proof of Hutton's success in self-education is given by the fact that at the age of 66 he was a much better horseman than he had been at 30. Of his acquaintance with equine anatomy, a remarkable proof was given at some 'Mounted Infantry' sports near Aldershot. A horse had been so badly injured that the Veterinary Surgeon ordered it to be shot on the spot. Hutton, coming up, passed his hand up and down the horse's forequarter and exclaimed, 'Rubbish, take it back to the stables.' And the horse walked away sound.

come near him as commander of a battalion, and he gave evidence of a certain indescribable reserve of power that leads to the belief that he would have been a successful general in the field. But his service was almost entirely regimental, and he never had a chance of taking part in war. At Newcastle, Natal, in 1881, he had, however, some months' experience of Staff work under many of the conditions of active service, and his work is stated to have been very good indeed. Whereas the judgment of Sir Redvers Buller was occasionally, and that of Sir Edward Hutton more often, at fault, Donald Browne's was always reliable.

To make an actual comparison between the merits of these four men is difficult, but—taking the analogy of an electric power chart—it may be said that whereas the abilities of Buller and Hutton perhaps reached a higher peak, those of Grenfell and Browne showed a better average level. All were great readers and men of high general education, but none showed much aptitude for games.[1] All were gifted with the artistic sense, and—excepting Buller—painted well in oils or water colours. Grenfell in his earlier days was intensely fond of playing the violin, and Browne the piano. Hutton was perhaps the only one who in the ordinary acceptation of the term would be called imaginative, yet Buller's creation of the Army Service Corps could never have been achieved by any one devoid of imagination in its highest sense.

All four would have readily acknowledged that their success in life was primarily due to Colonel Hawley's initiative and instruction.

[1] At Eton Redvers Buller rowed in 'The Victory.'

EPILOGUE

HAVING brought the regimental story up to the date of Colonel Hawley's retirement from the 4th Battalion, the writer lays down the pen which he took up in 1908 at the request of Sir Redvers Buller, and Lord Grenfell, Sir Redvers' successor as senior Colonel Commandant.

He hopes that as time goes on new information regarding the earlier years of the Regiment may come to light, and that it may be embodied either in a new edition of the present work or in some future one of wider scope and greater value. Any such information bearing upon the first seventy years of its history must be sought, either across the Atlantic in the U.S.A. and in Canada, or among the papers of private individuals in Germany and Switzerland.

Each of the three volumes published has, to some extent, contained the story of a great regimental Colonel, whose life, abilities, example, and instruction have had so deep an effect upon the Regiment that they may be said to have formed the model upon which its history and performances have been founded.

To these three men we owe a debt of gratitude which can never be repaid. Many regiments in the British Army have perhaps had no commanding Officer of similar calibre, and few probably, if any, have been fortunate enough to have such a trio as Bouquet, De Rothenburg, and Hawley, while the fact that of these three two were of foreign birth has been no detriment to The K.R.R.C.[1]

It is a little curious that none of the battalions which they respectively commanded are still in existence. Nevertheless the spirit of the trio pervades, and it may be hoped will continue to pervade, the Regiment for centuries to come.

In the foregoing pages have been mentioned the names of many other remarkable men in our regiment, who to a greater or lesser extent impressed their personality thereon or added to its prestige. Among those who became General Officers may be recalled the names of the two Field-Marshals, Sir John Forster FitzGerald and Lord Clyde, as well as those of John Stanwix, Charles Laurence, Lord Howe, William Haviland, who earned distinction in the Seven Years' War, of Augustin Prevost, the defender of Savannah in the American War of Independence, of Robert Lethbridge, Edward Codd, George Mackie, Anson Bonham, all of whom made a reputation in the West Indies during the Revolutionary War with France.[2] Sir George Prevost was the subject of alternate praise and blame for his conduct as C.-in-C. in the defence of Canada during the second American War in 1812–14, Sir George Townsend Walker and Sir John Hope were Generals of Division under Wellington, Sir James Schoedde was

---

[1] Colonel Henry Donald Browne, who commanded the 3rd Battalion at a later date, may well have been the equal of these three; but his period of command, limited to a bare four years, was less than half that enjoyed by those predecessors; and his influence, although all in all to the Battalion which he commanded, could from force of circumstances hardly permeate the whole Regiment to the same extent. In one particular he was also under peculiar disadvantage. Bouquet, De Rothenburg, and Hawley all commanded newly raised battalions which may be compared with virgin soil. Donald Browne was under the necessity of digging up weeds before he could sow his seed. It was not the least of his merits that, although aware of the short time at his disposal, he was determined not to build up his battalion until he had laid a secure foundation. The one that he commanded has shared the fate of those of the Trio.

[2] General Bonham did good service as D.Q.M.G. not only in the attack in Martinique, etc., but also in the Walcheren Expedition.

MEN OF DISTINCTION 305

distinguished in the war of 1842 with China, and Lord Melville, Sir John Jones, Adrian Hope, and Sir Arthur Cunynghame did great service in more recent times.

Among Officers of lower rank will be remembered John Bradstreet, capturer of Fort Frontenac, Jean Marc Prevost, the hero of Briar's Creek, Gordon, who captured Tobago, Charles de Salaberry, the victor of Chateauguay, William Williams, who commanded the 5th Battalion at Bussaco, Fuentes de Oñoro, Ciudad Rodrigo, Badajoz, and Salamanca, J. P. Galiffe, commander of the same Battalion at Vitoria, the Nivelle, Orthez, and Toulouse, the Hon. R. H. Molyneux, the Hon. A. F. Ellis, Joseph Bradshaw and C. L. Nesbitt. Webbe Butler, a man of quiet determination, commanded a Battalion with credit, and the names of Thomas Mitchell and G. C. Kelly, celebrated Adjutants of the 1st Battalion, also deserve mention.

Major-General Peter Hunter served in our Regiment from 1781 to his death in 1804, beginning as a Major and ending as Colonel Commandant. He is said to have been the son of a landowner in Ayrshire. His career is little known, but he probably served at all events in the latter phases of the American War of Independence, and he had a command during the Irish rebellion in 1798. In 1799 General Hunter was appointed Lieut.-Governor of Upper Canada and commander of all the troops in both Provinces. Mr. A. G. Bradley, in ' The Making of Canada,' says :—

'Hunter ruled Upper Canada for six years without friction ; and that is almost all that is known of this most shadowy figure on the whole record of Canadian Governors, though evidently not a shadow in fact, but rather an energetic, military man, who got himself obeyed and earned no bad name. There are plenty of his letters, but they tell nothing except that he was diligent, blunt, and straightforward, and met with little opposition. He describes Toronto in 1804 as being without a single public building. His Council of nine and his Legislature of sixteen met in two rooms, erected as the nucleus of Government House. . . . Hunter was unmarried, and in his 60th year he died at Quebec, during one of his frequent visits that as Commander-in-Chief he was compelled to make. He was buried in the new cathedral, where a tablet may be seen erected to his memory.'

Small as is the record of General Hunter, he seems to have had many of the qualifications of a Rifleman, for he kept himself out of sight, shunning self-advertisement, while insisting on obedience to his orders.

It will be remembered that when the Battalion was raised it contained, in addition to the ordinary officers, twenty engineers. Of these the most distinguished was Major Samuel Holland, a member of an English family which for a good many years had resided in the Netherlands. It was at Nimwegan that S. Jan Holland was born in 1728. At the age of 17 he joined the army of the Dutch, whose country was then invaded by the French, but obtained a commission in the 60th when raised in 1756, and appears to have been attached to the staff of Lord Loudoun.

During the Siege of Louisbourg Lieut. Holland was attached to Wolfe's Brigade as an engineer and entrusted with the attack on the section from the North-East harbour to the West gate, resulting in the capitulation of the town. Holland was then employed in making a survey of the fortifications, etc., being assisted by the Master of H.M.S. *Pembroke*, later known as the celebrated Captain James Cook. Holland then accompanied Lord Rollo, who took possession of the Isle St. Jean, at the present day known as Prince Edward's Island, which he was directed to prepare for the accommodation of the French families who had hitherto resided in Cape Breton. In the year following, 1759, he was present at the battle of Quebec, and held up the wounded hand of the dying

General Wolfe, with whom he was on terms of intimacy.[1] At the end of the Seven Years' War the North American Colonies were for purposes of survey divided into two portions; and of that north of the Potomac River, including the whole of Canada, Captain Holland was made Surveyor-General. His services in this capacity were of the greatest importance to the State, and the basis on which his surveys were founded has been continued to the present day.

When the War of Independence broke out in 1775, Holland, having peremptorily refused tempting offers to join the rebel army, had some difficulty in making his way to England, but was sent back again with the title of Surveyor-General of Canada. He died in 1801.

Other of the regimental engineers were J. F. des Barres, whose career has been described in Vol. I. of these Annals, and Bernard Ratzer, who became Surveyor-General in Jamaica, where in 1784 he died while in temporary command of our 1st Battalion.

But notable as were the abilities and services of these members of our regiment during the period embraced by the first three volumes of these Annals, namely 1755 to 1873, we find one name only that could be fairly claimed as that of an Empire builder. General Sir Frederick Haldimand, born at Yverdun in Switzerland, began his military career under Frederick the Great of Prussia. When our Regiment was raised he was appointed Lieut.-Colonel of the 2nd Battalion. Being transferred to the 4th Battalion he commanded the Grenadiers of Abercrombie's army in the sanguinary repulse at Ticonderoga,

---

[1] Four persons only were actually present when Wolfe expired, viz. Holland, Lieutenant Brown of the 28th, the Assistant Suregeon of the 48th, and a Grenadier named James Henderson. A picture of the General's death by Penny shows these four only. The better-known picture of Benjamin West is purely a work of imagination.

defeated the French with 8 Companies of his Battalion at Oswego, and in 1760 was present at the capture of Montreal.[1] Haldimand would seem to have been a man of tact. At Oswego on the death of General Prideaux he became senior officer of the regular army present; but rather than imperil the success of the operations by a personal dispute he resigned his claims to command in favour of Sir William Johnson.

It is possible that Sir Jeffrey Amherst had heard of his tactful disposition, for on entering Montreal he appointed Haldimand Governor of the city. The fact that French was his native language was of course an immense advantage; and Haldimand, probably more than any other officer in the British Army, was better able to sympathise with the views, predilections, and prejudices of its French inhabitants. He was largely responsible for the fact that the French Canadians were allowed to maintain their old custom and, more particularly, their own code of law. In this way the Colonel sowed the seed which enabled French and English to intermarry and live together harmoniously.

After retaining command of the Trois Rivières district until the year 1764, Colonel Haldimand was transferred to a new sphere of labour at Pensacola on the death of Colonel Bouquet, whose valuable papers, at present deposited in the British Museum, are being collected and collated. In Florida Haldimand remained until about 1775, when he went for three years to England. On the resignation of Sir Guy Carleton (afterwards Lord Dorchester) in 1778, Haldimand, who six years previously had been promoted to the rank of Major-General, was made Governer and Commander-in-Chief in Canada.

---

[1] Haldimand's action at Oswego was the subject of high praise from Colonel Bouquet, who considered that his friend had shown great powers of generalship.

The post was one of difficulty. Invasion by the rebels was constantly threatened, and powers of resistance were very limited. The French Canadians, although preferring the Crown to Congress, were—naturally enough —not over-enthusiastic in the cause of people who had annexed their territory less than twenty years previously. They were also well aware that not only was France at war with England, but had despatched a contingent of regular troops which was now fighting side by side with the rebels.

It is therefore no matter for surprise that complaints should have been occasionally made against the measures deemed by General Haldimand essential for the defence of the province.

It is more than likely that, surrounded as he was by intriguing foes and lukewarm friends, the General may at times—and rightly—have displayed something of the iron hand. But Kingsford, the historian of Canada, observes that:

'The vindication of his Government is completely established by the records in which his acts are recorded. It was fortunate for the tranquillity of the province that a man of his well-regulated and administrative capacity was placed in the position which he held. . . . His high sense of duty, his truth, and his honourable life will obtain for him the distinguished mention in Canadian history to which he is fully entitled.'

And of General Haldimand, Bradley, in his well-known work 'The Making of Canada,' writes : ' He served through the French war in America with more than credit. . . . After the war he held chief command in Florida, New York, and at Three Rivers.'

The historian goes on to describe the General's administration in glowing terms.

The defence of Canada was Haldimand's first care.

His regular force consisted of but three regular battalions only 1,200 strong, and 2,000 not very efficient Brunswickers. To meet the danger of a French fleet sailing up the St. Lawrence the General applied in vain for a ship or two to winter at Quebec, but by equipping merchant vessels he successfully hunted privateers and maintained some sort of communication with the outer world. He strengthened the frontier by the erection of Blockhouses at La Chaudière, St. Francis, and other points. He destroyed the American trade of supplies on Lake Champlain. He improved the navigation of the St. Lawrence by originating the system of canals, thereby avoiding the long and difficult portages at the rapids. On the recognition of the independence of the United States, Sir Frederick Haldimand, who received the K.B. in 1784, provided land and shelter for the large quantities of loyalists driven from their homes in the south and seeking the protection of the British flag. These refugees, known as the United Empire Loyalists, and their descendants have proved themselves a tower of strength to Great Britain. Ontario, described as being at that time a shaggy wilderness but with great possibilities, was selected as their main settlement. A territory for the Indian tribes known as the Six Nations was also established with fair success. The arrival of the Loyalists is pronounced by Bradley to have been 'the weightiest event in Canadian History,' and the success of their settlement owes to its Swiss Governor more than words can describe.[1]

Sir Frederick resigned his appointment in 1784. He returned first to England, then to his home in Switzerland, and in 1791 died at Yverdun on the shore of the Lake of Neuchatel.

[1] 'The Making of Canada,' p. 157.

SIR F. HALDIMAND

In England the services of Sir Frederick Haldimand—as is the case with those of many Empire Builders—are forgotten, and his very name is unknown. In Canada his memory is ever fresh; and the importance of the parts played by him in the administration and establishment of the then newly acquired country receives its full meed of recognition. Our Regiment has every reason to feel pride in its Swiss Colonel Commandant.

'In the Chapel of Henry VII. Westminister Abbey there is a brass plate bearing a coat of arms in colours, with the circular motto "Tria juncta in uno" on a shield supported by an Indian on either side, while at their feet is a scroll, "Mitivs jubetur exemplo;" and beneath is the inscription "Du chevalier Frederick Haldimand, Général et Colonel d'un Regiment d'Infanterie au service de sa Majesté; cy-devant Général Commandant en chef dans L'Amérique septentrionale; Gouverneur de la Province de Québec; Inspecteur Général des Troupes dans les Isles Occidentales, et Chevalier du très honorable Ordre du BAIN.

'"Installé le 19me Jour de May MDCCLXXXVIII."'[1]

So much for the deeds of the Regiment in the past. But the Riflemen of the future must not forget that it has, on occasion, met with failure as well as success, and that however well the Regiment may have done in the past, perfection on this earth is unattainable. It cannot rest on its oars, but must hope in the future to do even better and greater work for King and country. It may therefore be well to end these lines as they began, viz. with the words of the dying General Braddock; 'We shall know better how to do it the next time.'

[1] 'Makers of Canada' series, 'Sir Frederick Haldimand,' by Jean N. McIlwraith, p. 346.

APPENDIX A

SUMMARY OF REGIMENTAL EVENTS BETWEEN 1873 AND 1918

LIEUT.-COLONEL H. F. WILLIAMS, a distinguished veteran of the Punjaub and Mutiny campaign, and at a later date a Colonel Commandant, was appointed as successor to Colonel Hawley in the 4th Battalion [1]; but neither he, Major A. J. Fitzgerald nor R. J. E. Robertson, successively gazetted, took up the command, which eventually fell to Major Charles Williamson. Williamson's health soon necessitated his retirement, and in 1875 his place was taken by Major R. W. Hinxman, who had gained distinction in the 1st Battalion at Delhi.

In the autumn of 1873 Sir Garnet—afterwards Lord—Wolesley appreciatively asked that the 4th Battalion might be included among the regiments detailed for his expeditionary force to Ashanti. The request was refused. He then asked for the services of Captains Young and Buller. The former had quitted the service, but Buller distinguished himself in the subsequent operations, and received not only a Brevet Majority but the C.B. as well.

After a period spent at Portland and Devonport [2] the Battalion in 1875 moved to Ireland and was quartered in Dublin, where it found itself once more under the command of General Sir John Michel, C.-in-C. in Ireland. Sir John in his younger days had been a member of our Regiment, but for so short a time that he could

---

[1] At Delhi Williams had been so badly wounded that his leg was barely saved from amputation. He was sent to the Hills, but his wound would not heal. One day he slipped and fell down. In most cases such an accident would have been the *coup de grâce* for the leg; but in the present instance exactly the reverse occurred, and recovery was thenceforward continuous.

[2] At Devonport a rather remarkable feat by one of the Officers deserves perhaps passing mention. Lieut. the Hon. Alwyne Greville made a bet that he would walk blindfolded from the Raglan Barracks to the Royal Hotel, a distance of about two miles. He performed the feat successfully and apparently without much difficulty.

THE 4TH BATTALION

hardly be called a Rifleman. He had, however, as we have already seen, been associated with the Regiment in a Kafir war, in China, and at manœuvres. Sir John was a man of exceptional ability. At Eton he had been Captain of the Eleven, and it was perhaps then that he laid the foundation of a certain independence of character, of great advantage to those serving under his command but which perhaps did not entirely ingratiate him on all occasions with higher military or civil authorities. His services in South Africa, the Indian Mutiny, and in China were of the highest order. In 1885 Sir John received the rank of Field-Marshal, but died a few weeks afterwards.

Next year the Battalion went on to Fermoy, and thence on November 2, 1876, embarked in H.M.S. *Serapis* for India. In the absence of Colonel Hinxman, the Battalion, 673 of all ranks, was commanded by Major J. S. Algar, who had with him the following officers : Captains C. M. Calderon, J. H. H. Croft, E. W. H. Crofton, B. Frend, and P. A. Robinson ; Lieuts. H. S. Marsham, E. T. Hutton (Adjutant), A. G. A. Martin, H. Vere, R. Story, G. H. Wells, G. T. Campbell, H. E. C. Upton, R. S. Buchanan-Riddell, Hon. C. G. S. Canning, R. E. C. Crawford ; Sub.-Lieuts. G. C. Kitson and L. W. G. Butler ; Paymaster Major A. G. Anderson ; Quartermaster J. W. H. Riley ; Medical Officer Surgeon W. M. Harman.

The voyage was calm and the Battalion reached Bombay on December 6. Thence it proceeded to its allotted station at Agra.

Its term of service in India was extended to 16 years, during which it took part in the Chin Lushai expedition. Soon after its return to England in 1892 it was quartered at Aldershot, where, under command of Colonel H. R. Mends, it had the distinction of winning for three years in succession the Evelyn Wood competition, one which involved a long distance run and target practice by selected squads.

The outbreak of the Boer War found the Battalion in Ireland, where it acted as a reservoir to the supply of drafts for the other three Battalions in the field, and it was not until the close of the war that it was despatched to South Africa and took part in the last phase.

2

The 1st Battalion was brought by Colonel Gordon to England from Halifax, N.S., in a state of splendid efficiency. Its Captains and Subalterns were in many cases men of exceptional zeal and ability.

At the end of 1877 Colonel Gordon became A.A.G., Southern District, and was succeeded in command of the Battalion by Lieut.-Colonel J. D. Dundas, a veteran of the Indian Mutiny.

In 1878 difficulties with Russia entailed the calling out of the Reserves for the first time since the institution of short service in 1870. On what principle they were appointed to regiments on this occasion is not known, but the result was rather remarkable. The Cambridge Barracks, occupied by our Battalion, were filled with men in red jackets but with Rifle equipment! The neighbouring barracks were, on the other hand, filled with Rifle Militiamen in black serge and white belts! After some months H.R.H. The Duke of Cambridge, Commander-in-Chief, came down to inspect the troops. The Rifle Battalion appeared on parade wholly in green, but only after recourse of every kind of shift and borrowing. The red battalions, much to the annoyance of the C.-in-C., appeared partly in red, partly in green. But numerically and physically the Brigade presented a splendid appearance. Our Battalion, although deprived of H Company, which was on detachment, made up eight Companies of 46 file for this parade, and its gross strength was almost 1,100.

The Reserves were shortly afterwards demobilised, and in the autumn the Battalion was sent to Winchester with two Companies detached at Tipner and Marchwood respectively. Tipner in the war with France had been used for the detention of prisoners of war, and it is said that at the time of which we are speaking there was still in existence an order for sentries to fire on any person speaking French after sunset!

Meanwhile a draft of 100 men was despatched to reinforce the 2nd Battalion, which had been detailed for service in the second Afghan War. In the first days of 1879 the 3rd Battalion was detailed for active Service in South Africa, and the 1st Battalion was called upon to furnish it with two drafts, one of 225 and the other of 150 men. The inevitable result was that the latter Battalion, although rapidly filled up with recruits, was for practical purposes reduced temporarily to the status of a depôt; but in the following year, although composed of very young soldiers, it had been made up to a respectable strength, and on going to Aldershot in the summer of 1880 was again in a condition of efficiency. Had the Battalion remained at Aldershot it would certainly have been selected for service in the Egyptian campaign in 1882, but its services

1ST AND 2ND BATTALIONS 315

were needed in Ireland, on account of the chronic disturbances in that country, and to Ireland it was despatched at 48 hours' notice, just before the Christmas of 1880.

In 1886 the Battalion was brought back to England, and in 1891 embarked for India in the *Crocodile*, a worn-out old vessel, the main shaft of which broke in the Indian Ocean. The Battalion, which thus kept up its reputation for misfortune at sea, drifted about until the appearance of a vessel which towed the old *Crocodile* into Bombay.

The Battalion served in one or two Frontier expeditions, but after a few years was transferred to S. Africa and remained there until the outbreak of the Boer War in 1899. It was engaged therein, from the first action at Telana Hill until the peace in 1902.

3

In the autumn of 1878 war broke out in Afghanistan, and the 2nd Battalion, commanded at the outset by Major C. Ashburnham, and later by Lieut.-Colonel J. J. Collins, formed part of the force under General Sir Donald Stewart which passed through the Bolan Pass and occupied Kandahar without opposition. In 1880 Stewart's force marched to Kabul, but in the autumn of the same year was included in the force under Major-General F. S. Roberts, detailed for the relief of the garrison at Kandahar, which had been besieged after the defeat of an Anglo-Indian army at Maiwand. The task having been successfully accomplished and the Afghan War terminated, the Battalion, after operations in the Murree country, returned to Meerut. It had undergone a great deal of hardship and kept up the reputation of the Regiment in all respects, but of actual fighting had had but little.

In December of the same year (1880) the Battalion was sent to Natal as a reinforcement of the British force engaged in the first Boer War. This quickly terminated, and in 1882 the Battalion came to England. Its tour on service at home was uneventful. In 1890 it was sent to the Mediterranean and later on to India, whence in 1899 it proceeded for the second time to Natal, where the second Boer War had just broken out. The Battalion took part in the defence of Ladysmith.

4

The 3rd Battalion, which in 1872, as we have already seen, landed in England after 15 years of foreign service, sailed for

S. Africa in February 1879 to take part in the Zulu War, at the termination of which it was quartered at Pietermaritzberg with four Companies on various detachments.

In December 1880 H.Q. and four Companies, under Lieut.-Colonel Ashburnham, were ordered up to the Transvaal in conjunction with the 58th Regiment for the purpose of subduing the revolt which had broken out among the Boers, whose country had been annexed to the British Empire three years previously. The British force under Major-General Sir George Colley was brought to a standstill at Laing's Nek, a strong position just within the Natal frontier. Reinforcements were sent for, but before they could arrive in sufficient force an attempt made to clear the communications with Newcastle brought on an engagement in unfavourable circumstances. The Battalion, although nearly surrounded near the Ingogo river, gallantly held its ground for a whole day, despite severe losses; and at nightfall carried off the guns and regained its camp at Mount Prospect.

In the occupation of Amajuba Hill on February 27, which resulted in the defeat of our force and the death of General Colley, the Battalion had no share. The war terminated shortly afterwards.

In 1882 the Battalion was brought to Malta, whence in August it proceeded to Egypt and took part at the Battle of Tel-el-Kebir. Although the war proper quickly ended, affairs on the Red Sea littoral and in the Sudan were in a most unsettled state. Further military operations consequently ensued; and in 1884 the Battalion was present in two engagements at El Teb and Tamai, in which the insurgent tribes were heavily defeated. In 1891 the Battalion was brought home to be quartered at Gosport, and was still on home service when in the autumn of 1899 it received orders to embark for S. Africa with a view to taking part in the second Boer War. Under command of Lieut.-Colonel Buchanan Riddell it took a distinguished part in the operations for the relief of Ladysmith and those of subsequent date until the end of the war.

The South African War, 1899–1903, taught us a great many useful lessons; and the twelve succeeding years were a period of intensive training for the Great War which broke out in 1914.

6

Shortly after the termination of the S. African war a Veterans' Institution was formed in our Regiment, with a view to linking up

THE WAR, 1914-1918 317

the association between past and present Riflemen of all ranks, and of still further extending the happy relations existing from time immemorial between officers, N.C.Os. and Men. The result of this development showed itself conspicuously on the outbreak of the Great War, when men crowded to join our Regiment. Nineteen new battalions were actually formed; and but for the fact that it was considered inadvisable to extend the Regiment still further, even more battalions could have been raised, for several thousand men who had enlisted for the K.R.R.C. were transferred to other units.

In 1914 the whole of the Regular Army was in the highest condition of training and efficiency. What it achieved during the War may be best left to the judgment of a German general whose lot it was to come in contact with the British Expeditionary force during the first days of the campaign. That General gave it as his matured opinion that in the whole history of warfare the Services of the British army had never been surpassed, perhaps had never been equalled.

In August 1914 the 1st and 2nd Battalions were stationed at Aldershot, the 3rd and 4th in India. In the B.E.F. the 1st Battalion formed part of the 6th Brigade in the 2nd Division, and the 2nd Battalion was a unit of the 2nd Brigade in the 1st Division. Both battalions took part in the retreat from Mons and subsequent advance to the Aisne; both suffered enormously during the titanic contest, known as the first battle of Ypres. In this battle H.H. Prince Maurice of Battenberg, first cousin to the King, among many others laid down his life while fighting in command of his platoon. Prince Maurice might no doubt, without discredit to himself, have accepted an appointment promising greater security; but since attaining manhood his life had been spent in the 1st Battalion. His whole interests and happiness were bound up therein and, at whatever personal risk, he decided to share its fortunes, its perils, and the fate of his brother Riflemen.

The 3rd and 4th Battalions were brought home from India in the same ship and attached to the 27th Division, which reached France during the last days of the year. The change from the warmth of India to the wet and cold climate of northern France could not fail to be singularly trying to these two battalions, and of necessity their sufferings were very great. In April 1915, during the second battle of Ypres, the 27th Division under General T. D'O. Snow greatly distinguished itself. The battalion was posted on the Ypres-Menin Road close to the ground held by the 2nd and 1st

Battalions in the former battle, and its losses were hardly less. At Hooge, where the four battalions were almost destroyed, a plain monument has been erected to their memory.

In the autumn the 27th Division was sent to Salonika. The 4th Battalion was brought back to France in 1918 during the last three months of the war. The 3rd Battalion remained with the Salonika force until the Armistice.

The 1st and 2nd Battalions, constantly recruited by drafts from home, served in France during the whole period of the war, and subsequently formed part of the Army of Occupation at Cologne.

Of the newly raised battalions of the Regiment, twelve fought in France, one of them also in Italy. These Service Battalions, as they were called, worthily maintained the traditions of the old Regiment. They were all disbanded at the end of the war, and the same fate befell the 3rd and 4th Battalions.

> 'Not once nor twice in our rough-island story
> The path of duty was the way to glory.'

APPENDIX B

REGIMENTAL INSTITUTIONS

CELER ET AUDAX CLUB

THE story of a regiment is hardly complete unless it contains a word on the subject of its institutions. Of these the earliest is the Celer et Audax Club, originally formed in about the year 1859, for Rifle Officers past or present. It was purely a dinner Club, its object being that at the Annual Regimental Dinner—first instituted, as already mentioned, by Lord Melville—members should get their dinner at a cheaper rate than non-members. In the early years of the present century a feeling gradually developed that the time had arrived for the Club to extend its activities and undertake the administration of all regimental affairs other than those of a purely military character. Largely through the exertions of the late Sir Edward Hutton the Club was in 1908 reconstituted on an enlarged basis. Its annual subscription was raised from ten shillings to one pound, its committee was numerically increased and placed on a representative basis, and an Annual General Meeting instituted.

At meetings held in July and October of that year Lord Grenfell, as Chairman, pointed out the need of a Central Organisation to take action on behalf of the Regiment as a whole, and of a General Fund to be utilised for purposes in which Officers, past as well as present, are interested.

The proposal having been carried a Committee was elected to supervise the business of the Club in general, assisted by Sub-Committees dealing with individual subjects, *e.g.* the annual Point-to-Point Races, the publication of *The Chronicle*, etc.

In 1923 a further step was taken. Following the example of the Riflemen's Aid Association, and after taking legal advice, the Club became an Incorporated Body. 'The Celer et Audax Club General Committee, Limited,' is consequently now in a position to receive bequests and administer Trusts. This act was completed but shortly before the death of Sir Edward Hutton, who had done so much to bring it about.

Under the new organisation the Club has been successfully carried on, and is prepared to extend the scope of its activities as circumstances may from time to time require.

THE RIFLEMEN'S AID ASSOCIATION AND GREENJACKET CRICKET CLUB.

These were formed in co-operation with the Rifle Brigade in 1884. The success of both is well known and needs no further reference here. The Greenjacket Club owed its foundation largely to Colonel N. Willoughby Wallace, C.M.G., who was himself one of the most brilliant cricketers that our regiment has ever produced, and played in the Gloucestershire County team under the captainship of the famous W. G. Grace in its most palmy days.

THE CHRONICLE

The *K.R.R.C. Chronicle* produced its first annual number in 1901. It was compiled and edited by a Committee which at the outset included Colonel H. R. Mench, Sir Guy Campbell, Captain the Hon. A. R. M. Stuart-Wortley, and Major T. Riley (Hon. Sec.).

A comparison of the recent issues with the earliest numbers will show the improvement gradually made.

The *Chronicle* had been preceded by at least two monthly periodicals, neither of which however had more than a brief existence. The *Celer et Audax,* edited by Lieut. E. O. H. Wilkinson, was produced by the 3rd Battalion from 1878–1880; and the *Maltese Cross* by the 1st Battalion—under Colonel Astley Terry's editorship—from 1883–1889. Of these two newspapers, one or two numbers of the former, and a complete set of the latter, have been deposited among the archives in Eccleston Square.

REGIMENTAL POINT-TO-POINT RACES

There appears to be no allusion to this race in the *Chronicle* until the issue for 1907, in which year they took place on March 13 near Maldon in Essex. But they had been already held on previous occasions.

In 1911 H.M. The King most graciously presented a Challenge Cup for hunters, the property of members of the Celer et Audax Club which have never won a race under National Hunt Rules,

REGIMENTAL INSTITUTIONS

or Rules of Races (Point-to-Point excepted). It was won that year on the Smeeth (Kent) course by Major S. F. Mott.

LADIES' NEEDLEWORK GUILD

This Guild, composed of ladies connected with the Regiment, was instituted in 1907 for the purpose of making and collecting garments, particularly of underclothing, for the benefit of the wives and children of married Riflemen. Splendid work was done by all connected, but our compliments are perhaps specially due to the Hon. Secretary, Mrs. F. A. Fortescue, whose untiring energy enabled the Guild to deal with the enormous additional requirements during the war.

The Guild, of which Mrs. Price Davies is now Hon. Secretary, is in a flourishing condition, and has earned the most hearty gratitude of the Regiment.

VETERANS' DINNER [1]

This annual institution was founded at the suggestion of Corporal Clemens : a retired Rifleman of the 1st Battalion occupying a good position at the Law Courts. The proposal was warmly taken up by Sir Redvers Buller, senior Colonel Commandant, and the first dinner took place at the Drill Hall of the Victoria Rifles, kindly lent for the purpose, on February 28—the anniversary of the Relief of Ladysmith—1906. The *Chronicle* of that year mentions the gathering of 365 veterans of all ranks. It was presided over by Sir Redvers, supported by 44 officers. The General and Major T. Riley made memorable speeches, and the party could hardly have been more successful.

The pleasure of old friends meeting after many years can hardly be described in terms of exaggeration. But the dinner has done much more ; for it has not only cemented the traditional regard and fellowship between all ranks, but has undoubtedly given a great stimulus to the recruiting of our Regiment. On the outbreak of the Great War its fruits were clearly shown in this respect.

It is hoped that in future similar gatherings will take place annually in the great cities where old Riflemen reside : possibly also in the great Dominions.

[1] So far as is known, the senior (in age) Rifleman who has attended these dinners was T. Skinner, who joined the Regimental Depôt—then at Chatham—in the year 1846. Skinner served with the 2nd Battalion in the Kafir War, 1851–1853, and helped to build the well-known town of Harrismith, which took its name from the celebrated G.O.C. in South Africa.

APPENDIX C

Battle Honours

Up to the outbreak of the war with Germany the four battalions of our Regiment could claim to have been individually instrumental in obtaining the following honours :

1st Battalion. Louisbourg ; Quebec ; North America ; Roliça ; Vimieiro ; Talavera ; Bussaco ; Fuentes de Oñoro ; Albuera ; Ciudad Rodrigo ; Badajoz ; Salamanca ; Vitoria ; Pyrenees ; Nivelle ; Nive ; Orthez ; Toulouse ; Peninsula ; Punjaub ; Mooltan ; Goojerat ; Delhi, Chitral ; South Africa, 1899–1902 ; Defence of Ladysmith.

2nd Battalion. Martinique, 1762, 1809 ; Havana ; South Africa, 1851–3 ; Taku Forts ; Pekin ; Ahmad Kehl ; Kandahar ; Afghanistan, 1878–80 ; South Africa, 1899–1902 ; Defence of Ladysmith.

3rd Battalion. South Africa, 1879 ; Egypt, 1882, 1884 ; Tel-el-Kebir ; South Africa, 1899–1902 ; Relief of Ladysmith.

4th Battalion. South Africa, 1899–1902.

APPENDIX TO VOL. I OF THE ANNALS

I

ANY person looking at old Army Lists will find that during the years 1773–1785 inclusive the battalions of the 60th are listed separately. In previous and in subsequent years the regiment is shown on one list only.

When the regiment was first raised Colonels Commandant were appointed to command a battalion not specified. The other officers were gazetted in the same way to the regiment as a whole. But in 1773—for some unexplained, and probably unauthorised, reason—an alteration was made, and officers were gazetted to a specific battalion. When however in 1883, on the disbandment of the 3rd and 4th Battalions, the question arose, the Board of General Officers assembled for the purpose decided that the regiments must be considered as one and indivisible. In accordance with that decision, which amounted practically to a censure on the recent separation of battalions, the precedent of 1763 was followed and the junior officers throughout the regiment—irrespective of their particular battalion—were placed on half-pay. Thenceforward the Regiment, whatever the number of its battalions, has invariably been shown on one list.

The question arose a second time in 1845, when the 1st Battalion was ordered on service in India. The Indian Government, unaccustomed to a double battalion regiment, wished to prevent interchange between the two battalions, but was politely told to mind its own business!

II

The following supplementary notes are the results of information acquired since the publication of Vol. I. The marginal references apply to its pages.

P. 40. Casualties of the 3rd Battalion at Fort William Henry. The French claimed to have captured 1 Lieut.-Colonel, 1 Captain, 1 Lieutenant, 1 Ensign, 7 Sergeants, 5 Corporals, 104 Privates.

P. 73. l. 2, insert. 'During the month of March the 60th found a Light Company at Albany. Each Company provided for the purpose 1 Sergeant, 1 Corporal, and 12 Privates. Hitherto the 22nd, 40th, and 45th had been the only regiments with Light Companies. These had been raised during the previous year.' (*Vide* the Journal of the R.U.S.I., November, 1918.)

,, 93. During the whole of the operations against Quebec the casualties of the 60th were :

	Officers.	*Other Ranks.*
2nd Bn.	4 killed, 13 wounded.	22 killed, 176 wounded.
3rd Bn.	1 ,, 2	,, 30 ,,

,, 217. The entire loss of the Franco-American armies at the siege of Savannah amounted to 1,200 men.

,, 225. At the surrender of Pensacola the garrison comprised 32 Officers and 828 O.R., of whom 2 Officers and 220 O.R. were on the sick list. The casualties had been 90 killed and 46 wounded. The state of the three Companies R.A.R. showed 1 Captain, 1 Lieutenant, 1 Ensign, 123 O.R. fit for duty.

,, 238. On July 24 the cadre of the 3rd Battalion landed at Southampton and marched to Winchester, returning on the 28th to Southampton, where it embarked for Guernsey. This was probably the first visit to Winchester of any part of our regiment.

,, 246. During the operations against Guadeloupe, April, 1794, the casualties of the 60th amounted to 2 Officers and 6 O.R. killed, and 107 wounded.

,, 268. In his inspection report dated July 2, 1805, General F. Maitland writes : 'Nearly all the Captains and Subalterns with the 2nd Battn. 60th are foreigners who have come from Hompesch's or Löwenstein's Corps. These have been effective for 8 or 9 years, and have been the stand-by of the Battalion. They are industrious and good Officers, and deserve notice for their good conduct and *want of friends.*'

,, 278. Brig.-General Harcourt, writing to the G.O.C. about the misconduct of the Flank Companies, says : 'It is due to the Officers of these Companies to add that no shadow of censure attaches to them ; those of the 4th Battalion (Lieuts. Regnier and Bidgood) having to retire wounded, and Captain Howard, commanding the Grenadiers of the 2nd Battalion, having displayed a spirit, zeal, and skill which entitle him to every praise.'

P. 371. In addition to the names given, Lieut. D. Forbes was killed at St. Foye. The unknown Officer killed in 1762 was apparently Lieut. R. Schuyler, who fell in the re-capture of Newfoundland.

„ 372. Add to the names of officers killed in 1794 those of Lieut. F. G. Montmollin and Quartermaster Belt.

APPENDIX TO VOL. II

I

ON p. 6 the reasons for which Baron Ferdinand von Hompesch abandoned the completion of his new battalion are discussed. But it appears that having been elected Grand Master of the Knights of St. John at Malta, he was unable to complete the battalion that he was raising. To Malta he accordingly repaired, but his term of office came quickly to an end. In June, 1798, General Bonaparte, on his way to Egypt, summoned the town of Valetta. Several of the Knights had already agreed to surrender it; and Hompesch, on being promised a pecuniary compensation, acquiesced in the capitulation. The island remained in French hands for two years, and was then captured by the British fleet.

II

ALLUSION TO THE 60TH IN THE PENINSULAR WAR BY A GERMAN COMMISSARY

The following extracts referring to our regiment are taken from the translation of 'On the road with Wellington' (Wm. Heinemann & Co., Ltd., London, 1924), written by A. L. F. Schaumann, a D.A. Commissary General in the English Army during the Peninsular War, 1808–1814. The description of his experiences is vivid, and throws light on many subjects unnoticed by official historians.

P. 75. November 29, 1808. Schaumann, having reached Siete Carreros in Spain on his way to join Sir John Moore's army at Salamanca, describes the extremely hostile manner in which he was received by the Spaniards, despite the fact of them being our Allies. He continues, 'Meanwhile a small detachment of the 60th Yägers marched through, escorting a convoy of baggage, women, and children,[1] My billet was the last house in the

[1] This was a detachment from the 5th Battalion, which had been sent back from Salamanca to Portugal.

village, and the yard was full of chickens. In a moment there was a wild outcry. The 60th, all Germans, had killed some of the fowls and taken them away with them. My hosts and some of the muleteers wanted to attack one of the soldiers. With cold-blooded phlegm, however, this man dropped on one knee and raised his rifle to his shoulder, whereupon at least twenty of the Spaniards fled for their lives!'

P. 112. On January 2, 1809, during Sir John Moore's retreat to Corunna, Schaumann found himself at Villafranca. 'I took possession of a minute room which I shared with a Hussar Officer of the King's German Legion. The rooms below were occupied by about thirty Yägers of the 60th Regt.[1] When I woke one morning it was to find that the hams previously hanging in the chimney were all gone, and also that some of the Yägers who were lodged below, and who had marched before dawn that day, had crept up to my room before leaving; and while I was asleep, had not only robbed me of one of my pistols, but had also taken the sausage, a bottle of rum, my biscuits, and my gloves, as well as the provisions and many other things belonging to the officer of the 3rd Hussars who shared the room with me —a discovery which upset us both very much!'

,, 132. On January 11, Schaumann reached Burgo, close to Corunna. 'Here was a detachment of the 60th Regiment established here—which all this time had been acting as a bodyguard over the stores. God! how well-fed and smart the fellows beside us.'[2]

,, 162. July 27, 1809. On this, the day before the battle of Talavera, the 3rd Division, forming the Advance Guard, was attacked by greatly superior numbers of the French. 'Their retreat was carried out in a highly exemplary manner by Anson's Cavalry, Colonel Donkin's Infantry Brigade, and the German sharpshooters of the 60th Regiment.' On the next page Schaumann further describes the facts of the incident, which was a ticklish one, as mentioned in Vol. II., pp. 94–5 of this book.

---

[1] In view of the fact that the Battalion had been detached from Moore's Army a month previously, it is difficult to account for the presence of this detachment.

[2] Our 2nd Battalion—about 250 strong only—had been left in garrison at Corunna.

P. 274-5. October, 1810. 'At Rio Mayor were three Companies of Portuguese Caçadores, under the command of that brave German soldier Captain Schwalbach.' (This Officer, who had been originally a N.C.O. in our 5th Battalion, joined the Portuguese service, in which he eventually became a Major-General.) . . . The French having suddenly advanced in overwhelming force, 'Our Yägers took post at the entrance of the town and all around it. Brave old Schwalbach stationed himself with his foremost outposts, and coolly explained to his men how close they were to allow the French to come before they aimed and mowed them down.' By the ruse of a dummy battery the enemy was kept for some time at bay; but being eventually outnumbered Schwalbach's men fell back to Caldas.

III

The following is extracted from Dalton's 'Waterloo Roll': 'Captain Horace B. Seymour' (60th, alluded to in Vol. II., p. 290), 'the strongest man in the British Army, who is said to have slain more men at Waterloo than any single individual.

'Taken prisoner during the battle he was rescued by a party of Cavalry sent by Wellington himself for the purpose. He is the original of the "Captain Trevanion" in Lever's story "Harry Lorrequer," who was grossly insulted by a French Officer—a noted bully—at a restaurant in Paris a few weeks after Waterloo. After repeated insults the French bully ordered a glass of brandy, and while sitting opposite Trevanion drank it off, saying in a loud voice that could be heard all over the Café, " A votre courage, Anglais." Trevanion slowly rose from his chair, displaying to the astonished Frenchman the immense proportions and gigantic frame of a man well known as the largest officer in the army.

'With one stride he was beside the chair of the Frenchman, and with the speed of lightning seized his nose by one hand while with the other he grasped his lower jaw; and wrenching his mouth open with the strength of an ogre, he spat down his throat. The bully's jaw was broken by his adversary's iron grasp; and he disappeared to be seen no more.'

INDEX

A

ADVENTURE of officers at Gibraltar, 9
Albert, H.R.H. Prince, Colonel-in-Chief, 215
Andrews, Captain F., death of, 109
Anson, Hon. G., C.-in-C. in India, 87
Ashburnham, Lieut. C., at outbreak of Indian Mutiny, 94
Austin, Lieut. F., seizes the Treasury at Meerut, 97

B

BAREILLY, capture of, 175
Barnard, Sir H., commands Delhi Field Force, 111-115; thanks our regiment, 118; death of, 128
Battle Honours, gained by the various battalions, 322
Bedford, W. F., in Kaffir War, 67 *et seq.*; commands 3rd Batt., 83, 231
Beresford, Lord, Colonel-in-Chief, 215
Bertrand, Rev. Father, touching address of, 140
Biggs, Major T., commands troops in a cyclone, 235
Bingham, H., commands Rifle Companies in Euzoffzie Expedition, Lieut.-Colonel of 1st Batt., 216
Birkenhead, wreck of H.M.S., list of Riflemen in, 72
Bloomfield, Lord, his letter on 1st Batt., 14; his G.O., 15
Bonham, General P., 304 *n.*
Bouquet, H., one of our great C.Os., 303
Bradley, A. G. (historian), his opinion of Sir F. Haldimand, 304
Broughton Bridge, accident at, 18
Browne, H. D., Adjutant to 4th Batt., his opinion of Colonel Hawley, 295; characteristics of, 301; comment on, 304 *n.*

Bradshaw, Lieut.-Colonel J., joins 1st Batt., 32; commands battalion at Mooltan, 44; commands a brigade, 48; commands force in Euzoffzie country, 50; and infantry of Kohat Expedition, 55; his liberality, 56 *n.*; death of, 59
Buller, Redvers, anecdotes of, 256-257; joins 1st Batt. at Thunder Bay, 272; his allusion to Colonel Hawley, 297; remarks on, 298; initiates Regimental History, 308
Burke, Rifleman M., captures Pathan flag, 52
Butler, Webbe, takes 2nd Batt. to India, 188; in China, 201; commands 3rd Batt., 211
Buzdara Valley, 51

C

CAMBRIDGE, Adolphus, Duke of, Colonel-in-Chief, inspects 1st Batt., 15; death of, 215
Cambridge, George, Duke of, Colonel-in-Chief, 260; his opinion of Redvers Buller, 299
Campbell, General Sir Colin (afterwards F.M. Lord Clyde), inspects 1st Batt., 50; relieves Lucknow, 164; enters Bareilly, 176
Campbell, Colonel, 52nd L.I., commands a column of attack at Delhi, 138; his success, 143
Campbell, Captain Sir E., 125-127; exploit at Koodsia Bagh, 134; covers attack on Cashmere Gate, 140
Cathcart, General, succeeds Sir H. Smith in Cape Colony, 77
Celer et Audax Club formed, 319
Centrepiece in Officers' Mess, 1st Batt., 54
Chartist movement in 1848..62
China, situation in, 191; campaign in, 198 *et seq.*; 2nd Batt. quits, 212

330 INDEX

Chronicle, the *K.R.R.C.*, 320
Cockburn, Lieut.-Colonel W. T., in command of 2nd Batt., 27 ; retires, 28
Colonel-in-Chief, title of, 3
Colonels Commandant, origin of, 1 ; names of, 215
Cross, Lieut. W. J., captured by brigands, 9
Cunynghame, Lieut. A., in China, 192 ; commands Dublin District, 219

D

DAVY, Sir W. G., becomes Colonel Commandant, 16
Delhi, bloodshed at, 106 ; siege of, 114–138 ; malaria in camp at, 135 ; siege train reaches, 133 ; siege batteries at, 137 ; columns of attack on, 138 ; assault on and capture of, 141 *et seq.* ; its importance, 154, 156 ; distinguished officers at, 158
Depôt, regimental, its various stations, 214
Douglas, Captain, commands detachment of riflemen in expedition to Kohat, 55
Douro, Marquis of, 9
Dover Town Council erects monument to 1st Batt., 216
Dublin, 1st Batt. at, 16, 239 ; 2nd Batt., 19, 20, 227 ; 3rd Batt., 231 ; 4th Batt., 245
Dundas, Colonel Hon. H., commands 1st Batt., 30 ; his complaint to Sir C. Napier, 36 ; commands troops in Scinde, 36 ; Brigadier, 60 ; at Goojerat, 67 (*vide* Melville)

E

EAST India Company, 88
Elgin, Lord, British Commissioner in China, 202 ; enters Peking, 209
Ellis, Lieut.-Colonel Hon. A. F., character of, 13 ; death of, 24
Enamels, set of, presented to 2nd Batt., 209
Ensign, rank of, substituted for that of 2nd Lieut., 82
Euzoffzie Country, expedition to, 50

F

FEILDEN, R. J., commands 1st Batt., 219 ; his B.O. on joining, 221 ; in the Red River Expedition, 264 ; retires, 287

Fenian conspiracy, 230, 266
Flagstaff Tower, piquet at, attacked, 117
Fort William Henry, casualties at, 323
Fraser, Simon, Commissioner at Delhi, 101

G

GARVIN, Sergeant S., receives V.C., 121
Goorkhas, *vide* 'Regiments'
Gomm, General Sir W., G.O.C. at Jamaica, 22 *et seq.* ; C.-in-C. in India, 87 ; forms Camp of Exercise, *ibid.*
Governor-General of India (Lord Canning) fails to appreciate situation at Delhi, 129 ; his compliment and G.O. to 1st Batt., 185
Grant, Sir Hope, commands force in China, 192 ; Lord Wolseley's praise of, 210
Grenfell, F. W., his adventure at Malta, 222 ; characteristics of, 300
Grey, Major Hon. C., 8
Guadeloupe, casualties at, 324
Guides, Corps of, *vide* 'Regiments'

H

HALDIMAND, Sir F., an empire builder, 307 *et seq.*
Hare, Captain J., captures 'Sammy House,' 121
Hare, Colonel, fortifies Delhi, 130 *n.*
Hawley, Lieut.-Col. R. B., commands 4th Batt., 84 ; his system of training, 252 ; encourages sport, 255 ; attacked by 10th Hussars at manœuvres, 292 ; relinquishes command, 294 ; Colonel Browne's view of, 295 ; farewell order, 295 ; comments on his character, system, and pupils, 296 *et seq.* ; one of our great regimental C.Os., 303
Heathcote, Ensign A. S., seizes the arsenal at Meerut, 98 ; his description of Delhi after the assault, 148
Hindun, action at the, 109–110
History, regimental, sources of, in America, 303
Hodson, Captain, captures King of Delhi, 148
Holland, S. J., a distinguished engineer, 306
Hompesch, Baron F. von, Grand Master at Malta, 325
Hope, Hon. Adrian, Brevet-Major, 79 ; in the Crimea, 81 ; death of, 173
Hudson Bay Company, its claims, 261

INDEX

Humphries, Lieut., attached to 60th, killed, 119
Hunter, General P., career of, 305
Hutton, E. T. H., characteristics of, 301

I

INDIA, Sikh power in, 35
Indian Native Troops refuse to receive the new cartridges, 92
Innes, Surgeon Kerr-, his advice *re* uniforms, 116
Ionian Islands, 1st Batt. at, 11 *et seq.*; 2nd Batt. at, 21
Iron Mountain, capture of, 75

J

JONES, Brigadier, 61st Regt., commands a column of assault, his altercation with J. Nicholson, 143
Jones, Lieut.-Colonel John, at outbreak of Indian Mutiny, 95; drives the mutineers out of the Subzee Mundee, 124; commands Reserve Column at assault of Delhi, 146; his success, *ibid.*; captures King's Palace, 147; commands Roorkee Field Force, 167; captures Bareilly, 175; relieves Shahjehanpore, 178; his great success, 180

K

K.C.B., list of recipients while still commanding battalions, 95 *n.*
King of Delhi compelled to head the revolt, 104; captured, 148; court martial on, 153
Kingsford, historian of Canada, his opinion of Sir F. Haldimand, 309
Kingston, Jamaica, conflagration at, 28
Kissen Gunge, destruction of mutineers' battery at, 118
Kohat, expedition to, 55
Koodsia Bagh, captured by Sir E. Campbell, 134

L

LADIES' Needlework Guild, 321
Leslie, Captain Charles, 7
Light Company formed, 324
Lindesay, H. P., gallant conduct of, 237
Loch, H., released by the Chinese, 207

M

MAINODIN HUSSAN KHAN, his narrative, 114, 152
Maitland, General, his report on 2nd Batt., 324
Malta, 1st Batt. at, 11
Markham, Lieut.-Colonel C., takes command of 2nd Batt., 27; his death, *ibid.*
Medals for India and China given to 2nd Batt., 213
Melville, Lord, appointed to command of Sinhind Division, 58; his character, 59; becomes Colonel Commandant, 217; President of Celer et Audax Club, 319. (*See also* Dundas.)
Mess jacket, first worn in the Ionian Islands, 13
Michel, Colonel (afterwards Sir John), in manœuvres of 1872, 292; C.-in-C. in Ireland, 312; character of, 313
Mitchell, T., Adjutant, his book on Light Drill, 15, 87
Molyneux, Lieut.-Colonel Hon. H. R., commands 1st Batt., 11; his character, 13; death of, 15
Montauban, General, commands French in China, 194
Monument to 1st Batt. at Dover, 216
Mooltan, outbreak of revolt at, 37; description of, 40; siege of, 43; its capture, 45
Munro, 2nd Lieut. J., captured by brigands, 9
Munshi Jewan Lal describes action on the Hindun, 110; and panic of Sepoys, 114
Muter, Capt. D. D., saves the Treasury at Meerut, 94; brings reinforcement to Delhi, 135; at the assault, 142; D.A.A.G., 167; joins 2nd Batt., 211
Mutineers from Meerut march on Delhi, 100

N

NAPIER, Lieut.-General Sir C., commands army of the Indus, 38; his appearance, 36 *n.*; in expedition to Kohat, 55
Napier, Colonel Robert, at Mooltan, 45; at Delhi, 90
Napier, Ensign W. H., killed at the Hindun, 110
Nesbitt, Lieut.-Colonel C. L., in command of 2nd Batt., 31; in Kaffir War, 65 *et seq.*; drowned, 80

332 INDEX

Nicholson, Brigadier J., arrives at Delhi, 129; commands a column of attack, 138; death of, 148
North, C. N., takes 1st Batt. to Malta, 220; his career, *ibid.*

O

ORDER of battle in Delhi Field Force, 131
Oude, campaign in, 181

P

PALMER, F. R., commands wing of 1st Batt., 166; and the battalion in Rohilcund, 167; Lieut.-Colonel of 2nd Batt., 189; retires, 230
Parkes, H., taken prisoner by Chinese, 202; released, 207
Pensacola, parade state of 60th at, 224
Phillips, E., carries the Water Bastion at Delhi, 141; his death and character, 147
Point-to-point races, the regimental, 320
Pretyman, W., commands 4th Batt., 84
Pullee, Pathan flag captured at, 52

R

RECORDS, origin of regimental, 5
Red River, its situation, 262; expedition to, decided on, 263; difficulties of route, 264; comments on, 282 *et seq.*
Regiments mentioned:
  Carabineers, 101
  9th Lancers, 113
  8th Regt., 133
  52nd L.I., 128-129, 142
  61st, 139
  75th, 113
  Royal Dublin Fusiliers, 45
  1st European Fusiliers, 113
  2nd P.W.O. Goorkhas, 111-115; at Kissen Gunj, 108-120, 152; made Riflemen, 165; appreciation of, *ibid.*
  Guides, Corps of, 116, 120, 139, 152
Reid, Major (afterwards Sir Charles), commanding 2nd Goorkhas, 115; at Hindoo Rao's piquet, *ibid.*; repulse of enemy by, 124, 127; commands a column of attack, 129; wounded, 142; his letter to the C.-in-C., 183

Riel, L., raises flag of rebellion, 262; his escape, 280
Rifle, Brunswick percussion rifle issued to 1st Batt., 15; to 2nd Batt., 25; short Enfield-Pritchett rifle issued to 2nd Batt., 82; long ditto, to 3rd Batt., 83; to 1st Batt., 88; short E.-P. rifle to 1st Batt., 121; Whitworth rifle issued to 2nd Batt., 225; short Enfield rifle issued to 3rd Batt., 232; to 4th Batt., 245; Martini Henry to 1st Batt., 288
Riflemen's Aid Association, 320
Rohilcund, campaign in, 167 *et seq.*
Rosser, Captain, 6th D. Gs., offers to pursue mutineers, 100
Rothenburg, Baron F. de, a great C.O., 303

S

'SAMMY HOUSE' captured, 121
Savannah, enemy losses at, 322
Schaumann (German Commissary), his stories of 60th in Spain, 326
Schoedde, Sir J., in China, 191
Seaton, Sir T., organizes campaign in Oude, 181
Second Lieutenant, rank of, abolished, 82
Seymour, Captain H. B., 328
Shaw, Lieut. G. K., at Tang Ku, 200
Sibthorpe, Captain R. N., at Mooltan, 44
Sikh Wars, 35, 37
Sikhs, surrender near R. Pindee, 49
Sixtieth Rifles, compilation of Records ordered, 5
  1st Battalion: at Malta and Ionian Islands, 11; at Woolwich, 14; at Manchester, 16; at Dublin, *ibid.*; meets 2nd Batt., 21; ordered to India, 30; at Fermoy, 31; sails, 32; at Poona, *ibid.*; its frequent misfortunes at sea, 33; at Karachi, 35; attacked by cholera, 36; at Siege of Mooltan, 40; joins army of Lord Gough, 47; at battle of Goojerat, *ibid.*; its forced marches, 47, 49; in Euzoffzie expedition, 55; in expedition to Kohat, 58; its musketry system, 86; inspected by Sir W. Gomm, 87; at Meerut, *ibid.*; attacked by cholera, *ibid.*; armed with Enfield rifle, 88; at outbreak of Indian Mutiny, 94; clears the Bazaar, 96; at the Hindun, 109

INDEX 333

joins Delhi Field Force, 111; at Budlee-ka-Serai, 113; at Hindoo Raos' piquet, 118, 120; reinforced from Meerut, 135; at the assault of Delhi, 141; captures Jumma Musjid, 147; its casualties, 149; General Wilson's G.O. on, *ibid.*: honours for, 150; its operations near Meerut, 161 *et seq.*; curious mirage encountered by, 166; forms part of Roorkee Field Force, 167; at Bareilly, 174; at Shahjehanpore, 180; in Oude, 182; at Allahabad, 184; Governor-General's complimentary G.O. to, 185; honours for, 186; returns to England, 187; monument to at Dover, 213; at Aldershot, *ibid.*; at Tower of London, *ibid.*; receives Alexandra, Princess of Wales, 217; at the Curragh, 218; in Dublin, 219; at Malta, 220; at Montreal, 224; at Ottawa, 260; detailed for Red River Expedition, 264; list of officers engaged, *ibid.*; description of route, 270; Lord Wolseley's comments on, 271-272; on the Winnipeg river, 278; on the Red River, *ibid.*; reaches Fort Garry, 279; on the return voyage, 281 *et seq.*; reaches Toronto, 286; at Quebec, *ibid.*; at Halifax, N.S., 287; commanded by Colonel Gordon, *ibid.*; Martini rifles issued to, 288; embarks for England, 289; commanded by Lieut.-Colonel Dundas, 314; in Ireland, India, and South Africa, 315; in Flanders, 317

2nd *Battalion*: at Manchester, 18; accident at Broughton Bridge, *ibid.*; in Ireland, 19; at Gibraltar and the Ionian Islands, 21; meets 1st Batt., *ibid.*; at Jamaica, 22; decimated by yellow fever, 24; conduct at fire in Kingston, 26; at Quebec, 28; at St. John's. *ibid.*; at Halifax, 29; embarks for England, *ibid.*; movements of its depôt, *ibid.*; at Royal Review in Hyde Park, 60; in Lancashire and Ireland, 62; embarks for South Africa, 64; in Kaffir War, 65-80; capture of Iron Mountain, 75; armed with Enfield rifle, 82; Headquarter Companies sail for India, 188; forms part of Flying Column at Arrah, 189; remainder of battalion reaches India,

ibid.; forms part of Expeditionary Force to China, 191; lands at the Pehtang, 198; at capture of Tang Ku Fort, 200; at funeral of murdered prisoners, 208; enamels presented to officers of, 209; guard of honour to Lord Elgin, *ibid.*; at Tien Tsin, *ibid.*; embarks for England, 212; encounters hurricane, *ibid.*; quartered at Portsmouth, 213; receives medals for India and China, *ibid.*; at Aldershot, 224; at Dover, 226; in Dublin, 227; breech-loading rifles issued to, 228; embarks for India, 229; inspected by C.-in-C. at Calcutta, *ibid.*; at Rawul Pindi, 230; in Afghan War, 315; in Natal and at home, *ibid.*; in South Africa, 315; in Flanders, 317; report on, by General Maitland, 324.

3rd *Battalion*: raised, 85; list of its officers, *ibid.*; notes on, 84; in Dublin, 231; embarks for India, 233; at Bangalore, *ibid.*; in Burmah, 233; at Rangoon, 234; embarks for Madras, 234; in a cyclone, 235 *et seq.*; at Bangalore and Bellary, 240; embarks for Aden, 242; returns to England, *ibid.*; sails for South Africa, 315; in Zulu and Boer Wars, 316; at Malta, in Egypt, and South Africa, *ibid.*; in Flanders, 317; at Salonika, 318; first visit to Winchester, 324

4th *Battalion*: raised, 83; notes on, 84, 243; list of officers in, 244; its strength, 245; embarks for Canada, 246; at Montreal, 250; trained by Colonel Hawley, 252; returns to England, 258; at Aldershot, 290; at Colchester, *ibid.*; at the manœuvres, 291; at Winchester, 292; incident on Salisbury Plain, 292; Colonel Browne's remarks on, 294 *et seq.*; sails for India, 313; its success at Aldershot, 313; sails for South Africa, *ibid.*; in Flanders, 317; returns to France, 318

Slyfield, Lieut.-Colonel, death of, 25

Smith, General Sir Harry, C.-in-C. at Cape Colony, 65 *et seq.*; his farewell order, 77

Spence, Lieut.-Colonel G. A., commands 2nd Batt., 80

Subzee Mundee, piquet at, 120; cleared, 123

INDEX

T

TAKU Forts, captured, 201
Tang Ku fort captured, 200
Taylor, Alexander, at Mooltun, 45; his plan for assault of Delhi, 129; his reconnaissance, 133
Thompson, Rifleman, gains V.C., 124
Toole, J., Quartermaster, 289

V

VETERANS Association instituted, 316; annual dinner of, 321
Victoria Crosses, 150, 183

W

WELLINGTON, the Duke of, his last notice of the regiment, 57
Williams, Captain H. F., on outbreak of Indian Mutiny sounds the Assembly, 95; in command of 1st Batt., 220, 224; declines command of 4th Batt., 312

Willoughby, Lieut., barricades the magazine at Delhi, 101; blows it up, 105
Wilmot, Captain, narrow escape of, 124
Wilson, Brigadier, Bengal Artillery, takes command of the white troops, 96; ordered to join Delhi Field Force, 107; assumes command at Siege of Delhi, 124; his view of the situation, 129; his G.O. prior to the assault, 135; his brilliant services, 158
Winchester, 3rd Batt. at, 324
Wolseley, F.M. Lord, on the Siege of Delhi, 156 n.; in China, 199; finds the French in the Summer Palace, 206; commands Red River Expedition, 262; his success, 283; receives the K.C.M.G., 284; his farewell address, 285; at the manœuvres of 1872..298

Y

YONGE, Captain W. J., at Siege of Mooltan, 44
Young, J. O., in Red River, 267; forces his way to Matawan, 269; his reputation, 285; his popularity, 388

www.ingramcontent.com/pod-product-compliance
Lightning Source LLC
Chambersburg PA
CBHW050329230426
43663CB00010B/1796